In memory of
Selwyn and Sybille

CONTENTS

*... j'ai seulement fait ici un amas de fleurs étrangères, n'y ayant
fournis du mien que le filet à les lier.*
       Montaigne (Michel Eyquem Montaigne 1533–92)

Translated by John Bartlett (1820–1905) as:
*I have gathered a posie of other men's flowers, and nothing
but the thread that binds them is mine own.*

PREFACE

I have dedicated this book to my father, Selwyn Gummer, who had the greatest possible influence on his three sons.

A parish priest, Selwyn was a charismatic preacher with an abundance of what is known in Wales as *hwyl*, loosely translated as passion. His sermons were spellbinding.

We three brothers were all imbued with the same passion for the English language. It has been an essential part of my life and my career in media and communications. Any communication skills that I may claim to have, I owe to my father. John's rhetorical flair played a huge part in his political life. Mark, now working in the voluntary sector, having managed manufacturing companies for 30 years, is the English scholar of the family.

In a business in which words are our stock in trade, I have, over the years, become increasingly convinced of the importance of preserving the English language in all its idiomatic richness and peculiarity. It is important to keep alive Miss Blinda Blurb, Dr Samuel Mudd, Smart Alec and sweet Fanny Adams. We must preserve the memory of the Marquis of Waterford, painting the town red, recount the antics of James Gordon Bennett Jr and recall the skulduggery of Mickey Finn.

Standard reference books like the *Oxford English Dictionary* and even *Brewer's Phrase and Fable* only indirectly address idiomatic English. We need a single volume, a compilation of all the sources, which explains the origins of the many idioms and phrases which we use in everyday English.

While writing this book, I was pleasantly surprised that recently published books have generated so much interest in the subject, but I have been dissatisfied and disappointed that they continue to perpetuate many of the myths about the origins of English idioms.

I have included as many explanations of the phrases as I could find, and acknowledged them in the list of sources. It seems that every generation has come forward with suggestions that become accepted without question.

Like everyone else, I enjoy these attractive theories even if they are unfounded. I have included them because they can be fascinating and delightful. I have, however, tried to be rigorous and if they do not stand up to scrutiny, I say so. I have chosen the most commonly accepted definitions, and where there are two or more I have included them all. I do not claim that my preferred definition is correct, and some are lost in time.

I am sometimes asked to select my favourite idiomatic phrases. It is difficult among so many, but I find fascinating the way 'all things to all men' has come to mean the exact opposite of St Paul's original meaning. Similarly, 'cheap at half the price' should surely mean expensive, not cheap? I love 'Is that Mr Reilly (they speak of so highly)' and the poem by Edna St Vincent Millay about burning the candle at both ends. I like very much also 'spill the beans', 'nineteen to the dozen', the 'clapped out' hare, 'raining cats and dogs' and of course, 'the Real McCoy'!

The book is as comprehensive as possible, but the dynamism and richness of the language necessarily mean that there will be some omissions. While we strive to preserve the hoard of phrases from England's era of sailing ships, we must also capture idioms coined every day in the modern computer age.

Readers are invited to add to the scope of the book by accessing the website www.rmccoy.com and sending details of phrases which have been omitted, or suggesting definitions other than those I have provided.

I would like to thank all my family including our extended family, Alun and Mona Chalfont, for their advice and support, especially my daughter, Naomi, for helping me research the book and my wife, Lucy, for encouraging me to make this long-cherished project a reality. We often reflect on how fortunate we are. We have decided that any profits from this book will be donated to Action on Addiction, the only UK charity which funds research on addiction of all kinds.

Peter Chadlington
June 2005

A

A little bird told me – *a secret source told me*

This phrase has been known since the
16th century and its origin is the Bible,
Ecclesiastes 10:20: 'Curse not the
King, no, not in thy thought; and
curse not the rich in thy bedchamber: for a
bird of the air shall carry the voice, and that
which hath wings shall tell the matter.'

There is a charming story about King
Solomon and the Queen of Sheba. All the
birds were summoned before the King. Only
the lapwing did not appear. When he was
questioned about his disobedience, the lapwing
explained that he was with the Queen of Sheba and
that she had resolved to visit King Solomon.

The King immediately began preparations for the
visit. Meanwhile, the lapwing flew to Ethiopia and
told the Queen that King Solomon had a great
desire to see her. The magnificent meeting,
as we know, then took place.

John Heywood, *Dialogue Conteynyng
the Nomber in Effect of all Proverbes in the
Englishe Tongue* (1546): 'I did lately here … By one bird that in my eare
was late chauntyng.'

Charlotte Brontë, *Villette* (1853): '"Who told you I was called Carl
David?" – "A little bird, monsieur."'

Abominable snowman – *anyone or anything indescribable and unpleasant*

Originally an unidentified creature of the Himalayas, the name 'abominable snowman' derives from the Tibetan *meetoh kangmi* or, in the Sherpa language, *yeti*. It is said to raid mountain villages and to be tall, powerful and bear-like, with a near-human face. The name became known to European mountaineers attempting to climb Mount Everest in the 1920s and was popularised by climbing expeditions in the 1950s. In 1960 Sir Edmund Hillary found footprints which seemed to be those of an animal such as a bear. The mystery surrounding this creature gave rise to the detective novel *The Case of the Abominable Snowman* (1941) by Nicholas Blake.

In 1832, a report from the UK representative in Nepal (B.H. Hodson) described a hirsute creature which reportedly had attacked his servants. The natives called the beast *rakshas*, which means 'demon'. This appears to be first report of the snowman made by a Westerner. Then, in 1913, reports surfaced that a group of Chinese hunters had wounded and captured a hairy, man-like creature which the locals soon named the 'snowman'. This creature was supposedly kept captive in Patang at Sinkiang province until it died five months later. It was described as having a black, monkey-like face and a body covered with silvery yellow hair several inches long; its hands and feet were man-like and the creature was incredibly strong. It grunted and made guttural noises, but mostly made loud whistling sounds (incredibly, no photographs were ever reported taken or produced from this report).

In 1921, an expedition led by Colonel Howard-Bury climbing the north face of Mount Everest reported seeing a group of large creatures moving in the snow at the Laptha-la pass. Two years later another Mount Everest climbing expedition, this time led by Major Alan Cameron, observed a line of huge and dark creatures moving along a cliff face high above the snowline. Pictures of the creatures' tracks were taken two days later, when the expedition reached the area where they were seen. In 1925 a Greek photographer and member of the Royal Geographical Society named N.A. Tombazi glimpsed a creature he later described as 'exactly like a human being, walking upright and stopping occasionally to uproot or pull some dwarf rhododendron bushes'. Tombazi, who was at about 15,000 feet up in the mountains, later reached the spot where he sighted the creature, only to find some intriguing tracks in the snow.

In 1953, David Eccles, Minister of Works responsible for the Coronation decorations in London, became known as the Abominable *Showman*. General de Gaulle, having obstructed British entry to the European Common Market in the 1960s by saying 'Non!', was dubbed the Abominable *No-man*.

Above board – *honest, concealing nothing*

This phrase was originally a gambling expression indicating that one was expected to keep one's hands 'above the board [i.e. the table]' to avoid any suspicion of cheating. According to Dr Johnson, the expression was 'borrowed from gamesters, who, when they put their hands under the table, are changing their cards'.

Richard Carpenter, *The Conscionable Christian* (1620): 'All his dealings are square and above board.'

Ace in the hole – *a hidden advantage, secret source of power*

This American phrase comes originally from the game of stud poker. The card in the 'hole' is not shown until after the betting. With an ace in the hole, a player has an advantage of which the other players are unaware.

The phrase was used as the title of a Cole Porter song in the show *Let's Face It* (1941) and of a Billy Wilder film (US 1951).

The nearest equivalent in British English would be to 'have an ace up one's sleeve'.

Florance Willoughby, *Alaskans All* (1993): 'If she [the Arctic] doesn't get you with trick currents and shifting ice, she tries smothering you with blizzards or starving you. If these fail, her ace in the hole is the cold.'

Achilles heel *or* tendon – *a vulnerable spot, weakness, flaw*

According to Homer's *Iliad*, Achilles' mother, Thetis, immersed her baby son in the Styx, the river of the underworld, to make him invulnerable. To do so, she held him by his heel, which, as it was untouched by the waters, remained the only part of his body vulnerable to mortal attack.

Legend recounts that Paris, the Trojan prince, knew this and killed Achilles by firing a poisoned arrow into his heel.

A person's 'Achilles heel' is, therefore, his most vulnerable spot or fatal weakness. The Achilles tendon – between heel and calf – takes its name from its position and, as every athlete knows, its vulnerability.

Samuel Taylor Coleridge, *The Friend* (1810): 'Ireland, that vulnerable heel of the British Achilles!'

Acid test – *an absolutely sure way of discovering if something is genuine*

Gold is one of the few precious metals not affected by the majority of acids. It does, however, react with a mixture of hydrochloric and nitric acids which have therefore long been used to test whether a metal is genuine gold. In the Middle Ages this mixture was given the Latin name *Aqua Regia*, meaning 'royal water', because it dissolved the king of metals.

Woodrow Wilson, *The Times* (1918): 'The treatment accorded Russia by her sister nations in the months to come will be the acid test of their good will.'

Across the board – *wide-sweeping, all-encompassing*

The phrase comes from placing a combination wager on a racehorse. Race-tracks, particularly in the USA, display on notice boards the odds for first, second and third places. If you place money on all three options, you make an 'across the board' bet.

R.D. Hopper in *New Sociology*, edited by Irving Lewis Horowitz (1964): 'Job displacement is occurring right across the board.'

Adam's ale – *water*

Water is so called because it was all Adam had to drink in the Garden of Eden. The phrase is thought to have been introduced by the Puritans. Albert J Hyamson refers to a work by William Prynne entitled *Sovereign Power of Parliaments* (1643) to support this theory.

Thomas Brown, *Works* (1760): 'A cup of cold Adam from the next purling brook.'

Add insult to injury – *to follow one personal disaster with another, to wound by word or deed someone who has already suffered an act of violence or injustice*

The source here may be the Aesop's fable in which a bald-headed man suffers the indignity of hitting himself on the head in a vain attempt to swat the fly which has just bitten him.

The fly says: 'You wished to kill me for a mere touch. What will you do to yourself since you have added insult to injury?'

The earliest reference to this precise phraseology in English literature is to be found in *The Foundling* (1748) by Edward Moore.

Adonis – *an exceptionally beautiful young man*

Adonis, in classical mythology, was a Phoenician deity of exceptional beauty adored by Aphrodite, the Greek goddess of love. Despite Aphrodite's warnings that tragedy awaited him, Adonis went hunting and was killed by a boar. The name is thus applied to any handsome young man.

Both John and Leigh Hunt were sent to prison for libelling the Prince Regent, calling him 'a corpulent Adonis of fifty' (*Examiner*, 1831).

In the 18th century the name was adopted for a particular kind of wig.

> She who call'd thee once her pretty one
> And her Adonis, now inquires thy name.
>
> > William Cowper, 'On Female Inconstancy' (1800)

Against the grain – *not by the easiest route; against one's natural inclination*

In common use for over four centuries, the phrase derives from wood-work. It is obviously much easier to work with the grain of the wood than to work against it.

> Your minds,
> Pre-occupied with what you rather must do
> Than what you should, made you against the grain
> To voice him consul.
>
> > Shakespeare, *Coriolanus* (1608)

Albatross around one's neck – *an oppressive liability*

The mariner in Coleridge's 'The Rime of the Ancient Mariner' shot an albatross when his ship became ice-bound.

Because the albatross was regarded as a token of good fortune, the ship's crew hung the bird around the mariner's neck as punishment. Nevertheless a curse fell on the ship and all the crew died.

The albatross fell from the mariner's neck only when he accepted his responsibility for what had happened. He returned home to teach by example reverence for all God's creatures.

Strictly speaking, therefore, the expression refers to the personal guilt that one carries following an inappropriate act, which can be alleviated only by recognising the error of one's ways. However, in modern English, it now refers to any oppressive burden from which it is hard to escape.

Samuel Taylor Coleridge, 'The Rime of the Ancient Mariner' (1798):

And lo! the Albatross proveth a bird of good omen, and followeth the ship as it returned northward through fog and floating ice.

And a good south wind sprung up behind;
The Albatross did follow,
And every day, for food or play,
Came to the mariner's hollo!

In mist or cloud, on mast or shroud,
It perched for vespers nine;
Whiles all the night, through fog-smoke white,
Glimmered the white Moon-shine.

The ancient Mariner inhospitably killeth the pious bird of good omen.

'God save thee, ancient Mariner
From the fiends, that plague thee thus! –
Why look'st thou so?' – With my cross-bow
I shot the ALBATROSS.

Martin Amis, *The Rachel Papers* (1973): 'I am a member of that ever-dwindling minority ... the child of an unbroken home. I have carried this albatross since the age of eleven.'

Alive and kicking – *full of life*

There is no substantiated single source for this expression. It is, of course, often used by a pregnant woman who will say, reassuringly, that she can feel the unborn child, alive and kicking, in her womb.

In William N. Glascock's *Sailors and Saints*, the phrase is used to describe a ship's rolling motion: 'And there she is, all alive and kicking.'

Less likely is the suggestion that it was an idiom used by fishmongers to claim that their fish were so fresh that they were still jumping and flapping about.

All hell broke loose – *pandemonium broke out*

During the 16th century, there were several instances of similar expressions in English literature. In Robert Greene's *Friar Bacon and Friar Bungay* (1594) is found the phrase 'Hell's broken loose'.

The exact words first appear in John Milton, *Paradise Lost* (1667). Gabriel inquires of Satan, 'But wherefore thou alone? Wherefore with thee came not all hell broke loose?'

All mouth and trousers – *over-confident (especially of young men)*

This is a 19th-century expression, from the north of England, which was used to put down pushy, over-confident young men.

'Mouth' refers to a cheeky, sharp kind of insolence and 'trousers' implies a young man's confidence in his sexual prowess, best described perhaps as being cocksure.

In the 20th century, the phrase has been reinterpreted by southern writers as 'all mouth and *no* trousers' in the sense of 'all talk and no action'. In December 1999, Christian Aid unveiled a poster to highlight Third World debt. It depicted European Finance Ministers, their upper bodies normally attired but underpants and bare legs superimposed on their trousers. The caption read: 'All mouth.'

Guardian (2002): 'Bloody men. All mouth and no trousers.'

All my eye and Betty Martin – *a lot of nonsense*

There are several suggestions for the etymology of this phrase. An actress in the 18th century, called Betty Martin, and apparently fond of exclaiming 'My eye!', lived around the same time as the first recorded reference,

S. Crispe, letter in W.H. Hutton, *Burford Papers* (1781): 'Physic, to old, crazy Frames like ours, is all my eye and Betty Martin – (a sea phrase that Admiral Jemm frequently makes use of).'

Alternatively, this may be an English sailor's garbled version of the prayer heard in an Italian church: *Ah mihi, beate Martini*, 'Ah grant me, blessed St Martin'. This is supported by the well-attested practice of Englishmen turning the unfamiliar into something at least superficially recognisable. The Elephant and Castle is believed to have come from the Spanish *Infanta de Castilla*.

Another Betty Martin, a gypsy woman who gave a black eye to a policeman who arrested her, has also been offered as the origin.

Finally, 'all my eye and Betty Martin' may just be rhyming slang for 'fartin''.

Walter de la Mare, *On Edge* (1930): 'You might be suggesting that both shape and scarecrow too were all my eye and Betty Martin.'

All over bar the shouting – *almost completely finished, as good as decided, consider it done*

The phrase is of sporting origin, as for example in boxing, the shouting referring to the cheers for the victor and/or the jeers of those objecting to the result. The meaning is that something is over except for the talking and argument which will not alter the outcome.

The phrase has been known since 1842 in the form 'all over *but* the shouting'.

Groucho Marx in *The Cocoanuts* (1929) says 'all over but the *shooting*', and a Cole Porter song of 1937 has the title 'It's All Over But the Shouting'.

Western Morning News (1976): 'But if the Rhodesia affair is all over bar the shouting, can the same be said about South Africa?'

The Times (1995): 'Fewer than half the trusts had made 3 per cent offers and only half of those were without strings. "He seems to be giving the impression the pay round is all over bar the shouting. He couldn't be more wrong," she said.'

All things to all men – *pandering to the crowd*

In the 21st century, this phrase is employed critically to describe someone lacking personal conviction and with no firm views of his own.

However, St Paul, who originated the phrase, used it in a totally different and more positive sense:

> And unto the Jews I became as a Jew, that I might gain the Jews; to them that are under the law, as under the law, that I might gain them that are under the law;
>
> To them that are without law, as without law, (being not without law to God, but under the law to Christ,) that I might gain them that are without law.
>
> To the weak became I as weak, that I might gain the weak: I am made all things to all men that I might by all means save some.
>
> 1 Corinthians 9:20–22

Also ran – *a loser*

Racing results in newspapers record the first three horses in any race and then list the rest of the field under the title 'also ran'. Originating in Australia, the phrase was in general use from 1918.

P.G. Wodehouse, *The Mating Season* (1949): 'Dobbs ... was more laboured in his movements and to an eye like mine, trained in the watching of point-to-point races, had all the look of an also-ran.'

Ambrosia – *something divinely sweet, food, drink or perfume*

Derived from the Greek adjective meaning immortal, 'ambrosia' is the food or drink of the gods and also the gods' fabled unguent or anointing oil.

John Florio, *Montaigne* (1603): 'It is for Gods to mount winged horses, and to feed on Ambrosia.'

Richard Bradley, *The Family Dictionary* (1725): 'This Juice being well fermented and prepar'd with Clove, Cinnamon &c., would prove an Ambrosia, that would not be esteem'd indifferent, by those who do not care to drink Water.'

Annus mirabilis – *a year of wondrous events*

John Dryden, in his poem 'Annus Mirabilis', refers to the extraordinary events of 1666 when the Great Fire destroyed so much of London, the plague spread so catastrophically and the English won victories over the Dutch. Written in 1667, this poem gave rise to any very special year being called an 'annus mirabilis'.

The Nineteenth Century, a monthly review (1940): 'In 1848, the annus mirabilis of European history, a movement arose which shook the core of Europe.'

On 24 November 1992 in a neat variation of the phrase, Queen Elizabeth II said: '1992 is not a year I shall look back on with undiluted pleasure. In the words of one of my more sympathetic correspondents, it has turned out to be an *annus horribilis.*'

Answer's a lemon! – *an answer that is really no answer*

Thought to be of American origin, the phrase derives from the bitter acidic taste of the lemon. It means something unsatisfactory or not working properly.

One usage in the USA applies to the so-called 'Lemon Laws', statutes that require car manufacturers (not dealers) to remedy defects. Most statutes define 'lemon-ness' in terms of a car that continues to have a defect that substantially impairs its use, value or safety after a reasonable number of attempts to repair it.

Michael Arlen, *Piracy* (1922): '"What would happen if *we* went on strike?" … No-one among them … dreamed of answering. The answer was a lemon.'

Guardian (1963): 'The French nuclear deterrent … is a military lemon of the first order.'

Any Tom, Dick or Harry – *any ordinary person*

In *Henry IV Part 1*, Shakespeare refers to 'Tom, Dick and Francis'. This demonstrates how the three names changed in this expression depending on their popularity at the time. The trio Tom, Dick and Harry did not appear before 1815.

The *Watchtower* booklet, 'Should you believe in the trinity?', on Matthew 28:19: 'Do those verses say that God, Christ, and the holy spirit constitute a Trinitarian Godhead, that the three are equal in substance, power, and eternity? No, they do not, no more than listing three people, such as Tom, Dick, and Harry, means that they are three in one'.

Anyone we know? – *a straightforward request for information; a catchphrase*

As a request for information, for example in the context of someone announcing an engagement, the phrase increasingly acquired humorous overtones: 'She's going to have a baby.' – 'Who's the father – anyone we know?'

These overtones existed as early as the 1930s. In the film *The Gay Divorcee* (US 1934), Ginger Rogers states: 'A man tore my dress off.' A woman asks: 'Anyone we know?'

The Times (1986): 'The moment from which many of us date the genre was when the curtain rose on a production by Harry Kupfer in the late 1970s – I think of a work by Richard Strauss – to reveal a set dominated by a huge phallus, occasioning, from one male in the stalls to his gentleman friend, the loud whisper: "Anyone we know, duckie?"'

Apple of one's eye – *a particular favourite person or thing*

This phrase is a literal translation of a Hebrew expression, and through the immense influence of the Authorised Version of the Bible, it has been popular for centuries: 'He led him about, he instructed him, he kept him as the apple of his eye.' (Deuteronomy 32:10)

There is some doubt about the meaning of the Hebrew word *tappuah*, thought to mean 'apple', but which could equally mean another fruit. It may be that the phrase should be the 'apricot', 'Chinese citron' or 'quince' of one's eye!

The apple of the eye was the pupil and thought to be, like an apple, hard and round, essential to a healthy eye and in need, therefore, of special protection to safeguard sight.

W. Somerset Maugham, *First Person Singular*, 'The Alien Corn' (1931): 'George was the apple of his father's eye. He did not like Harry, his second son, so well.'

Apple-pie bed – *a practical joke in which a bed is made using only one sheet, folded over part way down the bed, thus preventing the would-be occupant from stretching out*

This is either a corruption of the French *nappe pliée*, folded cloth (see **Apple-pie order**), or a reference to apple turnover, which is a folded piece of pastry with an apple filling.

James Woodforde, *Diary of a Country Parson* (1781): 'Had but an indifferent night of Sleep, Mrs Davie and Nancy made me up an Apple Pye Bed last night.'

Apple-pie order – *with everything neatly arranged, in its proper place*

Several suggestions exist. Two folk corruptions are suggested from the French. The idea of the Old French *cap à pied*, meaning clothed in armour from head to foot, is that of an immaculately ordered and fully equipped soldier.

Others suggest that *nappe pliée*, folded linen, is the source, conveying the concept of neatness and tidiness.

In the 19th century, a learned discussion in *Notes and Queries* concluded that 'in apple-pie order' was a corruption of 'in alpha, beta order', i.e. as well ordered as the letters of the Greek alphabet.

Americans have tried to lay claim to the phrase, suggesting that it derives from New England, where housewives made pies of unbelievable neatness. The phrase, however, was current in English long before it was used in the USA.

David Garnett, *The Golden Echo* (1953): 'In the hall, drawing room and dining room everything was always gleaming and solidly in apple-pie order in its right place.'

Arcadian – *innocently pleasurable, usually associated with countryside*

Virgil (1st century BC) in his *Eclogues* chose Arcadia as the setting for his idealised world of shepherds, clear blue skies, love and songs. Arcadia is, in fact, a rather barren mountainous peninsula in southern Greece.

The Arcadia, written in the late 16th century by Sir Philip Sidney, was typical of the English prose style of the time. It led to 'Arcadian' becoming a description rather than a geographical reference.

Oliver Goldsmith, *An Enquiry into the Present State of Polite Learning* (1759): 'The wits even of Rome are united into a rural group of nymphs and swains under the appellation of modern Arcadians.'

Robert Southey, *Oliver Newman* (1829): 'Peopling some Arcadian solitude with human angels.'

Armed to the teeth – *heavily armed*

This means so fully armed that one is even carrying a weapon in one's teeth. It brings to mind a pirate with a cutlass clenched between his teeth.

'To the teeth' means 'completely', and has been in common use for six centuries or more, as in the Middle English metrical romance by an unknown author entitled *Sir Ferumbras* (1380): 'They wern y-armed in-to the teth & araid wel for the fight.'

In more recent times, Richard Cobden used the expression when speaking of the defence budget in 1849. He said: 'Is there any reason why we should be armed to the teeth?'

Arms akimbo – *a defiant stance*

'Arms akimbo' describes a man with his hands on his hips, elbows pointing outwards, and a defiant look on his face.

'Akimbo' is normally used only with the word 'arms'. It may have derived from the Old Norse word meaning 'bent into a bow' or 'curved'. It has been variously written 'in kenbow' or 'a kembo' before its current spelling, which gained currency in the 18th century.

Very recently (e.g. the *Daily Mirror* in July 2002), reference is made to 'legs akimbo', redefining the word as meaning 'apart' or, more strongly, 'flung out widely or haphazardly'.

As sure as eggs is eggs – *absolutely certain*

In logic or mathematics, 'x is x' is an irrefutable proof. 'Eggs is eggs' may have developed as a misunderstanding or a mis-hearing of this logical truth.

Thomas Hughes, *Tom Brown's School Days* (1857): 'I shall come out bottom of the form as sure as eggs is eggs.'

As the actress said to the bishop – *a saying of innuendo*

The innuendo lies in comparing the rectitude of the bishop with the reputation of some actresses for loose living. Indeed, at the beginning of the 20th century, 'actress' was used as a euphemism for 'prostitute'.

Throughout the 20th century, the phrase 'As the ... said to the ...' appeared in music hall acts, and the dots were filled in with appropriate choices of the day.

Innocent phrases are greeted with one version or another, as in: 'It's too stiff for me to manage it (as the actress said to the bishop)'; or 'I can't see what I'm doing (as the bishop said to the actress)'.

As the crow flies – *the shortest distance between two places, the measure of the straight distance between two points*

Although it has since proved false, country people used to believe that crows flew directly to their destination. There was a similar belief, also unfounded, that bees, being single-minded in their work, always flew in a straight line back to the hive. Hence the expression **Make a bee line**.

Charles Dickens, *Oliver Twist* (1838): 'We cut over the fields straight as the crow flies.'

At a loose end – *without anything to do; uncertain what to do next*

The nautical phrase 'at loose ends' referred to an untied rope which was, therefore, not fulfilling its intended job. To 'tie up the loose ends' is to settle the outstanding points of detail of any agreement or transaction.

William H. Mallock, *In an Enchanted Island* (1889): 'Excepting myself he was the only stranger in Cyprus who was thus at a loose end, as it were, and not on some professional duty.'

At one fell swoop –
all at once

'Fell' is an adjective derived from the Old French word *fel* (as in 'felon') meaning savage, cruel or terrible. 'Swoop' refers to a bird of prey suddenly descending on its victim.

The first time the phrase is used in writing is in Shakespeare's *Macbeth*, when Macduff says, on hearing of the murder of his wife and children: 'What! all my pretty chickens and their dam / At one fell swoop?'

The 21st-century expression does not carry this sense of savagery.

At sixes and sevens – *in confusion*

There is much dispute about the origin of this phrase. Some say that it comes from dicing. Nicholas Udall, in *Erasmus' Apophthegmes* (1542) says: 'There is a proverb *Omnem jacere aleam*, to cast all dice, by which is signified to set all on six and seven … assaying the wild chance of fortune, be it good, be it bad.'

If this is correct, the game was probably 'hazard', in which the chance of winning was controlled by a set of rather arbitrary and complicated rules.

The pips on the dice, and later on playing cards, were described from the original French: *ace* for one, *deuce* (two), *trey* (three), *quatre* (four), *cinq* (five), and *sice* (six). To gamble on *cinq* and *sice* was to wager everything on the highest numbers and therefore, in a figurative sense, to act recklessly.

It is thought that as time went by, the origins of the numbers were forgotten. *Cinq* (pronounced 'sink') was thought to be six, and *sice* was thought, therefore, to be seven. The idiom of being 'at sixes and sevens' developed from meaning the reckless act itself to the confusion and disorder which would normally follow such an act.

An alternative theory suggests that the expression arose out of a dispute between two of the great livery companies, the Merchant Taylors and the Skinners, as to which was sixth and seventh in the order of companies in processions in the City of London. In 1494, the mayor, Sir Robert Billesden, judged that they should alternate, year on year 'ever more', thereby condemning them to be for ever 'at sixes and sevens'.

However attractive this explanation may seem, it is unlikely to be the origin, since a reference in Chaucer shows that the phrase was used and understood a century before the dispute between the livery companies was settled:

> Lat not this wretched wo thyne herte gnawe,
> But manly, set the world on six and sevene,
> And if thou deye a martyr, to go to hevene.
> *Troilus and Criseyde* (c. 1385)

At the drop of a hat – *immediately*

Dropping one's hat or holding it above one's head and sharply lowering it was a common signal to start a race or, in early days and particularly on the American frontier, to start a fight. It was a signal which demanded immediate action.

Margery Sharp, *Cluny Brown* (1944): 'Miss Cream's visit coincided with a week of superb weather. At the drop of a hat she stripped and sunbathed – or rather, a hat was the only thing she didn't drop.'

At the eleventh hour – *at the very last moment*

The eleventh hour was the end of the working day in biblical times, corresponding to our 5:00 pm. Time was measured from 6:00 am (or the hour of sunrise) to 6:00 pm. The third hour therefore corresponds to our 9:00 am, the sixth to noon, the ninth to 3:00 pm and the eleventh to 5:00 pm.

The reference is to the Gospel according to St Matthew (20:1–16), where it is said that labourers hired at the end of the day were paid the same as those who had 'borne the burden and the heat of the day'. In this parable, Jesus is saying that God accepts everyone who comes to him on equal terms, whether they have spent a lifetime as a Christian or they accept him at the last possible moment.

Robert Southey, *All for Love* (1829): 'Though at the eleventh hour Thou hast come to serve our Prince of Power.'

At the end of one's tether – *at the limit of one's patience*

A tethered animal's freedom is limited, but it may graze or move within the length of the rope by which it is secured. By the 16th century the image also implied that one was living within one's own financial resources and not going beyond them, as in Hugh Latimer's *Second Sermon before Edward VI* (1549): 'Learne to eat within thy teather.'

The sense of frustration which has been added through modern usage is rarely noted in early references.

Hammond Innes, *The Doomed Oasis* (1960): 'I didn't need the set, withdrawn look of his face, the occasional mumbling of his lips, to tell me that he was mentally very near the end of his tether.'

Aunt Sally – *an object of ridicule, or a target of abuse*

This was a fairground game in which the aim was to knock the pipe from a model of an old woman's head by throwing sticks at it. 'Aunt' was often used to describe old ladies, and 'Sally' is either a pun on 'sally' as in 'attack' or a common name chosen at random.

'Aunt Sally ... this fashionable and athletic sport ... is rather overdone than otherwise', *The Times*, Derby Day (1861).

Axe to grind – *a private interest to serve*

Benjamin Franklin (1706–90) in *The Whistle* relates how, as a young man, he had been flattered into helping someone turn a heavy grindstone. However, all the man wanted to do was to sharpen his axe and, once he had done so, his whole attitude changed towards the young fellow.

The moral is that one should be careful when people try to persuade with smooth talk. They may have another purpose in mind, as in the following from Charles Miner, *Essays from the Desk of Poor Robert the Scribe* (1815): 'When I see a merchant over-polite to his customers, begging them to taste a little brandy and throwing half his goods on the counter – thinks I, that man has an ax to grind.'

B

Back to square one – *back to the beginning*

This is a reference to board games, like snakes and ladders, where certain throws result in the player returning to the start, i.e. the first square.

Some have argued that it refers to the numbered squares in the *Radio Times* between 1927 and c. 1940, which enabled radio commentators to help listeners follow football commentary. Commentators may well have used the phrase 'return to square one', but rather than invent the idiom, it is probable that they merely popularised it.

Doris Archer's Diary, *Selections from Twenty-One Years of The Archers* (1971): 'He's been looking a bit better since he had his holiday in Pembroke, but if he isn't careful all the worry and bother will put him back to square one.'

Back to the wall – *in a desperate situation*

After being chased, when all other means of escape have been eliminated, a man must turn and face his pursuers with his back against whatever impedes his escape (e.g. a wall). In such desperate circumstances, the wall also provides protection from the rear.

An early example is William Stewart's *The Buik of the Croniclis of Scotland* (1535): 'That we may haif thair bakis at the wall, Without defend that ar oure commoun fa.' (That we may have their backs to the wall without defence, those who are our common foe.)

Theodore Dreiser, *The Titan* (1914): 'I'm in a position of a man with his back to the wall. I'm fighting for my life. Naturally, I'm going to fight. But you and I needn't be the worse friends for that. We may become the best of friends yet.'

Badger – *to subject (one who cannot escape from it) to persistent worry or persecution, to pester*

The expression comes from the way the badger is treated rather than the way it behaves. In badger baiting, a dog harasses the captured animal in an attempt to draw it out from its sett.

John G. Wood, *Sketches and Anecdotes of Animal Life* (1855): 'A "brock" [badger] … led such a persecuted life, that to "badger" a man came to be the strongest possible term for irritating, persecuting and injuring him in every way.'

Bag and baggage – *entirely*

This is a military term meaning to march away with all one's equipment. It is sometimes used to express a complete and final departure.

William Gladstone's approach to the Middle East in the 1870s was called his 'bag and baggage' policy. The implication was that the Turks should be completely cleared out of the Balkans.

Charles Spurgeon, *The Treasury of David, Psalm 119* (1870): 'The king sent them packing bag and baggage.'

Baker's dozen – *thirteen*

Dating from 1419, bakers gave thirteen loaves for the price of twelve to dealers and street vendors, allowing them one loaf as commission.

Henry T. Riley, *Liber Albus … of the City of London* (translated 1861): 'These dealers [hucksters] … on purchasing their bread from the bakers were privileged by law to receive thirteen batches for twelve, and this would seem to be the extent of their profits. Hence the expression, still in use, "A baker's dozen".'

Another explanation, but less likely, is that bakers in the 13th century were liable for very heavy fines if they gave short weight. They therefore added another loaf just to be on the safe side. The thirteenth was the 'vantage loaf'.

Balloon goes up –

*the action, the operation,
the excitement, or the
trouble begins*

Observation balloons were
used in the First World War to
identify enemy positions and
movements. The hoisting of these
balloons was therefore often a precursor
to military action.

In the Second World War the phrase was
still being used, as in: 'Suddenly the balloon went up. There were 110's
and 87's all around us, and the 87's started dive-bombing a jetty.' (Hector
Bolitho, *Combat Report*, 1943)

It then became a reference to the start of any action, not necessarily
military, as in:

> Merely because I let you give me a beery kiss in the Props Room,
> you think the balloon's going up.
>
> (John Braine, *Room at the Top*, 1957)

Ballpark figure – *approximate estimate*

The phrase derives from the field in which baseball is played. When a ball
is hit in the ballpark one can judge where it is and how far it has been hit,
but not with any great precision.

Wall Street Journal (1967): 'I gave them a guess of somewhere around
£1.5 billion ... I thought it was a ballpark figure.'

New Yorker (1984): 'How many times per week do you have sexual
relations? On the average – just a ballpark figure.'

Balls to the wall – *going all out for success*

While some suggestions of the origins of this phrase, used mostly in the
USA, have been less than polite, it actually derives from the two handles

on some aeroplanes, one for the accelerator and one for the fuel mixture, which are topped with balls. Naturally some pilots refer to these as 'balls' and when they are instructed to fly full speed ahead, they push them forward to the 'wall' of the cockpit.

The phrase dates to the early 1950s during the Korean War. The earliest written citation is a little later.

Frank Harvey, *Air War* (1966–7): 'You know what happened on that first Doomsday Mission (as the boys call a big balls-to-the-wall raid) against Hanoi oil.'

Ballyhoo – *blarney, bombastic nonsense, extravagant advertisement of any kind, noisy publicity*

This is an early American advertisement for a circus. The owner would stand on a small stage, called a 'bally', outside the main tent, and in stentorian tones announce the key acts about to perform under the Big Top, often with a few short vignettes from the main stars.

The word 'hullabaloo' has similar overtones, arising from a word often used to attract attention, 'halloo'.

Philadelphia Evening Post (1914): 'A live little park full of side show tents … with … barkers spieling before the entrances and all the ballyhoos going at full blast.'

The word is also popularly associated with Ballyhooly, a village in County Cork, Ireland.

Baloney – *nonsense, rubbish*

It is conjectured that this word has its origins in the American colloquial pronunciation of the Italian 'bologna', in which the 'g' is silent, as can be seen from the early English spelling 'bolonia'. It refers to Bologna sausage, filled with varied meats and named after the Italian city where it originated.

Discovery, a monthly popular journal of knowledge (1935): 'He even suggests that much of modern psychiatry is "hooey" and "baloney".'

Bandy words – *argue vigorously*

In Old French, the verb *bander* meant to hit a ball to and fro in an early form of tennis. The word in English became 'bandy', as in John Webster, *The White Devil* (1612): 'That while he had been bandying at tennis.'

By the 17th century the word 'bandy' had become the name for the Irish game of hockey, in which the ball was 'bandied' about. This was the origin of the notion of arguing to and fro. Bandy, a relative of hurling and shinty, has its oldest record in a 13th-century painted glass window in Canterbury Cathedral depicting a boy holding a curved stick in one hand and a ball in the other.

People with bowed legs were described as having 'bandy legs' rather like the hockey sticks used at the time.

Shakespeare, *Romeo and Juliet* (1597): 'The Prince expressly hath forbidden *bandying* in the Verona streets.'

Amelot de la Houssaye, *History of the Government of Venice* (translated 1677): 'When they had bandied Arguments at home, they went to fight their Enemies abroad.'

Bank on – *depend upon*

Until very recently, banks were regarded as the most dependable of institutions. The name arises from the first banks set up in the market squares in medieval Venice. The moneylender sat on a bench (*banco*, bank) and provided loans and change, and displayed currencies from other trading centres.

Dodie Smith, *I Capture the Castle* (1949): "'Don't bank on things too much," I begged. "Simon may not have the faintest idea of proposing.'"

Bark up the wrong tree –
to misdirect efforts, waste energy

This is an American expression arising from hunting raccoons, nocturnal animals, with dogs. On occasion, while hunting at night, the dog would bark at the foot of a tree indicating the location of a raccoon, only for the hunter to find the dog was mistaken.

The first references to this idiom are to be found in James Hall, *Legends of the West* (1832), and in Davy Crockett, *Sketches and Eccentricities* (1833): 'He reminded me of the meanest thing on God's earth, an old coon dog, barking up the wrong tree.'

Barmy – *mad, crazy, stupid*

'Barm' is the froth on top of fermenting malt liquors. The froth looks like insubstantial brains, but the phrase may also refer to the way in which inmates in English prisons used to feign madness by 'putting on the barmy stick', i.e. frothing at the mouth.

There is a popular misconception that the word comes from Barming, near Maidstone, Kent, because the county lunatic asylum was at Barming Heath.

'Ginger, you're barmy!' was a street cry, dating possibly from a song written by Fred Murray (1912). The phrase was either followed by 'Get your hair cut!' or 'Why don't you join the army?', as in:

> Ginger, you're barmy!
> You ought to join the army.
> You'll get knocked out
> By a bottle of stout.
> Ginger, you're barmy!

In David Lodge's novel, *Ginger, You're Barmy* (1984), Mike 'Ginger' Brady and Jonathan Browne meet for the first time on the way to doing their National Service. The story is about how they react when confronted with a loss of freedom and the harsh army regime.

In 1994, rowdy English cricket fans following the national team to Australia for the Ashes tour were affectionately nicknamed the 'Barmy Army', an obvious equivalent of Scotland's Tartan Army of football fans.

Sir Walter Scott, *St Ronan's Well* (1824): 'Cork-headed barmy-brained gowks!' (A 'gowk' is a cuckoo, a fool or a dim-witted person.)

Barrack – *to heckle and shout derisively at someone*

First heard in Australia in the 1880s, the phrase became common usage in the UK at the end of the 19th century, when English cricket teams first visited Australia and found that the home crowds expressed their views more vociferously than their sedate English counterparts. It was rapidly adopted by the cricket correspondents who sent their match reports back home to England.

In Australia, the word originally had two opposed meanings. The first (and probably the earlier) meaning was to jeer or mock at opponents. Hence, A. Lynn-Guist (T.E. Argles), *Pilgrim: A Sensational Weekly Pamphlet* (1878): 'Douglass mumbled over a "petition" … for the edification of assembled roughs and larrikins; but was received with noisy insult and cries of "cheese [stop] your barrickin'" and "shut up".'

This adversarial sense of 'barrack' is now obsolete in Australia. The second sense is 'to cheer, shout encouragement at, give strong support to' (especially a sporting team, a cause, a person, etc.). E.E. Morris in his *Austral English* (1898) explains the transition: 'The sense of jeering is earlier than that of supporting, but jeering at one side is akin to cheering for the other.'

It is popularly said to allude to supporters of the Victoria Barracks army team at South Melbourne cricket ground, who were greeted with shouts of 'Here come the barrackers!' It was also a widespread description in Melbourne of the rough teams that used to play football on the vacant land near the barracks.

Alternatively, the word may derive from the Aboriginal word *borak*, meaning 'chaff' or 'banter'. 'Barrack' may have come from the coster-monger Cockney *barrakin*, *barrikin*, 'gibberish, a jumble of words', influenced by *borak*.

The most probable derivation, perhaps, is from the Northern Irish word 'barrack', which means 'to brag, to be boastful of one's fighting powers' (*The English Dialect Dictionary*).

Pelham Francis Warner, *How we Recovered the Ashes* (1904): 'They will grow up into the type of man who "barracked" Crockett so disgracefully at Sydney.'

Basket case *– unable to cope mentally or emotionally, physically disabled; ruined, no longer functional*

The phrase now has two applications – firstly to describe someone unable to cope mentally or emotionally, or physically disabled, and secondly, a totally ruined enterprise, country or company.

Used in the first sense, the earliest citation is from the *US Official Bulletin* (1919): 'The Surgeon General of the Army … denies … that there is any foundation for the stories that have been circulated … of the existence of "basket cases" in our hospitals.' Another definition is a soldier who has lost all four limbs and presumably requires transport in something like a basket.

To complicate matters, it has also been suggested that the origin of the phrase is British army slang. Although unlikely, there may be a connection between mental disability and the fact that basket-weaving was an activity carried out in British and American mental hospitals of the time, such as the one at Deolali (see also **Doolally**).

The second usage, established about 1973, meaning ruined, no longer functional, sees the sense changed to something useless, fit only to be thrown into a waste-paper basket. It is applied to economic failure in commercial enterprises, and especially to a country that is unable to pay its debts or feed its people.

Saturday Review, US (1967): 'Kwame Nkrumah should not be written off as a political basket case.'

Mario Puzo, *Fools Die* (1978): '"Hunchbacks are not as good as anyone else?" I asked … "No, nor are people with one eye, basket cases … and chickenshit guys."'

Battle-axe – *a belligerent (old) woman*

While the word 'battle-axe', meaning the weapon, has been a part of the English language for six or seven hundred years, its metaphorical use appeared only in the late 19th century.

The choice of this particular weapon to mean a belligerent woman may be the association with the *sagaris*, or double axe, which is an androgynous symbol in matriarchal civilisations. It is not surprising, therefore, that an American women's rights magazine was called *The Battle Ax*.

The *labrys* ('lip'), or double-headed axe, was the central ritual symbol and tool prominent in the Cretan region, and was carried only by women. This same feminine association with the labrys is found in the later Amazonian cultures and in Paleolithic cave paintings.

The labrys is a symbol of the female labia at the entrance of the womb and also of the butterfly, which is connected with rebirth. The labrys was a female-only ceremonial weapon, also used by women in agricultural work and in battle.

George Ade, *Artie* (1896): 'Say, there was a battle-ax if ever you see one. She had a face on her that'd fade flowers.'

Be at large – *to be at liberty, free, without restraint*

This is now normally used of a prisoner who has escaped from custody. It is a strange phrase. In use since the 15th century, it has no basis in the English language. It derives from the French *prendre la large* which means to stand out and be free to move.

It has many now obsolete or rare meanings, for example, in an unsettled or unfixed state, in a general sense, to the open, away, off, in the open sea, over a large surface. It also has a nautical sense, meaning a wind that crosses the line of the ship's course in a favourable direction, especially on the beam or quarter (see also **By and large**).

Reginald Bosworth Smith, *Carthage and the Carthaginians* (1878): 'They felt also that Hannibal was still at large, and it might not be well to drive him to despair.'

Be at loggerheads – *to have a bitter argument*

A loggerhead was a long handled device with a spherical cup at one end which was filled with pitch for heating over a fire. Such implements were used in medieval naval battles, in which hot pitch was thrown at enemy sailors.

Loggerheads was also another name for the game 'loggat', in which a piece of wood was thrown at a stake fixed in the ground and the nearest to the stake won.

G.R. Cutting, *Student Life at Amherst College* (1871): 'The game of "loggerheads" has become obsolete in this part of the country ... A "loggerhead" was a spherical mass of wood, with a long handle, and the game consisted of an attempt to hurl this towards a fixed stake, in such a manner as to leave it as near as possible.'

William P. Frith, *My Autobiography and Reminiscences* (1887): 'The Lord Chancellor ... and the Bishop came to loggerheads in the House of Lords.'

Be on the side of the angels – *to agree with the Great and the Good, the orthodox authorities*

The phrase is from a speech given by Benjamin Disraeli at Oxford in 1864. Addressing the vexed issue of evolution, Disraeli declared himself opposed to the theory that our early ancestors were apes, and maintained that man was descended from God: 'Is man an ape or an angel? I, my lord, am on the side of the angels.'

Sunday Times (1991): 'The war brought its dividends, however. Iran and Syria, the two key players in the hostage saga, who had been regarded as virtual international pariahs for their links with terrorism and had no diplomatic relations with Britain, found themselves back on the side of the angels.'

Bean-feast – *a slap-up dinner*

A bean-feast was an annual dinner given by an employer to his employees, and possibly so called because beans were prominent in the meal.

A bean-feast was also called a 'wayzgoose', meaning 'harvest goose'. This suggests that goose was commonly on the menu, but the claim that 'bean-feast' comes from the traditional eating of the bean goose, so called because of a bean-shaped mark on its beak, is unlikely.

Sporting Magazine (1805): 'At a late bean feast, a Gentleman Taylor, celebrated for his liberality, gave a rich treat to his men, at his occasional country residence. It was called a Bean Feast; but, exclusive of the beans, the table literally groaned with bacon (etc.).'

The same origins are to be found in 'beano' and 'full of beans'. See also **Full of beans**.

Beat around the bush – *to approach a matter in a cautious or roundabout way, fail to meet matters head on*

If a beater does not beat the bushes where the birds are expected to be found, he will have the least possible impact on events.

'One beats the bush – another takes the bird' is a 14th-century saying meaning that the beater does the work but the employer takes the benefit and the profit.

The same sense is found in George Gascoigne, *A Hundreth Sundrie Flowres* (1572): 'He bet about the bush, whyles other caught the birds.'

Beck and call – *someone else's control*

'Beck' is a shortened version of 'beckon', meaning to make a mute signal to call someone. Beckon comes from an old German word from which is derived the English word 'beacon'.

'Beckon' first appears around AD 950 in *The Lindisfarne Gospels*, Luke 1:22: 'He waes becnende them.' (He was beckoning them.) The verb 'to beck' is used in 14th-century English as in Chaucer: 'Spek nat, but with thyn heed thou bekke.' (Speak not, but beckon with your head.)

The word 'call' simply means having the authority to call someone's name and they will do what is asked of them.

The phrase 'beck and call' appears to be widely used by the late 19th century.

Bedlam – *noisy chaos*

The London hospital, the Priory of St Mary of Bethlehem, was originally intended for the poor suffering from any ailment, and for such as might have no other lodging. Hence its name was *Bethlehem* – in Hebrew, the 'house of bread'.

During the 14th century it began to be used partly as an asylum for the insane; there is a report of a Royal Commission in 1405 as to the state of lunatics confined there. The word Bethlehem became shortened to

'Bedlam' in popular speech, and the confinement of lunatics gave rise to the use of this word to mean a house of confusion. In 1675 it was transferred from Bishopsgate to Moorfields, where it became an attraction for paying visitors.

Guardian (1713): 'Our house is a sort of Bedlam, and nothing in order.'

Bee in one's bonnet – *an obsession*

The idea that someone had just one pet subject, just one 'bee' under their bonnet or cap, and therefore on their mind, led to this alliterative phrase.

A scatterbrained or disorganised person was described as having 'his head full of bees', as in Nicholas Udall's *Ralph Roister Doister* (1553): 'Who so hath suche bees as your maister in his head?'

Between the 16th and 20th centuries it also came to mean that someone was very anxious and restless.

A connection between bees and the soul was also once generally accepted. Porphyry (c. AD 232–305) says of fountains: 'They are adapted to the nymphs or those souls which the ancients called bees.'

Bee's knees – *perfection*

This phrase derives from the roaring twenties, when music, dancing, dress, language, all came together in one frenetic combination. Phrases like cat's pyjamas, cat's whiskers and bee's knees – all meaning the same thing – became household phrases through the songs and music of the period. The first known reference is in a flapper's dictionary in Missouri (1922) where it is defined as 'peachy' or 'very nice'.

The phrase has also been explained as being from an Italian-American way of saying 'business'. Alternatively, it has been argued that it means 'Bs and Es', an abbreviation for 'be-alls and end-alls'. Both are without doubt wrong.

Before the 20th century, the phrase meant something small or insignificant, as in G.F. Northall's *Folk-phrases* (1894): 'As big as a bee's knee.'

Before *or* quicker than you can say Jack Robinson –
very quickly, almost immediately, very soon, before you know it

This expression originated in the 1700s, but the identity of Jack Robinson has been lost. 'Faster than you can say Jack Robinson' dates from at least 1778, appearing in Fanny Burney's *Evelina*.

Captain Francis Grose, in the 1785 edition of his *Dictionary of the Vulgar Tongue*, says it comes from 'a very volatile gentleman ... who would call upon his neighbours, and be gone before his name could be announced.' This theory seems improbable.

Another explanation is that Richard Brinsley Sheridan, the playwright, as a Member of Parliament, was making a speech about corruption in the government. He was called upon to name those he was accusing and, looking at Jack Robinson, the secretary of the treasury, said: 'Yes, I could name him as soon as I could say Jack Robinson.'

If the story is true, Sheridan was using the already coined phrase, as he did not become an MP until 1780.

A third explanation is that it comes from a play containing the lines:

A warke it ys as easie to be done
As tys to saye Jacke! robys on.

The play, however, has never been found; only the claim survives.

Finally, there was a very popular song by Thomas Hudson in the early 19th century that told the story of a sailor of that name who returns to find his lady married to another. Given the date, it is obviously not the origin.

In the 19th century 'Jack Robinson', like 'John Thomas', started to be used as slang for penis. This is probably influenced by the earlier, more common sense.

Mme Frances D'Arblay (Fanny Burney), *Evelina* (1778): 'I'd do it as soon as say Jack Robinson.'

Gladys Mitchell, *Laurels are Poison* (1942): 'It'll be all over College before you can say Jack Robinson.'

Beg the question – *to assume something which needs first to be proved; prompt the question*

The phrase 'it begs the question' is now colloquially used to mean 'prompts the question'. It is assumed that 'beg' means 'request', as in 'I beg your pardon' or 'I beg to differ'.

This is not the original sense. To beg the question was to commit a logical fallacy, to take for granted or assume something that as much needed to be proved as the assertion itself.

An example is 'capital punishment is necessary because without it murders would increase'. A closely related idea is that of circular reasoning, of assuming the conclusion as part of the argument, as in 'lying is always wrong because we ought always to tell the truth'.

This logical fallacy was described by Aristotle in 350 BC. The original meaning was lost in translation. His Greek name for it was translated into the Latin as *petitio principii*, and in the 1580s the Latin was translated into English as 'beg the question'. It would be better translated as 'assume something which needs first to be proved'.

Believe that all one's geese were swans – *to over-estimate; to see things in too rosy a light; to look too favourably at one's own offspring or possessions*

In literature, swans are often used as symbols of perfection. This saying probably developed in days when geese were common and used for everyday food, whereas swans were few and beautiful.

Bishop Richard Montagu wrote in 1624: 'With Catholikes every Pismire is a Potentate; as every Goose a Swan.' ('Pismire' means 'ant'.)

Bells and whistles – *all the extras or add-ons*

One suggested origin is the days of silent films, when the accompaniment came from mighty theatre organs which had, over and above the normal keyboards, twenty or more sound effects, called 'toys', including car horns, sirens and bird whistles.

When talkies arrived, the theatre organs were still used but these 'toys' were no longer needed to accompany the events on the screen. So the 'bells and whistles' ceased to be essential to the functioning of the organ.

The phrase is actually quite modern and may be a product of the American military. One of its earliest appearances was in an article in *Atlantic* in October 1982, which said it was 'Pentagon slang for extravagant frills'.

Some have suggested that the phrase relates to early US railroad locomotives which had both bells and whistles, as this extract from an article in *Appleton's Journal* of 1876 shows: 'You look up ... and see ... a train of red-and-yellow railway-cars, drawn by two wood-burning engines, the sound of whose bells and whistles seems like the small diversions of very little children, so diminished are they by the distance.'

Further support for this idea is found in a song by Blind Willie McTell, 'Broke Down Engine Blues No. 2' (1933). The relevant part of the lyric is:

> Feel like a broke-down engine, mama,
> ain't got no whistles or bells.
> Feel like a broke-down engine, baby,
> ain't got no whistles or bells.
> If you're a real hot mama,
> come take away Daddy's weeping spell.

Below the salt – *in a lowly position in society*

On a dinner table, the family 'saler' (salt cellar) was of massive silver, and placed in the middle of the table. It formed the division between, at the top, the important people, and those of lesser status who were at the bottom – 'below the salt'.

Thomas Dekker, *The Honest Whore* (1602): 'Set him beneath the salt and let him not touch a bit, till everyone has had his full cut.'

Best bib and tucker – *one's best clothes*

In the late 17th century, a kind of bib was worn by adults to protect their clothes from spills. A tucker was a woman's garment, a flimsy piece of lace or muslin tucked into the top of low-cut dresses and ending in a lacy frill at the neck.

Some authorities believe that the entire expression was originally used to describe a lady, and with the passage of time and changes in fashion the term came to be applied to men as well.

J. Williams, *Life of Lord Barrymore* (1793): 'The Butcher's Lady thinks that living in style is manifested in putting on her best bib and tucker on holidays.'

Best laid plans of mice and men (go oft astray) – *there is always something to upset the most careful of human calculations*

This is a reference to the poem 'To a Mouse' (1785) by Robert Burns:

The best laid schemes o' mice and men
Gang aft a-gley.

In this poem, Burns reflects on his sadness at disturbing a mouse's carefully constructed home, and muses on the lot of man and animal. Burns' source for this idea is thought to be the Japanese poet and novelist Ihara Saikuku (1642–93).

Of Mice and Men, a novel by the American author John Steinbeck, is about the fragility of people's dreams, as indicated in the title. The end of the novel confirms this pessimistic view. None of the characters achieves his or her dream.

John Steinbeck, *Of Mice and Men* (1939): 'Nobody never gets to heaven and nobody never gets no land.'

Between a rock and a hard place – *without a satisfactory alternative, in difficulty*

The phrase originates in the USA and appears first in *Dialect Notes* (1921): 'To be between a rock and a hard place ... to be bankrupt. Common in Arizona during recent panics; sporadic in California'. It may have some relationship to the story of Odysseus, who had to pass between Scylla (illustrated) and Charybdis, the former a monster on a cliff and the latter a whirlpool. Neither was a particularly attractive option.

CBS News (14 September 2004): 'As [Aron Ralston] scrambled through a narrow crevasse in a canyon, his arm became pinned by an 800-pound boulder. After five days of waiting to be rescued, Ralston decided to use a multi-purpose tool to amputate part of his own arm. ... He recounts the harrowing story in a new book titled *Between a Rock and a Hard Place*.'

Between the devil and the deep blue sea – *having equally unpleasant alternatives*

The first examples of this phrase have the form 'between the devil and the dead sea' and date from the 17th century. Later examples are phrased as 'between the devil and the deep sea', as in Tobias Smollett, *Sir Launcelot Greaves* (1762): 'The conjurer having no subterfuge left, but a great many particular reasons for avoiding an explanation with the justice, like the man between the devil and the deep sea, of two evils chose the least.'

Only in comparatively recent times does the 'deep blue sea' version appear. It is often claimed that the phrase is 17th-century nautical slang. The devil is the seam between the planks on a sailing ship, which were difficult to caulk, to make watertight. To do so, sailors had to hang precariously over the side of the ship, often in a boatswain's chair, 'between the devil and the deep blue sea'.

Dates and sources do not support this, and they have led scholars to believe that this interpretation has arisen from the desire of writers to romanticise sailing-ship days, or to assume that an expression that mentions the sea must refer to sailors.

Between you, me and the gatepost – *in strictest confidence*

Originally, in the days of four-poster beds, the phrase was 'Between you, me and the bedpost'. Whatever kind of post it may be, it has always been a symbol for something lifeless and therefore that could be relied upon not to betray a confidence.

Edward Eggleston, *Hoosier Schoolmaster* (1871): 'A-twix you and me and the gate-post, don't you never believe nothing that Mirandy Means says.'

Beware Greeks bearing gifts – *a warning against trickery*

This phrase is an allusion to the most famous Greek gift of all, the Wooden Horse of Troy. After besieging Troy unsuccessfully for ten years, the Greeks built a large wooden horse as an offering to the gods before returning home.

When it was taken within the walls of Troy, men leapt out from it, opened the gates for their fellow soldiers and destroyed the city.

In the first example found of the phrase in its modern sense, Virgil in the *Aeneid* has Laocöon warn the Trojans not to admit the horse, saying: 'timeo Danaos et dona ferentes', 'I still fear the Greeks even when they offer gifts'.

The phrase now seems generally to appear in humorous variations, notably the reference to Michael Dukakis, the vertically challenged Democratic opponent of George Bush in the 1988 US Presidential election: 'Beware Greeks wearing lifts.' The phrase 'Trojan horse' has entered the language in the field of computers, meaning a 'malicious, security-breaking program that is disguised as something benign'.

Beyond the pale – *completely unacceptable*

A pale (from the Latin *palus*, a stake) came to mean the fence made of wooden stakes enclosing an area of ground. Later it developed to mean an area subject to a particular jurisdiction. The territories of Calais and Dublin were both termed 'The English Pale', over which English jurisdiction was established in the 15th and 16th centuries respectively. It is an easy step to see that someone 'beyond the pale' was outside civilised society and, therefore, unacceptable.

Andrew Boorde, *Introduction to Knowledge* (1547): 'Irlande … is divided in ii partes, one is the Englysh pale & the other, the wyld Irysh.'

Charles Dickens, *The Pickwick Papers* (1837): 'I look upon you, sir, as a man who has placed himself beyond the pale of society, by his most audacious, disgraceful, and abominable public conduct.'

Big cheese – *an important person (usually derogatory)*

It was in America that the phrase gained popularity and where it has the slightly derogatory overtone when referring to the most important person in a company or an organisation.

Sir Henry Yule in *Hobson-Jobson* (1886), the Anglo/Indian dictionary, refers to the Persian or Hindi word *chiz* meaning 'thing'. Expressions such as 'My cheroot is the real chiz' were commonplace.

In England at about the same time, one of the favourite expressions was 'the real thing'. As the English returned from India, the two words were transposed, eventually leading to the English spelling 'cheese'.

John Masters, *The Road Past Mandalay* (1961): '"Where's the manager?" – "The manager?" – "The Bara Sahib. The Big Cheese. The Boss." – "The Brigadier is out."'

Raymond Chandler, *Black Mask* (1964): 'So the big cheese give me the job.'

Bill stickers will be prosecuted – *traditional British warning to anyone about to paste a poster on a wall*

The date of the phrase is unknown. The term 'bill-sticker' was current by 1774, but the earliest evidence found of the warning is in a *Punch* cartoon dated 26 April 1939. The graffito response, 'Bill Stickers is innocent', was current by the 1970s.

Westminster Magazine (1774): 'Bill-stickers, pickpockets and chimney-sweepers.'

Realm (1864): 'With … the progress of civilisation, bill-sticking has expanded into bill-posterism.'

Black hole of Calcutta – *small, very cramped surroundings*

In 1756, Surajah Dowlah, the Nawab of Bengal, attacked and captured Calcutta. He reputedly confined 146 British prisoners, including one woman, in the small prison of the East India Company's Fort William. The prison measured 18 feet by 14 feet 10 inches. Only 22 men and the woman escaped suffocation.

The term 'black hole' was defined as a military punishment cell by C. James in his *Military Dictionary* (1816).

It is used figuratively in literature, as in Thackeray's *Vanity Fair* (1847–8): 'Do you think Miss Pinkerton will come out and order me back to the black hole?'

Black Maria – *a police or prison van*

The origin of this phrase is disputed but it is certainly American. In Boston in the early 1800s, Mariah Lee, a black woman, kept a boarding house with such severity that she became more feared than the police. Her name has been attached to the phrase but it seems an unlikely connection because the first reference to such a vehicle in Boston is dated 1847, rather a long time after her heyday.

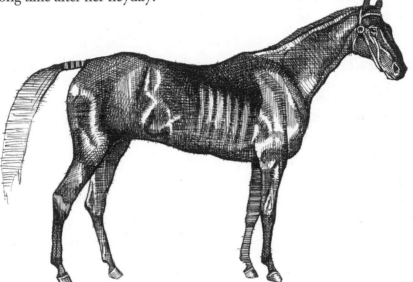

The term appears in the title of a short story, 'The Prison Van; or, The Black Maria', by Joseph Clay Neal in *Peter Ploddy, and Other Oddities* (1844). It refers to its usage in Philadelphia but there is now evidence that it was current in New York as early as 1835.

The chronology suggests that the most likely source is a famous black racehorse called Black Maria. Her best-known exploit was on 13 October 1832 when she won a race for the Jockey Club purse of $600 at the Union Course in New York. Three years later her name is used for a horse-drawn prison van in the same city, no doubt because it took prisoners to their unwanted destination rather more quickly than they would have liked.

Harper's New Monthly Magazine (1870) recounted Black Maria's triumph as follows: 'The track was heavy, and yet to achieve a victory, twenty miles had to be run. We wonder if there is a horse on the turf today that could stand up under such a performance as this.'

Black sheep – *odd one out in a family or group*

The most reasonable explanation is that a black sheep was worth less than a white sheep because its fleece could not be dyed. There have, of course, always been connotations that black was associated with the devil and therefore, if you were the black sheep of the family you were usually regarded as a disgrace.

James Joyce, *Ulysses* (1922): 'He was down and out but, though branded as a black sheep … he meant to reform.'

Blackball – *to exclude someone from a group*

Voting in the Greek and Roman civilisations was often by means of small black and white balls called 'ballots'. To vote for someone or something, a white ball was placed in a closed urn. To vote against, a black one was used. (See also **Spill the beans**.)

Benjamin Disraeli, *Vivian Grey* (1826): 'I shall make a note to blackball him at the Athenaeum.'

Blackguard – *scoundrel*

There is some doubt about the original application of the term 'black guard' which became the word 'blackguard'. The word is found in several contexts.

The 'black guard' were the menial workers in a household, responsible for the pots and pans, and so described because of their unkempt and dirty appearance.

Sir W. Fitzwilliams, *Calendar of State Papers* (1535): 'Two of the ringleaders had been some time of the Black Guard of the Kings kitchen.'

The phrase was also used for a guard of attendants, black in person, dress or character; a following of 'black' villains.

Richard Hakluyt, *The Principall Navigations, Voyages and Discoveries of the English Nation* (1589): 'The Captein now past charge of this brutish blacke gard.'

The phrase was also applied to the linkboys and torchbearers at funerals, and later to the army of vagrant children of great towns, the 'city Arabs' who ran errands and blacked shoes.

In the 16th and 17th centuries the phrase gained wider currency to encompass all forms of low life, as in John Stow, *A Survey of London* (first published in 1598, edited by John Strype in 1704): 'Such who are commonly known by the name of the Black Guard, who too commonly lived upon Pilfering Sugar and Tobacco on the Keys, and afterwards became Pickpockets and House Breakers.'

Blackleg – *someone who flouts strike action*

In the 16th century, a cheat was called a 'rook', reflecting the agricultural society's distaste for rooks and crows, which fed off cornfields.

The rooks had black legs and this seems to have developed into the expression 'blackleg', also meaning a cheat or swindler, particularly in gambling, as in Richard Cumberland, *The Note of Hand* (1774): '"Gentleman of the turf; what sort of gentlemen are they?" – "These fellows are gamblers, black-legs, sharpers."'

The word came to describe those breaking a strike, thereby cheating on their colleagues and friends.

Blacklist – *list of unacceptable people*

The phrase 'black list' first appears in the 17th century, as in Philip Massinger, *The Unnaturall Combat* (1639): 'The black liste of those / That have nor fire nor spirit of their own.'

When Charles II came to the throne in 1660, he drew up a list of all those who had conspired against his father, Charles I, executing thirteen and imprisoning many more. This was recorded in Joseph Washington, *A Defence of the People of England by John Milton* (1692): 'If ever Charles his Posterity recover the Crown … you are like to be put in the Black List.'

Today, the phrase usually refers to a list of people who are not acceptable members of a club.

Blaze a trail – *to pioneer*

Stripping a piece of bark off a tree to indicate a trail produced a white mark similar to that on the face of a horse, which is known as a 'blaze'.

John Henry, *An Account of Arnold's Campaign against Quebec* (1812): 'A path tolerably distinct which we made more so by blazing the trees.'

Blighty – *England*

This is a contraction of the Hindi word *bilayati* meaning foreign or far away. Soldiers in the First World War adopted the word and gave it their own specific meaning of 'England' or 'home'. They popularised it in language and song, as in: 'Take me back to dear old Blighty, put me on the train for London town.'

Patrick MacGill, *The Great Push* (1917): 'I'll send out the money and fags when I go back to blighty.'

Blot on the landscape – *anything that spoils a view; objectionable*

Both literally and figuratively, the phrase has been in use since the early 20th century. T.E. Lawrence used it in a 1912 letter: 'His two Kufti people … will be a blot on the landscape.'

It was also the title of a Tom Sharpe novel (1975) in which Blott is a character.

P.G. Wodehouse, *Jeeves in the Offing* (1960): '"And a rousing toodle-oo to you, you young blot on the landscape," she replied cordially.'

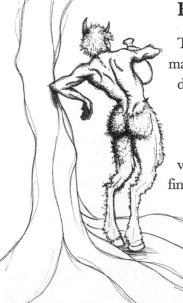

Blow hot and cold – *to vacillate*

The origin of the phrase is Aesop's fable about the man and the satyr. Satyrs were woodland gods or demons, in form partly human and partly bestial, companions to Bacchus, Greek god of wine.

The man and the satyr drank together in token of a bond of alliance being formed between them. One very cold wintry day, as they talked, the man put his fingers to his mouth and blew on them. When the satyr asked the reason for this, he told him that he did it to warm his hands because they were so cold.

Later on in the day they sat down to eat, and the food prepared was quite scalding. The man raised one of the dishes a little towards his mouth and blew in it. When the satyr again inquired the reason, he said that he did it to cool the meat, which was too hot.

The satyr said that he could no longer consider the man his friend. 'Says the satyr, "If you have gotten a trick of blowing hot and cold out of the same mouth, I've e'en done with ye."' (Sir Roger L'Estrange, *Fables*, 1694)

Blow the gaff – *to give away a secret or confidence*

Originally, 'gaff' was 'gab' which derived from gabble – meaning to talk too much and even indiscreetly. Gab may also be related to 'gob', slang for mouth. From this comes the idea of 'blowing' the mouth, letting out too much air, i.e. talking too much.

Frederick Marryat, *Peter Simple* (1833): 'I wasn't going to blow the gaff, so I told him, as a great secret, that we got the gun up with a kite.'

Blow to smithereens – *to shatter into tiny pieces*

Having an Irish diminutive ending, 'smithereens' is a borrowing from the Gaelic, *smidirin*, fragment, and means tiny pieces.

Daily Mail (1991): 'In *Lethal Weapon 3* ... Riggs and Murtaugh, Glover's character, have been demoted to walking the beat but that's still not enough to prevent the city from being blown to smithereens again.'

Blue blooded – *aristocratic*

'Blue blood' derives from Castilian families who claimed pure ancestry untarnished by Moorish ancestors. This is a direct translation from the Spanish (*sangre azul*), and probably refers to the blueness of their veins, which stood out so clearly against their paler skins compared with their hairier and darker Moorish compatriots.

Maria Edgeworth, *Helen* (1834): 'One (officer) ... from Spain, of high rank and birth, of the *sangre azul*, the blue blood.'

Blue Ribbon – *the highest distinction, the pick of the bunch*

The most desired Order of Knighthood in Britain is the blue ribbon of the Garter. Conferred only by the Sovereign, it was constituted by King Edward III in 1348. It is said that, while dancing, the King's partner dropped her garter. To the amusement of courtiers, he picked up the garter and put it around his own leg, saying 'Honi soit qui mal y pense' (shame on him who thinks this evil), which became the motto of the Order. Others say that the motto refers to his territorial designs on France.

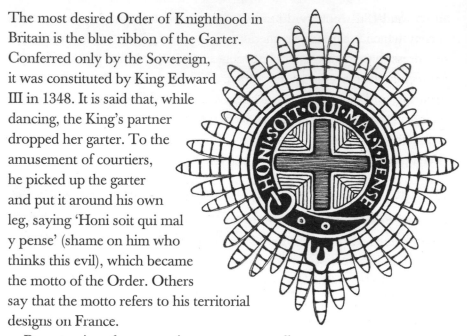

By extension, the expression connotes excellence.

There is an interesting parallel case in French. Honours conferred on knights of the Order of the Holy Spirit (L'Ordre du Saint Esprit) were also suspended by a blue ribbon. The phrase *cordon bleu*, blue ribbon, has come to denote excellence in cuisine.

'The Blue Ribbon of the Turf', for instance, is the Derby. It was coined in 1870 by Lord Beaconsfield (Benjamin Disraeli) in his biography of Lord George Bentinck in the quotation below.

'Lord George had given up racing to become leader of the Conservative party, and was defeated in Parliament a few days before the horse Surplice, which he had sold, won the coveted prize. The two events troubled him greatly.

'It was in vain to offer solace', says Disraeli. 'He gave a stifled groan. "All my life I have been trying for this, and for what have I sacrificed it? You do not know what the Derby is," he moaned out. "Yes I do; it is the Blue Ribbon of the Turf."

'"It *is* the Blue Ribbon of the Turf," he slowly repeated, and sitting down at a table he buried himself in a folio of statistics.'

Blue stocking – *intelligent woman – even pretentiously so*

In the mid-18th century, Elizabeth Montagu founded a London literary society which included as a member Benjamin Stillingfleet, who wore his day-dress blue stockings as he could not afford the black silk ones appropriate for evening wear. But his contributions to the debate were inspiring, and when he was unable to attend, Boswell commented that the members were lost 'without blue stockings'.

It is thought that Admiral Boscawan, whose wife hosted many of these evenings, dubbed the society 'The Blue Stocking Society'. Both women and men were members, but 'blue stocking' attached itself to women because they both organised the events and talked about subjects which, in the society of the day, women should not discuss.

William Hazlitt, *Table-talk; or Original Essays on Men and Manners* (1822): 'I have an utter aversion to *blue-stockings*. I do not care a fig for any woman who knows even what *an author* means.'

Blue-chip – *reliable, giving the highest return*

This phrase comes from the coloured counters used to represent money when playing games like poker. The blue chip has the highest value, and a blue-chip investment is one that promises to be the most lucrative.

National Association of Pension Funds, 'EC Bulletin' (1991): 'The group still has a blue-chip client list, however, and serves more than 300 of the Fortune 500 companies.'

Blurb – *promotional literature, particularly publishing literature on the dust jacket or cover of a book*

In 1907, Gelett Burgess, an American humorist, invented Miss Blinda Blurb – a parody of the archetypal woman featured in contemporary novels. The word caught on almost immediately.

Burgess, in *Burgess Unabridged* (1914), defined the word as follows: '1. A flamboyant advertisement; an inspired testimonial. 2. Fulsome praise; a sound like a publisher.'

'On the "jacket" of the "latest" fiction, we find the blurb; abounding in agile adjectives and adverbs, attesting that this book is the "sensation of the year".'

Bob's your uncle – *everything will be easy once you have done this*

A.J. Balfour was promoted in 1887 by his uncle, the Prime Minister, Lord (Robert) Salisbury, to be Chief Secretary for Ireland. Balfour had previously been made President of the Local Government Board in 1886, then Secretary of State for Scotland with a seat in the Cabinet. These promotions were viewed as nepotism. Hence the thought that everything would be all right if Bob was your uncle!

However, the phrase is not recorded until 1937 in Eric Partridge, *Dictionary of Slang and Unconventional English*. He suggested that the phrase had been in use since the 1890s, but nobody has found an example in print. It is also surprising that there is no contemporary reference to the phrase in any satirical magazine of the day.

It is more likely that it derives from 'all is bob', meaning that everything is safe, pleasant or satisfactory. This phrase is to be found as early as the 17th century, and is defined in Captain Francis Grose, *Dictionary of the Vulgar Tongue* (1785).

There have been several other slang expressions containing 'bob', some associated with thievery or gambling, and from the 18th century it was also a common generic name for someone you did not know. Any or all of these might have contributed to its genesis.

Boffin – *scientific expert; an intellectual*

A nickname used by the RAF in the Second World War for a research scientist, or one of the 'backroom boys'. It passed into general use in the 1940s. Its origin is unknown.

One theory derives it from the practice of a certain scientist to give his colleagues Dickensian nicknames, Mr Boffin being a character in *Our Mutual Friend*. Mr Boffin inherited his wealth from a dust contractor and became known as the 'Golden Dustman'. Another claim is that this is connected with early police fingerprint experts who brushed dust onto surfaces and who became known as 'boffins'.

There is also a family of Hobbits called Boffins. J.R.R. Tolkien wrote *The Hobbit* in 1937, contemporaneously with, or very shortly before, the word becoming common currency.

Bog-standard – *ordinary, basic, of average quality*

The suggestion that this is an acronym for 'British or German', referring to manufacturing standards set by these two countries in Victorian times, is unlikely to be true.

The most obvious link is with 'bog', the long-established slang term for a lavatory. It has a negative sense, as might be expected from anything that is linked to excretory functions.

A more convincing suggestion is that it is a corruption of 'box-standard', for something that is just as it was when it came out of the box, with no customisation or improvement.

Sir Clive Sinclair, *Computerworld* (1983): 'We cannot foresee the day when a computer becomes just a standard box. There will be box-standard machines along the road, but we do not simply have to make those.'

Bold as brass – *very bold, self-confident, fearless*

It has been recorded that the phrase refers to a London magistrate in the late 1770s called Brass Crosby (1725–93). It was illegal at that time to publish proceedings in Parliament, and one London printer who had done so was brought before Crosby's court. Crosby, reflecting public opinion, dismissed the case and was as a result himself arrested for treason.

There was a public outcry and Brass was released from prison as something of a hero. His brave stand against authority led to the term 'as bold as brass'.

George Parker, *Life's Painter* (1789): 'He died damn'd hard and as bold as brass. An expression commonly used among the vulgar after returning from an execution.'

Boot is on the other foot – *there has been a reversal of circumstances or opinion*

Up to the end of the 18th century, shoes were made to be worn on either foot. There were no 'right' and 'left' shoes. If one shoe pinched, the wearer would try the other foot.

Daily Express (1992): 'A few years ago Speelman – then ranked number five in the world – caused something of an upset when he beat number three ranked Short. This time the boot was on the other foot. "We all suspected that Nigel hadn't developed the degree of ruthlessness he needed to beat a friend," says Black. "Now he obviously has."'

Born on the wrong side of the blanket – *illegitimate*

The allusion may be to the consequences of hurried moments of illicit pleasure on the top of the blankets, whereas legitimate children would have been conceived in more leisure and with due propriety underneath them.

Alternatively, it might refer to the shame of illegitimate births that forced mothers to have their children in secrecy outside the marriage bed rather than in the comfort of it.

Sir Walter Scott, *Guy Mannering* (1815): '"Frank Kennedy," he said, "was a gentleman, though on the wrong side of the blanket."'

Bottle – *courage*

In the 19th and 20th centuries 'no bottle' meant 'no good', as in W.F. Brown, *Police Journal* (1931): 'When he got up the steps, he had a mouthpiece who was no bottle.'

The modern sense may simply refer to courage which comes out of a bottle (as in **Dutch courage**) and, as time went by, its meaning broadened to include genuine courage.

It may, however, be rhyming slang, as in 'bottle and glass', meaning 'arse'. To lose one's bottle is therefore to lose control of one's bowel movements through sheer fright.

Tony Park, *The Plough Boy* (1965): 'Spirits, guts, courage … it's the worst that could be said about you, that you'd lost your bottle'.

Other definitions, including references to the bottle held by a second in a boxing ring, have also been proposed.

Brand (spanking) new – *completely new*

This was originally a reference to the 'fire brand' and comes from the blacksmith's trade, meaning pieces of metal which were just out of the furnace. Shakespeare uses 'fire-new' in the same sense.

In 17th-century English, 'spanking' means something which was exceptionally good or fine, as in Sir Richard Fanshawe's *To Love Only for Love's Sake* (1666): 'What a spanking Labradora!'

The combined expression was first used in the mid-1800s and was defined in *Dialect Notes* (1905) as follows: 'Bran spankin' new … absolutely new.'

Break a leg – *good luck*

Many in the theatre believe that to wish someone good luck would bring about the opposite. It belongs with such other beliefs that it is bad luck to whistle in a theatre, that you should never say the final line of a play at a dress rehearsal, and that you must never say the name of 'the Scottish Play' (i.e. *Macbeth*) in the green room.

It is argued that the reference is to the actor John Wilkes Booth, who assassinated President Abraham Lincoln before leaping on to the stage at Ford's Theatre, breaking his leg in the process.

Another suggestion is that the old style of bowing, known as bending the knee, may have led to the thought that 'breaking a leg' was to bow a lot after a hugely successful performance.

However, these explanations may be discarded on the grounds of chronology. They assume that 'break a leg' is an old expression, whereas it has existed only since the 1930s.

Similar phrases appear in other languages, as in the German 'Hals und Beinbruch' (meaning 'neck and leg break') which is a way of wishing someone good luck without any fear of supernatural retaliation. It is sometimes said that the German expression is actually a corruption of the Hebrew 'hatzlacha u-brakha', meaning 'success and blessing'.

Whatever its source, the most plausible theory is that 'Hals und Beinbruch' was transferred, perhaps via Yiddish, into the American theatre (in which Yiddish- or German-speaking immigrant Jews were strongly represented) some time after the First World War. The English phrase 'break a leg' may therefore find its origin in Germany via America.

Break the mould – *to destroy utterly;* [current usage] *to create something completely new*

This is one of those curious and fascinating examples of a phrase that has come to be used in a sense opposite to the original meaning. (See also **Cheap at half the price**.)

It is, in its original sense, a destructive phrase, as in the days of the Luddites, when breaking the mould from which iron machinery was cast was intended to prevent the machinery from ever being produced again. The mould being completely destroyed, the machinery would have to be re-cast from scratch.

This was not the sense intended by the Social Democratic Party, established in 1981, when there was much talk of it 'breaking the mould of British politics', i.e. doing away with the traditional system of a government and one chief opposition party. The sense here was not of destroying the mould to return to the previous status quo. It was of creating something new, casting a new mould.

This is much more the sense of the phrase used by Andrew Marvell in his 'Horatian Ode Upon Cromwell's Return from Ireland' (1650):

> And cast the kingdoms old
> Into another mould.

A.J.P. Taylor, *English History 1914–1945* (1965): 'Lloyd George needed a new crisis to break the mould of political and economic habit.'

Roy Jenkins, leader of the Social Democratic Party, 8 June 1980: 'The politics of the left and centre of this country are frozen in an out-of-date mould which is bad for the political and economic health of Britain and increasingly inhibiting for those who live within the mould. Can it be broken?'

Bring home the bacon – *to succeed*

For hundreds of years, a pig was the sought-after prize at country fairs because the pig represented the only meat that many families ever ate.

The phrase probably refers to winning a competition such as bowling for a pig or catching the greased pig.

It may refer to the Dunmow Flitch, a custom instituted in 1111 by Juga, a noble lady. Anyone going to Dunmow in Essex and humbly kneeling on two sharp stones at the church door might claim a flitch (side) of bacon if they could swear that for the previous year and a day they had neither quarrelled nor wished themselves unmarried!

When Jack Johnson, the American boxer, won the World Heavyweight boxing championship in 1910, his mother exclaimed: 'He said he'd bring home the bacon, and the honey boy has gone and done it.'

Philip Larkin, *Jill* (1946): 'The College takes a number of fellows like him to keep up the tone ... but they look to us to bring home t' bacon.'

Broken reed – *unreliable support*

Isaiah 36:6 provides the key to this: 'Thou trustest in the staff of this broken reed, on Egypt: whereon, if a man leans, it will go into his hand and pierce it: so is Pharaoh King of Egypt to all that trust him.'

Iris Murdoch, *A Severed Head* (1961): 'A nervous shrinking which was not exactly dislike made me hesitate to probe the motives of such a being. Therewith some vague yet powerful train of thought led me to say, "I am a broken reed, after all."'

Bucket-shops – *shops where you can buy cheap tickets*

The Chicago Board of Trade in 1882 prohibited the sale of grain in less than 5,000 bushels. As reported in the *Leeds Mercury* (1886), a number of illegal brokerage houses were established to serve men of small means.

The 'Open Board of Trade' commenced business in an alley under the regular Board of Trade rooms. There was an elevator to carry the members of the board to their rooms, and occasionally a member, if trade was slack, would call out 'I'll send down and get a bucketful pretty soon', referring to the speculators in the 'Open Board of Trade' below.

The term bucket-shop was widened in the 20th century to include any retailer of cut-price goods aiming to undercut the market by working outside the official system, especially one selling cheap airline tickets.

Daily Telegraph (1982): 'The meeting will seek … co-ordinated airline action to stamp out bucket shop sales of tickets.'

Buggins' turn – *appointment by rotation rather than merit*

Admiral Fisher, in 1901, was the first to record this expression, in A.J. Marder, *Fear God and Dread Nought*: 'Favouritism was the secret of our efficiency in the old days … Going by seniority saves so much trouble. "Buggins's turn" has been our ruin and will be disastrous hereafter!'

Whether he invented it or it was already well established in Civil Service tradition is unknown.

Bulldog breed – *the British*

The bulldog originated in Britain. Its disposition is equable and kind, resolute and courageous (not aggressive or vicious) and its demeanour is pacific and dignified. Winston Churchill first made reference to the bulldog at the outbreak of the First World War in a 'Call to Arms' meeting at the London Opera House.

During the Second World War he came to symbolise the bulldog breed. Small model bulldogs were manufactured bearing Churchill's facial pout and wearing a tin helmet.

Manchester Guardian (1914): 'Mr Churchill has made a speech of tremendous voltage and carrying power. His comparison of the British navy to a bulldog – "the nose of the bulldog has been turned backwards so that he can breathe without letting go" – will live. At the moment of delivery, with extraordinary appositeness, it was particularly vivid, as the speaker was able by some histrionic gift to suggest the bulldog as he spoke.'

Charles Kingsley in *Two Years Ago* (1857) wrote of: 'The original British bulldog breed, which, once stroked against the hair, shows his teeth at you for ever afterwards.'

Felix McGlennon, 'Sons of the Sea' (1897): 'Sons of the Sea! All British born! / ... boys of the bulldog breed / Who made old England's name.'

George Orwell, 'Inside the Whale' (1940): 'The typical English boasting, the ... "bulldog breed" ... style of talk.'

Burn the candle at both ends – *to work, or play, from early in the morning long into the night*

The expression dates from pre-electricity times, when candles were an important consumable commodity in every household. The image refers to the candle itself, consumed too quickly because both ends are burning.

Excessive consumption is the key to this expression. Randle Cotgrave (1611) translated into English the French expression 'brusler la chandelle par lex deux bouts'. In modern French, in which the metaphor still thrives, 'brusler' has become 'brûler' and 'lex' is now the familiar plural article 'les'.

'Burn' can still mean 'to consume rapidly, squander', as in 'he has money to burn'. The double-sided quality inherent in the phrase 'burn the candle at both ends' led to the use of the expression when both husband and wife were spendthrifts.

This sense of the expression was not confined to household finances. The mismanagement of a railway line was described in a 19th-century American railway journal: 'They had been "burning the candle at both ends", and instead of holding in reserve a portion of their easily acquired earnings, they had been spending money with a lavish hand.'

There is a logical extension from using up one's financial resources to using up one's physical and mental resources.

Detroit News (2000): 'Our students are ... trying to burn the candle at both ends, they're not only studying, but most of them are working several jobs.'

Finally, the connotation of avid consumption of life's pleasures is exemplified in the poem 'First Fig' by Edna St Vincent Millay (1920):

My candle burns at both ends;
It will not last the night;
But ah, my foes, and oh, my friends –
It gives a lovely light!

Bury the hatchet – *to make peace*

When North American Indians smoked their pipe of peace they would, literally, bury their weapons of war.

Buried was the bloody hatchet,
Buried was the dreadful war-club,
Buried were all war-like weapons,
And the war-cry was forgotten.
There was peace among the nations.
Henry Wadsworth Longfellow,
The Song of Hiawatha (1855)

Iris Murdoch, *Under the Net* (1954): 'It is possible to break the ice without burying the hatchet.'

Busman's holiday – *doing on holiday what you do for a living; a holiday in name only*

This is believed to be a reference to the drivers of horse-drawn buses, who when they went on holiday, travelled with their horses to keep them company, or who could not go on holiday because they had to check on the well-being of their horses.

A typical story appeared in John Ciardi, *A Browser's Dictionary* (1980): 'British drivers of horse-drawn omnibuses, becoming attached to their teams, were uneasy about turning them over to relief drivers who might abuse them. On their days off, therefore, the drivers regularly went to the stables to see that the horses were properly harnessed, and returned at night to see that they had not been abused.'

Other writers are justly scornful of these stories. The horses on London buses in the 19th century were no better cared for than any working nags.

They were often sweated to death. Anna Sewell's descriptions in *Black Beauty* (1877) were not exaggerations.

The mundane truth is that a popular recreational activity among working-class Londoners in the late 19th century was an excursion by bus. A bus driver who went on such a trip was said to be taking a busman's holiday. The term is first recorded in *The English Illustrated Magazine* (1893).

Observer (1927): 'The USA Secretary for War … said … "No, I did not go to see the military manoeuvres. Busmen's holidays do not give me any delight."'

By and large – *broadly speaking, without entering into details, on the whole*

The phrase is a nautical one from the days of sail. Sailing 'by' means to steer a ship very close to the wind. The ship cannot sail directly into the wind, but by adopting a course 45 degrees into the wind it can make progress by 'tacking' at 90 degrees to and fro across the wind direction. Sailing 'large' means that the wind is on the quarter, that is to say, blowing across the boat or to the stern, giving a more constant course. The helmsman would use the technique of sailing by and large during changing winds and difficult conditions. The ship's course would thus be set generally in the right direction but it would not be particularly accurate.

Large ships were assessed on their ability to sail 'by and large'. In its nautical sense the phrase was current by 1669 and in wider use by the turn of the following century.

Samuel Sturmy, *The Mariner's Magazine, or Sturmy's Mathematical and Practical Arts* (1669): 'Thus you see the ship steered in fair weather and foul, by and large.'

The Times (1955): 'The virtue of sound broadcasting was that, by and large, the content mattered more than anything else.'

By hook or by crook – *by any means possible, special or extraordinary, fair or foul*

The origin of the phrase is obscure, although it has often been said that it referred to the billhook, a chopper with a hook on the end, and a shepherd's crook, used for catching sheep. An old manorial custom authorised tenants to take as much firewood as could be reached down by the crook and cut down by the billhook.

Sadly, chronology does not bear this out. Examples of the phrase appear as early as the 14th century, which would pre-date the establishment of such a manorial custom.

John Wycliffe, *Selected Works* (1383): 'Thei sillen sacramentis ... and compellen men to bie alle this with hok or with crok.' (They sell the sacraments and compel men to buy all this by hook or by crook.)

John Gower refers to false witness and perjury in *Confessio Amantis* (1390): 'What with hepe and what with croke they make her master oft winne.' (By hook and by crook they make their master often win.)

By Jingo – *an exclamation of surprise*

A mild oath, it was colloquially used from around 1694 as an exclamation but in 1670, and probably much earlier, it was a piece of conjurer's gibberish, used like 'abracadabra'.

The word comes probably from the Basque word *J(a)inko*, meaning God, which was introduced by Basque harpooners on British whalers.

Oliver Goldsmith, *The Vicar of Wakefield* (1766): 'One of them ... expressed her sentiments ... in a very coarse manner when she observed, that by the living jingo she was all of a muck of a sweat.'

'We don't want to fight but, by jingo, if we do / We've got the ships, we've got the men, we've got the money too', went the music-hall song during the Baltic crisis of 1877–8. This led to the word 'jingoism' to refer to aggressive patriotism.

By Jove – *an exclamation of surprise*

'By Jove' is a mild oath, referring to the Roman god Jupiter, who in Old Latin was termed 'Jovis'; this, in the classical period, was substituted with the compound 'Juppiter' or 'Jupiter' (= *Jovis-pater*).

Shakespeare, *Love's Labours Lost* (1588): 'By Ioue [Jove], I always took three threes for nine.'

'By Jove – I needed that!' was a late 1960s/early 1970s catchphrase used by the Liverpool comedian Ken Dodd. It is readily adaptable, but is most applicable perhaps to alcoholic refreshment.

By the seat of one's pants – *doing something without planning, by instinct*

Pilots, before the sophisticated technology of today's aircraft, judged the progress of the flight by 'feel'. The largest part of their bodies in touch with the plane from which to get that 'feel' was, naturally, the seat of their pants. The phrase was first used about 1930, perhaps earlier.

Robert Sheckley, *The Game of X* (1966): 'Flying *was* in fact extremely difficult, but ... I was just one of those seat-of-the-pants naturals who instinctively do everything right.'

By the skin of one's teeth – *surviving a very close run thing*

'My bone cleaveth to my skin and to my flesh and I am escaped with the skin of my teeth.' (Job 19:20) Job meant that he had lost everything *except* the skin of his teeth. But this misquotation has continued down the ages.

The Nation (1893): 'His eldest son was implicated in the robbery ... and came off by the skin of his teeth.'

C

Cack-handed – *left handed; clumsy, awkward, inept*

Cacare (Latin) means to defecate and is the source of two Old English words, 'cack' meaning dung and 'cachus' meaning privy. As with many ancient cultures, the right hand was used for eating and the left for cleaning oneself after defecating.

Notes and Queries VIII (1859): 'If a man, at hay time or harvest, holds his fork with his left hand lowest, they say "Ah! he's no good! He's keck-handed!"'

Call a spade a spade – *to be blunt, straightforward*

An oddity of this phrase is that it is a mistranslation. The original was an ancient Greek proverb, 'To call a fig a fig, a trough a trough'. This appears in Aristophanes' play *The Clouds* (423 BC), and the Greek writer Plutarch also used it.

Plutarch's word was *skaphe*, a hollow object, meaning variously a trough, basin, bowl or boat. When he translated Plutarch into Latin, the medieval scholar Erasmus misread it as *skapheion*, the Greek word for a digging tool. Nicholas Udall copied him when making his 1542 English version, *Erasmus' Apophthegmes*: 'Philippus answered, that the Macedonians wer feloes of no fine witte in their terms but altogether grosse, clubbyshe and rusticall, as they whiche had not the witte to call a spade by any other name then a spade.'

The phrase has remained in the language ever since, as in Jonathan Swift, *Polite Conversation* (1731–8): 'I am old Tell-Truth; I love to call a Spade, a Spade.'

The phrase is avoided in the USA because of sensitivity to associations with a racial slur. However, the slang phrase 'spade' for an African-American comes from the spades suit of cards ('as black as the ace of spades') and derives from the Italian for a sword, not the digging tool.

Call one's bluff – *to challenge someone to prove his or her claims*

The phrase originates in the USA. A poker player 'bluffs' his opponents by claiming he has a better hand than in fact he does. To 'call' such a bluff means that the player has to reveal his hand.

The Times (1898): 'The policy of the Russian Foreign Office … has been a series of prodigious bluffs. Some of these Lord Salisbury has seen fit to "call"; others he has refrained from "calling".'

Carry the can – *to take responsibility*

In the late 19th century, this phrase was a naval expression meaning to be reprimanded, perhaps influenced by 'carry the keg', a pun on 'carry the cag' meaning to be vexed, sullen or low (*Lexicon Balatronicum*, 1811).

Perhaps romantically, it is suggested that the modern military origins lie in the custom of the rawest recruit carrying the can of beer for the rest of his section.

Others suggest that it may have involved 'carrying the can back' to the Quartermaster's stores.

The original RAF form, later common to all the services and current about 1920–45, is 'carry the can back', which meant to be made a scapegoat, to do the dirty work while another gets the credit, to accept the blame for one's own or another's error, or to be landed with (usually unwanted) responsibility for an unpleasant task.

Hector Bolitho in *The English Digest* (1941) noted 'the can-back king', one who was very good at it. Since about 1945, the phrase has reverted to the shorter original form, 'carry the can', but it retains all the senses listed above.

Evening Standard (1959): 'He has enough political *nous* not to wish to carry the can for … Aneurin Bevan.'

Carte blanche – *absolute freedom to act*

The French for 'blank paper', the phrase was first used, in this sense, in the 18th century to mean that the individual could write his own terms on a blank sheet of paper with only a signature on it, knowing that they will be accepted. Joseph Addison, *Spectator* (1712): 'I threw her a Charte Blanche, as our News Papers call it, desiring her to write upon it her own Terms.'

The expression is of military origin, referring to unconditional surrender, as in Lord Raby (1707) in Thomas Hearne, *Remarks and Collections* (1886): 'Who sent Chart Blanch to make a Peace.'

Since the 18th century it is used only in the figurative sense, as in *London Society* (1879): 'Our good easy vicar gave me carte blanche to use this organ.'

Cast aspersions – *to defame someone, spread stories*

Aspergere (Latin), to sprinkle, is the root of the English verb 'asperse' and noun 'aspersion'.

The notion of 'aspersion', sprinkling (usually water), is often used in a form of Christian baptism.

Bishop Gilbert Burnet, *An Exposition of the Thirty-nine Articles of the Church of England* (1699): 'Aspersion may answer the true end of Baptism.'

During the 17th century it was figuratively used to mean that someone was sprinkling the neighbourhood with damaging allegations, as in George Herbert, 'Charms and Knots' (1633):

Who by aspersions throw a stone
At the head of others, hit their own.

It was in Henry Fielding, *Tom Jones* (1749), that the expression was used for the first time in its full modern sense: 'I defy all the world to cast a just aspersion on my character.'

Cat has nine lives – *a cat has a seemingly endless capacity to escape danger or death*

A proverbial saying by 1546, it refers to the cat's well known capacity for getting out of scrapes, literally 'landing on its feet' in most cases.

The reason for nine, rather than any other number, originates from ancient Egypt, where cats were venerated for ridding the country of a plague of rats. They were linked to the trinity of Mother, Father and Son. To calculate how many extra lives the cat had, the Egyptians multiplied the sacred number three, three times and arrived at nine.

Shakespeare, *Romeo and Juliet* (1592):

> TYBALT: What wouldst thou have with me?
> MERCUTIO: Good king of cats, nothing but one of your nine lives; that I mean to make bold withal, and as you shall use me hereafter, drybeat the rest of the eight. Will you pluck your sword out of his pitcher by the ears? make haste, lest mine be about your ears ere it be out.

Catch red-handed – *to catch while committing an illegal act*

There are some early, now obsolete, Scottish legal expressions, 'red-hand' and 'with red hand', as in Sir George Mackenzie, *Criminal Law* (1678): 'If he be not taken red-hand the sheriff cannot proceed against him.'

This term was adapted to 'red-handed' by Sir Walter Scott in 'The Lay of the Last Minstrel' (1805), and it also appears in *Ivanhoe* (1819): 'I did but tie one fellow, who was taken red-handed and in the fact, to the horns of a wild stag.'

For an example in its literal sense, to catch a criminal even before the victim's blood could be washed from the culprit's hands, see Mabel Peacock, 'Academy' (1885):

> When Abel in thine arms lay dead,
> And Cain red-handed turned and fled.

The phrase in law has, however, long been applied to any crime, not exclusively murder, as in Earl Dunmore, *Pamirs* (1893): 'A notorious thief was caught red-handed in the act of breaking open a lock.'

Catch-22 – *two mutually exclusive conditions, a no-win situation*

In 1961, Joseph Heller's comic novel, *Catch-22*, introduced this phrase, meaning deadlock because the conditions for decision were mutually exclusive. From Chapter V: 'There was only one catch and that was Catch-22, which specified that a concern for one's own safety in the face of dangers that were real and immediate was the process of a rational mind. Orr was crazy and could be grounded. All he had to do was ask; and as soon as he did, he would no longer be crazy and would have to fly more missions. Orr would be crazy to fly more missions and sane if he didn't, but if he was sane he had to fly them. If he flew them he was crazy and didn't have to; but if he didn't want to he was sane and had to.'

An example of the phrase in general usage appears in the Sumter (South Carolina) *Daily Item* (1974): 'His Public Interest Group now finds itself in a Catch-22 situation. It cannot prove the device works without EPA funds, but EPA won't grant the funds unless they prove the device works.'

Chalk and cheese – *two completely different people or things*

John Gower in *Confessio Amantis* (1390) writes: 'Lo, how they [the Church] feignen chalk for chese', meaning that the Church preaches one course of action and practises another.

To the modern mind, cheese is a slab of bright yellow cheddar. To understand the strength of this idiom, one should think of cheese as fresh, white, young cheese, which in appearance is similar to freshly gathered chalk, but quite different in all other essential respects.

Samuel Rowlands, *The Letting of Humours Blood in the Head-vaine* (1600): 'Tom is no more like thee, than Chalks like Cheese.'

Chance one's arm – *to take a risk*

A military expression for breaking regulations which, if he were caught, could cost the offender his NCO stripes; these were, of course, worn on his arm.

Daily News (1899): '… to "chance your arm" means to risk a court-martial which has the power to take all the pretty pretties off a man's sleeve. I first heard the phrase in 1886.'

Later, it is used figuratively, as in the *Economist* (1959): 'Mr Macmillan may have no more by-elections in this Parliament by which to judge when to chance his arm.'

Charity begins at home – *love begins with one's nearest and dearest*

Charity has two distinct meanings. The first, from the Latin *caritas*, means love. The second, and more common modern definition, means the giving (primarily but not exclusively of money) to good causes. This saying uses the word in its original sense.

A biblical counterpart is from 1 Timothy 5:4: 'But if any woman have children or nephews, let them learn first to show piety at home.'

Robert Southey, *English Eclogues* (1798): 'But charity begins at home, / And, Nat, there's our own home in such a way / This morning!'

Che sera sera – *what will be, will be*

In English, the phrase can be found as far back as Chaucer but this foreign version is a curious mixture of languages. There is no such phrase in modern Spanish or Italian, although *che* is a word in Italian and *sera* in Spanish.

It is in fact an Old French or Old Italian spelling of what would be in modern Italian *che sara sara*. This is the form in which the Duke of Bedford's motto has always been written.

Doris Day had a hit song in 1956 with 'Che sera sera, Whatever Will Be Will Be', and in 1966, Geno Washington and the Ram Jam Band had a hit with 'Que sera sera'.

Geoffrey Chaucer, 'The Knight's Tale' (c. 1390): 'When a thyng is shapen, it shal be.'

J.W. von Goethe, *Faust* (John Anster's translation, 1835), 1.1: 'What doctrine call ye this, *Che sara, sara!*'

Victor Hugo, *The Man Who Laughs* (1869): 'In the centre, on the three stages of benches, each lord had taken his seat. … The dukes mustered strong … All were in order, according to right of precedence … Wrottesley Russell, Duke of Bedford, whose motto and device was *che sara sara*, which expresses a determination to take things as they come …'

Cheap at half the price – *very inexpensive, a bargain*

This is a confusing phrase which, when analysed, seems to mean the opposite of very inexpensive, the sense in which it is used. If something is cheap at *half* the price, it implies that it is not cheap at all.

It is in fact a play on the word 'cheap'. The phrase does not refer to money but to the quality of goods offered. Therefore something of very low quality would still be expensive even if it were half the price. The origin is thought to be a deliberate and humorous inversion of an old street trader's cry, 'Cheap at *twice* the price'.

An explanation for the confusion may be that once the phrase moved away from its London street-trader roots, it became less easy to understand.

Nineteenth-century money lenders were regarded as 'cheap' because of their job and the usurious rates they charged. They would still have been regarded as 'cheap' even if they had halved their interest rates.

Cheesed off – *fed up and bored; disgusted, disgruntled*

The original phrase, 'browned off', a reference to metal work that has gone rusty, was used in the regular army from about 1915 and was adopted by the RAF about 1929.

William Simpson, *One of our Pilots is Safe* (1942): 'Most of our time was spent moping about the aerodrome getting thoroughly "browned-off", and hoping against hope for some real action.'

'Cheesed off' probably also has an RAF provenance, and developed because cheese often goes brown when cooked.

Equally, it could refer to cheese going bad and becoming sour and unpalatable.

John Hunt and Alan Pringle, *Service Slang* (1943): '*Cheesed off*, more than *brassed off*, but not entirely *browned off*.'

Chew the fat – *to gossip, chat, pass the time in idle conversation, especially complainingly*

Some literal-minded stories have been invented to explain the origin of this phrase, from American Indians or Inuit in the north of Canada chewing hides in their spare time to soften them, to Elizabethan farmers in Britain hanging haunches of smoked pork by the hearth so that family and visitors could sit around talking and slicing off slivers of meat.

The evidence suggests that it might have originally come from the Indian Army, meaning a kind of generalised grumbling to stave off boredom. J. Brunlees Patterson, *Life in the Ranks of the British Army in India, and on board a Troopship* (1885) refers to 'chew the fat' in this context and to another phrase, 'chew the rag', which is synonymous.

Punch (1916): 'I got me woes … / An' she's got 'ers, the good Lord knows, / Although she never chews the fat.'

Chinese fire drill – *incompetent execution of a plan, a state or example of utter confusion*

In the early 20th century, when a British ship with a Chinese crew was on a fire drill, water had to be collected from starboard and taken down to the imaginary fire in the engine room, then pumped out and thrown over the port side. After initially going according to plan, hands were soon collecting water from starboard, running across the deck and throwing the unused water directly over the port side!

The phrase was first used in the military in the Second World War. Several expressions in common use in aviation since the First World War, such as 'Chinese landing', a clumsy landing, and 'Chinese ace', an inept pilot, derive from the English phrase 'one wing low', thought to resemble the Chinese language or a Chinese name.

The use of 'Chinese' to mean 'clumsy; inferior' may stem from these phrases, although there were earlier isolated examples which were based on ideas of the inferiority of the Chinese. Whatever the origin of the phrase, and whichever meaning is intended, it is now regarded as offensive to Chinese people, and should be avoided.

The other, rather specific, sense of the phrase is an American high-school or college prank where a group of students jump out of a car at a red traffic light, run around the car, and pile back in before the light turns green.

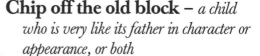

Chip off the old block – *a child who is very like its father in character or appearance, or both*

The reference here is to a chip hacked from the same wood as the block, as the child is the same stock as the parent. The metaphor is age-old: Theocritus in 270 BC preferred 'a chip off the old flint', which hints that one variant or other of the phrase might go back to the Stone Age.

John Milton used one English form in 1642: 'How well dost thou appear to be a chip off the old block?'

Edmund Burke commented on the occasion of the first speech in parliament of William Pitt the Younger (illustrated) on 26 February 1781, that he was 'not merely a chip off the old block, but the old block itself'. Pitt was the son of William Pitt the Elder, Earl of Chatham, and just 21 years old when he entered parliament. In 1783 he became the youngest Prime Minister on record, at the tender age of 24. As Prime Minister he is remembered for his tough policies against corruption, his fiscal reforms, the shifting of power towards the House of Commons and the union with Ireland.

Daily Express (1992): 'The West End's Eve Club, owned by Romanian émigré Helen O'Brien, (had) … its heyday in the pre-free love Fifties and early Sixties. Errol Flynn dropped by with his son, Sean, then aged 14. He was, Helen recalls, "a real chip off the old block. He disappeared and we found him in dressing room Number 2 ogling the girls."'

Chip on one's shoulder *a display of defiance or ill-humour; an unforgotten grievance; a sense of inferiority characterised by a quickness to take offence*

In the USA and Canada people looking for a fight would carry a block of wood on the shoulder and invite people to knock it off, signifying that they were ready for a fight.

Long Island Telegraph (1830): 'When two churlish boys were determined to fight, a chip would be placed on the shoulder of one, and the other demanded to knock it off at his peril.'

J. Cannan, *People to be Found* (1956): 'I got him the sack – months ago but all this time he's been carrying a chip on his shoulder.'

Chock-full; chock-a-block – *filled so as to leave no vacant space, crammed full to bursting, full to suffocation*

'Chock' is probably an old form of choke, referring to something so full that the throat is choked up. 'Choke-full' appears to be rather the more frequent spelling in literary use in England, but 'chock-full' is almost universal in spoken use.

Anon., *Le Morte Arthur* (?1400): 'Charottes chokkefulle charegyde with gold.' (Carts laden chock-full with gold.)

Chock-a-block is, however, a nautical expression, used to describe how two blocks of tackle cannot move because they are so close together – not unlike choking.

W. Somerset Maugham, *Then and Now* (1946): 'The city's two or three inns were chock-a-block and men were sleeping three, four and five in a bed.'

Chopping and changing – *constantly changing one's mind*

A 15th-century, repetitive expression where 'chop' (from Old English *ceapian*) means barter and 'change' means to exchange one thing for another. The two verbs, therefore, have roughly the same meaning and the repetition adds emphasis. Frederick Marryat, *Jacob Faithful* (1835): 'At last we were all arranged … although there were several chops and changes about, until the order of precedence could be correctly observed.'

Thomas Hood, 'To Kitchener' (1845): 'Like Fortune, full of chops and changes.'

Clapped out – *exhausted*

It has been claimed that the phrase refers to the hare. When being chased, a hare will stop, gather its breath and sit on its hind legs. Its front legs appear to 'clap' as they rise and fall in time with its laboured breathing. A hare which can run no more is said to be 'clapped out'.

It was also an RAF term from about 1942 and at first, especially in the Far East, applied to aircraft which were worn out and unserviceable. After the Second World War, it was applied derivatively, especially among racing drivers, to car engines. By the 1970s it was in widespread use, as in 'a clapped out old banger'.

It was used to refer to people, meaning exhausted or no longer effective, and especially among teenagers since about 1955, as noted by Michael Gilderdale in *A Glossary of Our Times* (1958). 'Clapped' was a variant of 'clapped out', as in I. Jefferies, *It Wasn't Me!* (1961): 'Bertie's cracking up … he's sort of clapped.'

In stark contrast to the rather romantic notion of the hare, the RAF term probably had to do originally with someone sexually incapacitated by '(the) clap' (gonorrhoea), and therefore useless.

Clean bill of health – *doctor's advice that there are no medical problems*

A ship's captain, on leaving a port which had a poor record for infection, would be granted a 'clean bill' stating that there was no infection at the port or on the ship and therefore, on presenting this clean bill at the next port, he would be free to dock.

John Evelyn, *Memoirs* (1644): 'Having procur'd a bill of health (without which there is no admission at any towne in Italy) we embarq'd on the 12th.'

Cleanliness is next to godliness – *cleanness and reverence for God are closely linked*

This proverb is said by some to have come from ancient Hebrew writings, in the work of the rabbi Phinehas ben Yair.

However, its first appearance in English, though in slightly altered form, is in the writings of Francis Bacon. In his *Advancement of Learning* (1605) he wrote: 'Cleanness of body was ever deemed to proceed from a due reverence to God.'

The saying was quoted by John Wesley in a sermon, 'On Dress' (1788): 'Slovenliness is no part of religion. Cleanliness is indeed next to godliness.'

Climb on the bandwagon – *to support a plan or cause for personal profit or advantage*

Political candidates in the USA, particularly in the south, would ride a huge horse-drawn wagon and their arrival would be heralded by a band playing on board.

Supporters would join the candidate, but only some were genuinely loyal; others were looking for some reward should the candidate be elected.

Although the practice is long-standing, the idiom itself is first recorded about the Presidential campaign of William Jennings Bryan early last century.

New York Evening Post (1906): 'Many of those Democrats ... who rushed into the Bryan band-wagon ... will now be seen crawling out over the tailboard.'

Close your eyes and think of England – *advice to succumb to unwanted sexual intercourse; to put up with any unpleasant action*

Although the document has never been found, the phrase is generally ascribed to the *Journal* of Lady Hillingdon (1912): 'I am happy now that Charles calls on my bedchamber less frequently than of old. As it is I now endure but two calls a week and when I hear his steps outside my door I lie down on my bed, close my eyes, open my legs and think of England.'

Some have suggested that the sense is to close one's eyes and think of the *future* of England, i.e. breeding good stock for the sake of the country.

Salome Dear, Not With a Porcupine, edited by Arthur Marshall (1982), states that the newly-wed Mrs Stanley Baldwin was supposed to have declared subsequently: 'I shut my eyes tight and thought of the Empire.'

In 1977, there was a play by John Chapman and Anthony Marriott at the Apollo Theatre, London, with the title *Shut Your Eyes and Think of England.*

Sometimes the phrase occurs in the form 'lie back and think of England', but this probably comes from confusion with the phrase 'she should lie back and enjoy it'.

Daily Mail (1991): 'It is bizarre to call a television programme *Think of England*, for that phrase is invariably preceded by "Close your eyes and ..." which really won't do for so visual a medium. And in any case, it denotes having to engage in something unpleasant.'

Cloud-cuckoo-land – *impossible, impractical plan*

This is the English translation of the Greek *Nephelokokkygia*, the city in the clouds between Athens and the heavens, devised by two Athenians who were fed up with city life and who feature in Aristophanes' satirical play *The Birds* (414 BC). Actually their endeavour proved quite successful and the current meaning has developed through misuse.

Economist (1964): 'They weigh their evidence and give their judgment in what seems ... a cloud-cuckooland.'

Cock a snook – *to show defiance, contempt or opposition*

The phrase describes 'snooks', the disdainful gesture of putting the end of the thumb of one hand on the tip of the nose and spreading out the fingers. The origin of the gesture is unknown. Today the expression can be applied to any show of contempt and need not be accompanied by the gesture.

The Times (1980): 'East German craft last spring embarked upon a new ploy ... to net a Danish torpedo ... cocking a snook at NATO's Baltic muscle.'

Cock and bull story – *far fetched story, a tale devised to serve as an excuse, a canard*

In the days of long journeys by stagecoach, passengers would exchange stories en route and at staging posts while the horses were being fed.

The 'Cock and Bull' inn sign is found in the 17th century, and both 'Cock' and 'Bull' as separate signs were always popular.

At Stony Stratford, Buckinghamshire, the pub called the 'Cock' was the staging post for the London-bound coach and the coach from Manchester stopped nearby at the 'Bull'. The travellers met and told probably rather exaggerated stories of their travelling adventures and this, it is said, gave rise to the expression.

The phrase possibly also derives from old fables in which cocks and bulls conversed, as in Richard Bentley, 'Boyle Lecture' (1692): 'That cocks and bulls might discourse and hinds and panthers hold conferences about religion.'

The 'hind and panther' allusion is to John Dryden, 'The Hind and the Panther' (1687), and 'cocks and bulls' probably had a familiar meaning at the time.

The final words in Laurence Sterne, *Tristram Shandy* (1759–67) are:

> 'L–d! said my mother, what is all this story about? – A Cock and a Bull, said Yorick – And one of the best of its kind, I ever heard.'

Cock-a-hoop – *in high spirits usually after success; jubilant, exultant*

A phrase of doubtful origin, obscured by subsequent attempts to analyse it; the following are suggestions.

The expression may derive from the phrase 'to set the cock a hoop', meaning to live luxuriously, from literally putting the bird on a hoop or full measure of grain.

Equally, the word could come from the tavern, where drinkers would put the 'cock' (i.e. the tap or spigot) on the 'hoop' (i.e. the top) of the barrel, so nothing would inhibit the flow of the beer.

> Your eyes, lips, breasts are so provoking
> They set my heart so cock-a-hoop
> Than could whole seas of crayfish soup.
> John Gay, Poems (1720)

Charles Greville, *Memoirs of George IV* (1834): 'The Tories have been mighty cock-a-hoop.'

Codswallop – *nonsense*

The word is of uncertain origin but the following story is sometimes offered to account for it. In 1875, Hiram Codd (who was British despite his American first name, working in Camberwell) developed a new mineral water bottle which had a glass 'marble' as a stopper. As beer was known as 'wallop', so 'codswallop' became the disparaging name for non-alcoholic drinks, and in due course, gained a more general application.

Comparisons have also been made between the two synonymous phrases, 'a load of (old) codswallop' and 'a load of (old) cobblers', both meaning a lot of utter nonsense, i.e. 'balls'. The testicular parallel of 'cods' and 'balls' may be accidental. However, codswallop is also written as 'cod's wallops', where 'cod' means 'scrotum' and 'wallops' suggests 'bollocks'. This produces a tautology in which the repetition serves to reinforce the idea of utter (double) nonsense.

Allan Prior, *The Operators* (1966): 'All that stuff about mutual respect between police and criminal was a load of codswallop.'

Cold enough to freeze the balls off a brass monkey –
extremely cold

Many definitions have been put forward for this saying, suggesting that a monkey was a pyramid of cannon balls on deck, or a young boy on look-out at the top of a mast. However, there is no real evidence that these, and similar nautical definitions, are well founded.

Its earliest recorded reference is in 1929, well past the age of sail, and the earliest written form is 'cold enough to freeze the tail of a brass monkey'.

Even when weather was involved, it was often heat rather than cold that was meant, as in the oldest example known, from Herman Melville, *Omoo* (1847): 'It was so excessively hot ... that labor in the sun was out of the question. To use a hyperbolical phrase of Shorty's, "it was 'ot enough to melt the nose h'off a brass monkey."'

The images of sculpted groups of three wise monkeys – hear no evil, see no evil, speak no evil – were common throughout the 19th century, although the term 'three wise monkeys' is not recorded before the 1920s. It is more likely that the phrase came from them, as an image of something solid and inert that could be affected only by extremes.

Cold feet – *a state of fear or apprehension, so nervous one thinks about withdrawing*

In the early 17th century, Ben Jonson in *Volpone* refers to 'having cold feet', but in the context it means very poor, probably from not having shoes to wear. It is unknown how the phrase developed into today's meaning.

During the First World War, some have said, 'cold feet' referred to trench fever, but the term did not have widespread currency. There is no evidence that fear of 'going over the top' might have been the origin of the phrase.

In an 1862 novel by Fritz Reuter, a card player backs out of a game on the grounds that his feet are cold. One can imagine that he was fearful of losing all, and his cold feet were as good an excuse as he could think of to help him get out of the game.

Ian Hay, *The First Hundred Thousand* (1915): 'It seems that the enemy have evacuated Fosse Alley again. Nobody quite knows why: a sudden attack of cold feet probably.'

Cold shoulder – *a show of indifference; an intentional snub or slight*

In the early 19th century Sir Walter Scott used this expression in two of his novels, *The Antiquary* (1816) and *St Ronan's Well* (1824), as in the following: 'I must tip him the cold shoulder or he will be pestering me eternally.'

Its origins suggest that it refers to that dismissive movement of the shoulder to indicate rejection.

Similar references are found in the works of the Brontës, Dickens, Trollope and Galsworthy, and suggest that Scott either invented or popularised a little known idiom.

'Cold shoulder of mutton' was also a mid-Victorian variant of cold shoulder, giving rise to the idea that the phrase refers to cold food offered to a guest who has outstayed his welcome.

Cold turkey – *reaction to stopping certain drugs suddenly, particularly heroin*

During heroin withdrawal, the skin of an addict goes white and is covered with goose bumps like a plucked, uncooked turkey.

'If you've ever seen a smack-head handcuffed to a bed gibbering uncontrollably because he can't get a fix, then be afraid, because that's what you'll look like after two weeks of internet-free cold turkey.'

That, at least, is according to an 'Internet Deprivation Study' carried out by Yahoo! and advertising outfit OMD. Participants in the human experiment were deprived of the web for fourteen days, and found themselves quickly succumbing to 'withdrawal and feelings of loss, frustration and disconnectedness'.

Cold-blooded – *calculating and calm, unemotional, pitiless*

The ancient theory of the four humours included the qualities of hot and cold, dry and wet. The two humours associated with cold were phlegm and black bile. The characteristics of the phlegmatic temperament were calmness and lack of emotion, and of the melancholic temperament (from black bile), despondency and irritability.

The two humours associated with hot were blood and yellow bile, producing sanguine and choleric temperaments respectively. A sanguine temperament was courageous and hopeful, a choleric temperament easily angered.

It was generally believed therefore that hot-blooded people act rashly while the cold-blooded act coolly and calmly. The French 'sang-froid' has the same derivation.

In animals, cold-bloodedness distinguishes fish and reptiles from other animals and humans. In being applied to humans, the word is used to describe someone whose circulation is slow, and therefore figuratively, without emotion, cool, unfeeling and even deliberately cruel. An action in cold blood is done with deliberation, without the heat of passion. Something done excitedly or rashly is said to be hot-blooded.

Bishop William Stubbs, *The Constitutional History of England* (1875): 'As king we find him [Henry IV] suspicious, cold-blooded and politic.'

Edward A. Freeman, *The History of the Norman Conquest* (1868): 'The taking away of human life in cold blood.'

Come a cropper – *to fall or fail*

This phrase is derived from **Neck and crop**, 'crop' being another word for a horse's throat, and it describes a situation where the rider falls forward from the saddle, desperately clinging to the horse's neck and crop.

An example of its figurative use is Anthony Trollope, *The Way We Live Now* (1874): 'He would "be coming a cropper rather", were he to marry Melmotte's daughter for her money, and then find that she'd got none.'

Come Hell or high water – *come what may*

Attempts have been made to trace this phrase back to punishments meted out to witches in the Middle Ages. Miscreants were obliged to stand in boiling water, the depth of which was directly proportional to the crime. This supposedly gave rise to the phrase: 'From Hell and high water, may the good Lord deliver us.'

A similar saying, the so-called Thieves' Litany – 'from Hull, Hell and Halifax, good Lord deliver us' – has also been suggested as the origin. The phrase was known by 1653, because the gibbet was much used in these places in the 16th and 17th centuries.

Examples of 'come Hell or high water' have not been found, however, before the 20th century. One suggestion is that it comes from driving cattle. P.I. Wellman, *The Trampling Herd* (1939): '"In spite of hell and high water" ... is a legacy of the cattle trail when the cowboys drove their horn-spiked masses of longhorns through high water at every river and continuous hell between.'

Sunday Times (1962): 'A superb instinct for working with the camera guided her to rough out a public image which, come hell or high water, she was not going to change.'

Cook someone's goose – *to ruin someone's plans or chances of success*

The origin of this phrase is probably similar to that of **Kill the goose which lays the golden eggs**, in which the aspirations of the greedy peasants are frustrated.

However, there is a story which attributes it to King Eric XIV of Sweden, whose reign began in 1560. According to an old chronicle:

> 'The Kynge of Swedland coming to a towne of his enemyes with very little company, his enemyes to slyghte his forces, did hang out a goose for him to shoote, but perceiving before nyghte that these fewe soldiers had invaded and sette their chief houlds on fire, they demanded of him what his intent was, to whom he replyed, "To cook your goose!"'

No copy remains of the old chronicle to support this story as the origin. Furthermore, the expression does not seem to have been current before the middle of the 19th century, when a street ballad objected to the attempts of Pope Pius IX to revive the influence of the Catholic Church in England by the appointment of Cardinal Wiseman:

> If they come here we'll cook the goose
> The Pope and Cardinal Wiseman.

Daphne du Maurier, *Rebecca* (1938): 'They say Max de Winter murdered his first wife. I always did think there was something peculiar about him. I warned that fool of a girl she was making a mistake, but she wouldn't listen to me. Well, she's cooked her goose now all right.'

Cost an arm and a leg – *to be outrageously expensive*

This probably arises out of the phrase 'to give one's right arm for' (i.e. to want something so much that you would give up your most treasured possession).

Interestingly, the first reference to this phrase is in Billie Holiday's autobiography *Lady Sings the Blues* (1956), which suggests that she either made it up or popularised a little known expression. Similar earlier phrases were 'cost a bomb' or 'cost a packet'.

Cotton on – *suddenly to understand something, to catch on*

'To cotton' something, usually a fabric, is to raise the pile and generally improve its appearance. By the early 16th century, 'cotton' had the additional meaning of 'improve' or 'succeed'. Over the subsequent two centuries it included 'work well with someone' and 'to strike up a friendship'.

Clement Walker, *The History of Independency* (1660): '[The Parliament] and their Masters of the Army could not cotton together.'

An example of its modern usage is Nevil Shute, *Landfall* (1940): '"How long have they been doing this?" – "God knows. We've only just cottoned on to it."'

The noun, cotton, is a 13th-century English word derived from the French *coton* and the Arabic *qutun*.

Couldn't run a whelk-stall – *incompetent*

This phrase appears to have originated with John Barnes, the Labour MP: 'From whom am I to take my marching orders? From men who fancy they are Admiral Crichtons ... but who have not got sufficient brains and ability to run a whelk-stall?' (*South-Western Star*, 1894)

The phrases 'couldn't organise a piss-up in a brewery' and 'couldn't fight his way out of a paper bag' are modern equivalents.

Financial Times (1981): 'None of them [the 364 economists] has had enough practical experience to run the proverbial whelk-stall.'

Criss-cross – *a series of intersecting lines*

Originally, 'Christ's-cross', or sometimes 'Christ's cross row', was a term for the alphabet.

In the 18th century, the alphabet was preceded by a sign of the cross and children were therefore encouraged to learn their 'Christ's cross row', or their ABC.

SIR RALPH: I wonder, wench, how I thy name might know.
MALL: Why you may find it, sir, in th' Christcross row.
Henry Porter, *The Pleasant History of the Two*
Angry Women of Abington (1599)

The origins in time fell away and criss-cross, like zigzag and others, was thought to be a duplication (i.e. to cross and cross again). This may also be why, since 1935, a criss-cross has also been used to mean a crossword puzzle.

Crocodile tears – *a show of false sorrow*

The legend is that crocodiles weep, make moaning noises and sob to lure passers-by to the river bank before attacking them.

There is in fact sound evidence that crocodiles have large tear ducts which cause bubbles when the air gets into them and the animal is under water.

As the mournful crocodile
With sorrow snares relenting passengers.
Shakespeare, *Henry IV Part II* (1590)

An example of the figurative use is George Augustus Sala, *The Strange Adventures of Captain Dangerous* (1863): 'Saying with crocodile tears, that he was not the first to have an undutiful son.'

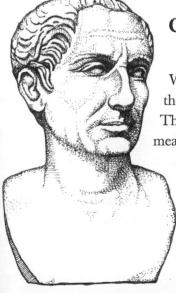

Cross the Rubicon – *to make an irrevocable decision*

When Julius Caesar crossed the stream named the Rubicon in 49 BC there was no turning back. The decision to cross from Cisalpine Gaul into Italy meant that he had revealed his intentions to invade Italy and attack the forces under Pompey's leadership.

Charlotte Brontë, *Jane Eyre* (1847): 'A pause – in which I began to steady the palsy of my nerves, and to feel that the rubicon was passed.'

Christopher Ogden, *Life of the Party* (1994): "'I've been to Paris with Fulke Warwick." – "Talk about crossing the Rubicon." Crossing the Rubicon was deb talk for going all the way.'

See also **Die is cast**.

Cuckoo in the nest – *a misfit or parasite*

The cuckoo uses the nests of other birds to bring up its young, by eating one of the eggs in the nest, leaving an egg of its own and then migrating. The nestling cuckoo, which hatches earlier than other birds, destroys all the other eggs in the nest and is fostered and fed until it is large enough to fly away.

Oliver Wendell Holmes, *The Poet at the Breakfast Table* (1872): 'We Americans are all cuckoos – we make our homes in the nests of other birds.'

The derivation of 'cuckoo' is the Old French *cucu*, from which 'cuckold' is also derived.

Curate's egg – *something which is a haphazard mixture of good and mediocre*

A curate, an assistant to a vicar or parish priest, is an ordained minister at the bottom of the priestly pecking order, poorly paid and with no job security.

The humorous British magazine *Punch* (9 November 1895) featured a cartoon drawn by George du Maurier. This showed a timid curate having breakfast in his bishop's home.

The bishop says: 'I'm afraid you've got a bad egg, Mr Jones.' The curate replies, in a desperate attempt not to give offence: 'Oh, no, my Lord, I assure you that parts of it are excellent!'

Readers liked this exchange so much that the cartoon led to the catch-phrases 'parts of it are excellent' and 'good in parts', which are recorded from the beginning of the 20th century.

Despite one American dictionary, the phrase does not mean 'something discreetly declared to be partly good but in fact thoroughly bad', which would be its literal interpretation.

Curry favour – *to seek someone's approval through flattery, to ingratiate oneself with someone*

The phrase is a corruption of the Middle English 'to curry favel' or 'fauvel', itself from the Old French *estriller fauvel*, meaning to rub down or groom a chestnut horse. *Fauvel* derives from the French *fauve*, fallow-coloured. In a 14th-century French allegory, *Le Roman de Fauvel*, a fallow horse, representing hypocrisy and deceit, is carefully curried, or smoothed down, in order to gain his favour. Through the closeness in pronunciation and the link in meaning, 'curry favel' became 'curry favour'.

Harold Nicholson, *The Age of Reason* (1960): 'In order to curry favour with the Grand Duke, who might at any moment become Tsar, the Schouvalovs encouraged him to bring to St Petersburg a detachment of his Holstein troops.'

Cut and dried – *completely decided; quite ready*

The phrase originally referred to herbs in herbalists' shops, as contrasted with growing herbs.

The first known use of the expression is in a letter to the Reverend Dr Henry Sacheverell (1710): 'Your sermon was ready Cut and Dry'd.' This was not praise. The (unknown) correspondent did not mean that the sermon was well prepared, convincing and authoritative. He meant that it had been prepared in advance and lacked freshness and spontaneity.

The next known use is in Jonathan Swift, 'Betty the Grizette' (1730): 'Sets of Phrases, cut and dry, / Evermore thy Tongue supply.' Again, Swift means that the phrases lack spontaneity – they are clichés.

Cut and run – *to make a quick getaway, to quit*

Formerly anchor cables on sailing vessels were made of hemp. If a naval warship at anchor were in danger of enemy attack and needed to make a speedy departure, the crew would not take the time to wind in the anchor but would simply *cut* through the cable and let the ship *run* before the wind.

Thus spake Bavaria's scholar king,
Prepared to cut and run:
I've lost my throne, lost everything,
Olola, I'm undone.
    Epigram, *Quarterly Review* (1887)

Cut no ice – *to make no impression on someone, to be powerless to influence someone*

This expression originated in America towards the end of the 19th century and came into British usage in the 1920s.

It refers to ice-skating. One can skate with ease only on keen blades which cut into the ice. Blunt blades make no impression and the skater makes no progress.

Erskine Caldwell, *God's Little Acre* (1933): 'We had him tied up in no time, just like you rope a calf to take to market. He yelled some and kicked a great deal, but that didn't cut no ice with the boys and me.'

Cut the mustard – *to reach a required standard, come up to expectations, succeed in an attempt*

The phrase is unlikely to have originated, as some have suggested, from a mis-hearing of 'cut the muster', a military phrase meaning well turned out.

For over three centuries, mustard has been used to describe what is best. It adds flavouring to even the tastiest of foods, and as a result the word is found in a number of different phrases – 'keen as mustard', 'the proper mustard' (the genuine article), 'all to the mustard' (sharp-witted, keen).

Every one of these forms was used by O. Henry, among the most famous writers in America in the early 20th century. He used the word in the sense of 'something excellent' in *Cabbages and Kings* (1904): 'I'm not headlined in the bills, but I'm mustard in the salad dressing just the same', a sentence which clearly points to where all these forms are rooted.

Also in *The Heart of the West* (1907), he uses the full phrase, recorded for the first time: 'I looked around and found a proposition that exactly cut the mustard.' O. Henry must be credited with popularising, perhaps even inventing, 'cut the mustard'.

Tennessee Williams, *Sweet Bird of Youth* (1959): 'Boss Finley's too old to cut the mustard [i.e. perform sexually].'

Cut to the chase – *Get on with it! Get to the point!*

A script direction in J.P. McEvoy's novel *Hollywood Girl* (1927) is the first literal use of this expression, and means cut from the dramatic scene to the dramatic action (i.e. the chase).

A 1929 novel about Hollywood has 'Jannings escapes … Cut to chase', for example. The figurative use, which is now quite common, is fairly recent; it seems to date only from the early 1980s.

San Francisco Chronicle (26 October 2003): 'Cut to the Chase – As a movie, *Bullitt* was confusing, but the strength of that driving sequence … was still enough to ensure that *Bullitt* would become a classic.'

Cut to the quick – *to cause searing (emotional) pain*

The 'quick' comes from the old English *cwicu* meaning 'living', and refers to the flesh under finger- and toenails, the most sensitive on the human body.

M.C. Self, *The Complete Book of Horses and Ponies* (1963): 'As with your fingernail, we must be careful not to trim too close to the "quick", or sensitive part of the horse's foot.'

Apart from 'cut' to the quick, there are many other phrases in English literature like 'touched', 'galled', 'stung' (etc.) to the quick, as in Daniel Defoe, *Moll Flanders* (1722): 'This stung the elder brother to the quick.'

Sir Thomas More, *Utopia* (1551) 'Their tenants … whom they poll and shave to the quick, by raising their rents.'

D

Dark horse – *a person about whom little is known*

This phrase is first found in writing in Disraeli's novel *The Young Duke* (1831): 'A dark horse which had never been thought of … rushed past the grandstand in sweeping triumph.'

It probably goes back much earlier and relates to a horse about which little form was available before a race.

A 'dark horse' in US politics is a person not named as a candidate before a convention, who unexpectedly receives the nomination when the convention has failed to agree upon any of the leading candidates.

Davy Jones's locker – *the destination of all sailors who die at sea*

Davy Jones is the old-time sailor's devil, and his locker is his storage place at the bottom of the sea. Many have tried to identify Davy Jones but the true source remains unfathomed.

One David Jones ran a pub in London. He also had a sort of privatised press gang. He would drug unwary patrons and store them in his ale lockers at the back of the pub until they could be taken on board a ship.

Another story tries to identify Davy Jones with Jonah of the Old Testament, who survived in the belly of a great fish. However, this connection seems tenuous because Jonah survived. No sailor ever returns from Davy Jones's locker.

A third theory says Davy Jones was a fearsome pirate, but no one has identified this alarming but stereotypical outlaw. A fourth names Duffer Jones, a notoriously myopic sailor who often found himself overboard.

'Davy' could also come from the Devil himself. The shortest sailor on board usually impersonates him during the Crossing of the Line, a bizarre naval cross-dressing ceremony.

Others have suggested a link with St David, the patron saint of Wales. Jones, again, is a corruption of Jonah.

Finally, *duppy* is a spirit in West Indian mythology that seizes souls. Duppy or Duffy Jonah became Davy Jones. Stranger things have happened but it seems far-fetched, and there is no evidence for it.

Tobias Smollett, *The Adventures of Peregrine Pickle* (1751): 'This same Davy Jones, according to the mythology of sailors, is the fiend that presides over all the evil spirits of the deep, and is often seen in various shapes, perching among the rigging on the eve of hurricanes, ship-wrecks, and other disasters to which sea-faring folk are exposed, warning the devoted wretch of death and woe.'

Dead as a dodo – *completely dead, obsolete*

To be found in Mauritius and Réunion in the Indian Ocean until the 17th century, a dodo (*Didus ineptus*) was a flightless, rather comical bird which sailors and colonists found easy to catch and tasty to eat.

Pigs, which were also introduced to the islands around the same time, foraged the nests and by the early 18th century the dodo was extinct.

H.O. Sturgis, *Belchamber* (1904): 'The Radicalism of Mill ... is as dead as the dodo.'

Figuratively, 'dodo' came to mean an old-fashioned, stupid, inactive or unenlightened person.

Dead as a door-nail – *lifeless; certainly dead*

There are numerous theories as to the origins of this phrase, and none of them offers real satisfaction.

Most popular is the suggestion that the door-nail is the section of metal under the knocker, which was thought to be 'dead' because of the number of times it was hit on the head, and the muffled sound it emits.

However, it has also been proposed that 'door-nail' describes a beam of wood placed across the inside of a door for security, and held in place by brackets. The fact that it was rigid suggested death.

A third option is 'clinching' – an expression in carpentry which describes how the tip of the nail, once hammered through a piece of timber, is flattened so that it cannot be used again. The nail is then considered 'dead'.

The phrase, which is very old, may simply refer to the large-headed nails with which doors were formerly studded for strength, protection or ornamentation.

William Langland, *Piers Plowman* (1362): 'Fey withouten fait is febelore then nought, / And ded as a dore-nayl.' (Faith without action is weaker than nothing, and dead as a door-nail.)

Dead ringer – *looking just like someone else*

A common way of testing whether a coin was counterfeit was to drop it on a hard surface. If it rang like a bell it was not the real thing. Counterfeit coins were, therefore, called 'ringers'. Later, a ringer was a good horse substituted for a bad horse to enable gamblers to make a dishonest profit. The word 'dead' is used here to add emphasis, as in 'dead centre' or 'dead on'.

It is also suggested that up to the 20th century, medical practice being less advanced, the certification of a person's death was sometimes mistaken. Comas were less well understood, and bodies were exhumed to find that a 'corpse' had regained consciousness after burial and tried to escape the coffin. To avoid this, a string was attached to the wrist of the body and connected to a bell above ground, giving rise to the phrase 'dead ringer'.

There is little support for this theory, although the fear of being buried alive is a common theme in 18th- and 19th-century literature, first in Germany and then in France, Britain and elsewhere. (Poe's 'The Black Cat' and 'The Fall of the House of Usher' are American examples.)

David Powis, *The Signs of Crime: A Field Manual for Police* (1977): Ringer 'originally meant horses or greyhounds that had been ... disguised. Not so common in this sense now. Also used to describe any genuine appearing fake.'

See also **Ring true *or* Have the ring of truth.**

Dead to the world – *deeply asleep; in a state of exhaustion or intoxication; unconscious of one's surroundings*

Before the 19th century, this term was exclusively used in the religious sense of giving up all worldly pleasures to devote oneself entirely to God. It probably derived from St Paul's phrase 'dead to sin'.

However, by the late 19th and early 20th centuries, it was used to mean unconscious and, hence, deeply asleep.

> A few Monks, a stern society
> Dead to the world and scorning earth-born joys.
> > William Wordsworth,
> > 'The Cuckoo at Laverna' (1837)

St Paul's Letter to the Romans 6:1–2: 'What shall we say, then? Shall we continue in sin, that grace may abound? God forbid. For we that are dead to sin, how shall we live any longer therein?'

George Ade, *'Doc' Horne* (1899): '"Our host is dead to the world," observed the actor … "Let him rest," said Doc.'

Devil to pay – *consequences of something one has done*

Making a pact with the Devil is deeply ingrained in Christian history. Jesus was offered such a pact and the idea has been perpetuated in the many stories about Dr Faustus.

It has also been attributed to 'paying' or caulking the seam called the devil, near a ship's keel, whence the expanded form 'the devil to pay and no pitch hot'. (See also **Between the devil and the deep blue sea**.) There is no evidence that this is the original sense, and it has never affected the general use of the phrase.

Lord Byron, from Thomas Moore, *Life and Letters* (1820): 'There will be the devil to pay, and there is no saying who will or who will not be set down in his bill.'

Devil's advocate – *a person who presents an argument which he does not himself support; a person who advocates an opposing or unpopular view; a person who injures a cause by his advocacy*

To ensure that a candidate for beatification or canonisation is properly considered, a Roman Catholic official is appointed, *Advocatus Diaboli*, to make the case against, so that all factors are given due weight. The supporter was until 1983 called *Advocatus Dei* (God's Advocate).

James Bonar, *Malthus and His Work* (1885): 'The father made it a point of honour to defend the Enquirer; the son played devil's advocate.'

Die is cast – *the fateful decision has been made, there is no turning back*

There are two possible interpretations. 'Die' is the singular of dice. When Julius Caesar crossed the Rubicon and advanced against Pompey (49 BC), he is quoted as saying 'Jacta alea est' – the dice have been thrown.

However, 'die' in this case may refer to pieces used in manufacturing for cutting, stamping or forming material (usually metal). 'Cast' here would then mean to form molten metal into a particular shape by pouring into a mould. Once the metal has been poured into the die it will set quickly, and the shape will be fixed.

This latter is almost certainly the origin of the phrase, 'straight as a die', referring to the straight edge achieved in moulding and pressing.

The expression has been known in English since at least 1634.

Winston S. Churchill, *The Second World War* (vol. 5, 1952): 'At 4 am on June 5 the die was irrevocably cast: the invasion would be launched on June 6 [1944: the D-Day landings in Normandy].'

See also **Cross the Rubicon**.

Die-hard – *resilient, determined*

The 'Die-hards' were the British 57th Regiment of Foot, later becoming the West Middlesex Regiment. Before the victorious battle of Albuera against the French in 1811, Colonel Inglis, badly wounded but refusing to be moved, roused them with the words: 'Die hard, my lads, die hard.'

The phrase has also come to mean someone who is extremely conservative, stubborn or irreconcilable, especially on a political issue.

The best-known die-hards were those who opposed home rule for Ireland in 1912, and the supporters of the Marquess of Salisbury in 1922, as in: 'Mr Chamberlain said: "Politics have many vicissitudes. A few days ago I was orthodox; today I am a Die-hard."' (*Daily Mail,* 1922)

Disgusted of Tunbridge Wells – *a reactionary person*

The title of a BBC Radio 4 programme in 1978, it was intended to evoke the sort of letter fired off to the press between the two world wars, in which the writer did not want to give his or her name and so signed 'Mother of Three', 'Angry Ratepayer', 'Serving Policeman', etc.

Royal Tunbridge Wells had acquired the reputation of being where stuffy, reactionary views were held, much to the 'disgust' of the residents (*Kent Courier,* 24 February 1978).

Guardian (1985): 'A paper must have the right to an editorial opinion. So must a columnist. If the columnist becomes too eccentric his editor will remove him. If a paper gets too far out of touch with disgusted of Tunbridge Wells or Dave Spart of Islington he will take his 23 pence a day elsewhere.'

Dog in a manger – *person unwilling to let others benefit from things he cannot use himself; churlish, spoiling*

One of Aesop's fables tells of a dog which sat in a manger full of hay and snapped at a hungry ox to prevent it from eating. The dog had no use for the hay but begrudged the ox its fodder. Another version has horses instead of oxen.

The meanest dog there ever was
Went looking for a nest
Where he could sleep by day or night
If he should need a rest.

The horses watched with fearful eyes
The cruel approaching stranger,
And sure enough, he went to sleep
Right in the horses' manger.

How MEAN that creature is, they cried,
To spoil our eating shelf!
He'll snap and bite if we come near,
Yet can't eat straw himself.

>   William Cleary, verse adaptation of
>   Aesop's fable 'A Mean Dog Nests in a Manger'

Frederick Marryat, *Japhet* (1836): 'Why, what a dog in the manger you must be – you can't marry them both.'

Dog-days – *hot summer weather*

Sirius, the Greater Dog or the Dog Star, was an object of wonder and veneration to all ancient peoples throughout human history. In the ancient Vedas it was known as the Chieftain's Star; in other Hindu writings it is referred to as Sukra, the Rain God, or Rain Star. The Dog is also described as 'he who awakens the gods of the air, and summons them to their office of bringing the rain'.

The Romans called the hottest weather, from the beginning of July to mid-August, *dies caniculares* (dog days). Their theory was that Sirius, being the brightest star in the constellation, rising with the sun (from about 3 July to 11 August), added to its heat.

For 35 days before and 35 days after the sun conjuncts it on 4 July, the star Sirius is hidden by the sun's glare. The ancient Egyptians refused to bury their dead during the 70 days that Sirius was hidden from view, because it was believed that Sirius was the doorway to the afterlife, and the doorway was thought to be closed during this yearly period.

E. Cooke, *A Voyage to the South Sea* (1712): 'Hotter in January, than Italy in the Dog-Days.'

Dog's life – *a dreadful existence, a life of misery*

Phrases such as 'it's a dog's life' hark back to a society in which dogs were not pampered, protected and domesticated pets.

There are many – 'not a dog's chance'; 'die like a dog'; 'give a dog a bad name'. In all cases the dog is seen to be pitiful and wretched. The full version of the reference above is 'give a dog an ill name and hang him', not exactly fair to the dog, as in Nathan Bailey, *Dictionarium Britannicum: or a More Compleat Universal English Dictionary* (1730–6): 'He who would hang his Dog first gives out that he is mad.'

Donkey's years – *a long time*

The long characteristic of the donkey is not his life but his ears. Formerly the phrase appeared as: 'I haven't seen you for as long as donkey's ears.' The original phrase was a mouthful and it became abbreviated to the modern, neater (if misleading) expression.

Edward Verrall Lucas, *The Vermilion Box* (1916): 'Now for my first bath for what the men call "Donkeys' ears" meaning years and years.'

Observer (1961): 'American influence and financial participation have been strong here for donkey's years.'

Doolally *or* Doolally tap – *mad*

In the late 19th century, the British army established a military base at Deolali about 100 miles north-east of Bombay. The base had an asylum, into which unstable battle-weary troops would be sent, but it also doubled as a transit camp for British soldiers waiting for ships home.

The ships, however, left for **Blighty** only between November and March. The consequent inactivity, boredom, stifling heat and disease meant that many men began to act strangely and eccentrically. They were said to be suffering from 'Doolally tap'.

'Doolally' is simply the British soldiers' way of mispronouncing a foreign name, and 'tap' is the Persian or Urdu for malarial fever (from Sanskrit *tapa*, heat or torment). So the whole expression might be loosely translated as 'camp fever'. By the 1940s it had already been shortened to doolally ('tap' didn't long survive the journey from India).

Rather curiously, in America, 'doolally' is also known as a term for something whose name one can't for the moment remember. It has the same pattern as other US words with the same meaning, like 'dohickey', 'doojigger' and 'doodad'. Doolally may have been imported, or it may be an independent local variation on one of these other words.

'Hell, No, I Won't Go', *Economist* (2002): 'As aid dwindled, Mr Mugabe made no effort to spend within his means. From 1997, public finances went doolally. The main result was graft.'

James Curtis, *The Gilt Kid* (1936): 'What's the matter with that bloke? Doolally?'

Dot the i's and cross the t's – *check and correct the detail, finalise the details of an agreement, be meticulous*

With the exception of the letter j, these are the only two letters requiring a separate dot or pen stroke in the English alphabet, details which may be overlooked by schoolchildren.

Daily Chronicle (1896): '[He] dotted our 'i's' and crossed our 't's' with a vengeance about the lack of men in the navy.'

Double whammy – *double blow*

The phrase originated in the *Li'l Abner* cartoon strip in the USA and referred to an intense stare which had a withering effect on victims. Al Capp, *Li'l Abner* (1951): 'Mudder Nature endowed me wit' eyes which can putrefy citizens t' th' spot! ... There is th' "*single whammy*"! *That*, friend, is th' full, *pure power* o' *one* of my evil eyes! It's *dynamite*, friend, an' I do not t'row it around lightly! ... And lastly – th' "*double whammy*" – namely th' *full power o' both eyes* – which I hopes I never *hafta* use.'

The phrase was popularised in the UK in the 1992 Conservative election campaign by an extremely successful poster which featured a boxer under the slogan 'Labour's Double Whammy'. In the foreground, on his boxing gloves, appeared two short statements: '1. More Taxes', and '2. Higher Prices', i.e. what voters would get under a Labour government. Chris Patten, the Conservative Party Chairman, came up with 'double whammy', which proved so successful that a new catchphrase entered the British political lexicon.

Double-cross – *to betray, to deceive*

The phrase is first recorded in 1834, and derives from thieves' slang. Around 1800, 'cross' came to mean something dishonest as opposed to 'square' or 'straight'. Something done 'on the cross' was crooked, and crooks sometimes attempted to improve their chances by going back on an illegal deal, so crossing the crossers.

The expression gained currency in horse-racing and bare-knuckle fighting, where throwing a race or a fight was a double-cross.

There is a story that the origin of the phrase was Jonathan Wild, who, at the end of the 17th century, employed a gang of thieves and, at the same time, ran a 'lost property' racket for the goods he stole, representing himself as an honest broker to the real owners. He kept a book and marked the thief's name with a cross when he had evidence of a crime. If the thief displeased him, he marked the name with a double cross and that meant he planned to shop him to the police.

His exploits were fictionalised in books by Daniel Defoe and Henry Fielding. He was also the inspiration for Mr Peachum in Gay's *Beggar's Opera*. He died on the scaffold at Tyburn on 24 May 1725.

The Referee (1887): 'A double cross was brought off. Teemer promised to sell the match, and finished by selling those who calculated on his losing.'

Doubting Thomas – *person who requires empirical proof before believing anything*

Christ's disciple, Thomas Didymus, would not believe that Jesus had died.

'The other disciples therefore said unto him, We have seen the LORD. But he said unto them, Except I shall see in his hands the print of the nails, and put my finger into the print of the nails, and thrust my hand into his side, I will not believe.' (John 20:25)

Elizabeth Gaskell, *Mary Barton* (1848): 'Mary, don't let my being an unbelieving Thomas weaken your faith.'

Down in the dumps – *dejected*

Most Northern European languages have words which in English translate into 'the dumps'. In Dutch it's *dumpig*, meaning damp or hazy; in German it's *dumpf*, meaning gloomy. It is certainly possible to trace 'dumps' to 15th-century English.

Sir Thomas More, *A Dialogue of Comfort Against Tribulation* (1529): 'What heapes of heaviness, hath of late fallen among us already, with which some of our poore familye be fallen into suche dumpes.'

Dressed up like a dog's dinner *or* breakfast – *dressed up in an extravagant or showy way*

Originally, 'dressed up like a dog's dinner' suggested something showy, and 'dressed up like a dog's breakfast' suggested something scrappy.

C.L. Anthony, *Touch Wood* (1934): 'Why have you got those roses in your hair? You look like the dog's dinner.'

Eric Partridge, *A Dictionary of Slang and Unconventional English* (1937): '*Dog's breakfast* – a mess.'

'Dressed up or done up like a dog's dinner' meant 'dressed to kill' or 'dressed stylishly', and some have associated this with the story of Jezebel and King Ahab. After many years leading Ahab astray, Jezebel 'painted her face and tired her head' but nevertheless failed in her attempt to impress Jehu. His messy disposal of her fulfilled Elijah's prophecy that the 'dogs shall eat Jezebel by the walls of Jezreel' (2 Kings 9).

Before the invention of tinned dog food, a dog's breakfast could well have consisted of the left-over scraps from the night before.

Both phrases came to be used interchangeably, and in the slightly pejorative sense of being over-dressed, glitzy, but the distinction was still being made as late as 1977 in a letter from Sir Huw Wheldon concerning his TV series 'Royal Heritage': 'It was very difficult, and I feared it would be a Dog's Dinner. There was so much … to draw upon … and I think it matriculated, in the event, into a Dog's Breakfast, more or less, & I was content.'

Dressed (up) to the nines – *dressed as smartly as possible*

There is some dispute about the origin of this phrase.

Some believe it may represent nine out of ten – implying near-perfection. Others suggest that in medieval English, the phrase 'dressed to the eyes' would have been 'to the eyne', but this is an unlikely derivation because 'to the nines' is not recorded until the end of the 18th century, as in Robert Burns: '"Twad please me to the nine.' ('Answer to Verses', 1787); or 'Thou paints auld Nature to the nines.' ('Pastoral Poetry', 1793)

The third suggestion is that the origin comes from the British Army's 99th Regiment of Foot, also known from 1874 as The Duke of Edinburgh's Regiment. In the mid-19th century they were so renowned for their smartness that other regiments based with them in Aldershot were constantly trying to equal 'the nines'. The 99th's sartorial perfection at this time is said to have given rise to the expression 'Dressed to the nines'.

'Dressed (up) to the nines' first appears in John Hotten, *A Dictionary of*

Modern Slang, Cant and Vulgar Words (1859): "'Dressed up to the *nines*", in a showy or recherché manner.'

Thomas Hardy, *The Hand of Ethelberta* (1876): 'when she's dressed up to the nines for some grand party'.

Drinking a toast – *proposing good health and loyalty, or a compliment to someone or something, marked by the raising of glasses*

An old custom is to put toast into beer to improve its flavour. In the reign of Charles II, a renowned beauty was bathing in the spa at Bath, and one of her admirers took a glass of the water in which she was standing and drank her health.

This prompted another to exclaim that he would jump in the water, for 'though he liked not the liquor, he would have the toast!', i.e. the lady herself (*Tatler*, no. 24). The person or thing, therefore, to which guests are invited to drink in compliment, as well as the drink itself, became known as toasts.

> Say, why are beauties praised and honoured most,
> The wise man's passion and the vain man's toast.
> Alexander Pope, *The Rape of the Lock* (1712)

Dumbing down – *attempting to make information more accessible, to the detriment of satisfactory standards*

The phrase was apparently coined to describe a tendency in the American education system in about 1986. The usage spread to Britain, most notably with regard to radio programming, in 1997.

Economist (1987): 'America's knowledge vacuum is largely caused by what has been called the "dumbing down" of school curricula and textbooks over recent years. Books have been made bland and easy, partly in an effort to appease militant interest groups, partly because the act of reading is given more importance than the matter that is read, partly in the name of "social relevance" (whatever that is).'

Sunday Times (1997): 'The BBC is about to axe 30 programmes on Radio 4 as part of the most significant shake-up in the network's history. The changes have already prompted critics to accuse the corporation of "dumbing down" large swathes of its output.'

Dutch courage – *false courage, courage induced by alcohol*

During the 17th and early 18th centuries, Anglo-Dutch enmity and trade disputes were at their peak, and therefore the word 'Dutch' became pejorative.

A 'Dutch uncle' gives heavy-handed advice. 'Double Dutch' means nonsense. 'Going Dutch' is paying only for oneself, and implies meanness. 'I'm a Dutchman' is a general expression of disbelief.

'Dutch courage' is false courage, normally brought about by the consumption of alcohol. It is another slur on the Dutch, who were reputed to be heavy drinkers. The phrase 'Dutch bargain', a bargain settled over drinks, arises from the same supposed Dutch failing.

Sir Walter Scott, *Woodstock* (1826): 'Laying in a store of what is called Dutch Courage.'

E

Eagle-eyed – *having excellent eyesight*

The phrase 'to keep an eagle eye' – a close watch – on some person or event has been used since the early 19th century, but the legend of the eagle's phenomenal sight goes back to the earliest records. It is said that the eagle has better sight than any other bird, but as age takes its toll and its sight weakens, the eagle flies towards the sun, which burns off the ravages of time and restores the eagle's sight.

Bishop Barlow, *The Eagle and the Body* (1601): 'Faith, being Eagle eyed, can … see the maiestie of God.'

Ear to the ground – *alive to rumour and gossip*

It is allegedly possible to hear the hooves of oncoming horses before their sound becomes audible, by putting one's ear to the ground and listening for their vibration.

Graham Greene, *The Quiet American* (1955): 'What's the gossip of the market, Tom? You fellows do certainly keep your ears to the ground.'

Earmark – *to designate*

Since the 16th century, farmers have cut notches in the ears of their animals to indicate ownership, but it was not until three centuries later that the word was used in today's slightly different sense. Nowadays, earmarking is figuratively not to do with ownership. It is deciding to reserve something for a certain purpose.

John Fitzherbert, *A New Tracte or Treatyse Moost Profytable for all Husbande Men* (1523): 'Se that they [the sheep] be well marked, both ear-marke, pitche-marke and radel-marke.'

Stephen McKenna, *Happy Ending* (1929): 'I need only earmark sufficient time in the summer for certain people whose hospitality I've accepted.'

Ears are burning – *one is being talked about*

In Roman times, it was believed that your ears would ring or burn if others were talking about you, or as Pliny said: 'When our ears do glow and tingle, some do talk of us in our absence.'

The left ear warns of evil intent while the right signifies praise. Sir Thomas Browne (1605–82) ascribes the conceit to guardian angels who touch the right ear if the talk is favourable and the left if otherwise.

> One ear tingles; some there be
> That are snarling now at me.
>   Robert Herrick, *Hesperides* (1648)

Eat humble pie – *to be humbled or humiliated, apologise*

'Umbles', sometimes 'humbles', are the edible offal of deer and other animals, and have been eaten for centuries. The idiom gained its current meaning only in the 19th century, as a play on the word 'humble'.

Some argue that 'umbles pie' was eaten only by the lower classes. When the lord and his family dined off venison at high table, the huntsman and his fellows took lower seats where they partook of the huntsman's perquisites, which were the heart, liver and entrails of the deer, made into a pie.

Thomas Love Peacock, *Maid Marian* (1822): 'Robin helped him largely to numble-pie ... and the other dainties of his table.'

William Makepeace Thackeray, *The Newcomes* (1855): 'You must get up and eat humble-pie this morning, my boy.'

To 'eat crow' in the USA has the same meaning, and has its origin in an anecdote from the Anglo-American war of 1812–14. A New Englander had unwittingly crossed the British lines in order to shoot a crow. An unarmed British officer, in order to punish him, praised his marksmanship and asked to see his weapon. Thereupon he forced him at gunpoint to take a bite out of the crow. When the officer returned his gun, the American compelled him in the same way to eat the remainder of the crow.

Eat your heart out – *to fret or worry, pine, brood or be jealous*

The phrase is often used frivolously as a taunt to a person one has bettered, or supposedly bettered, in some way. Thus someone who has had a first short story published might say 'Eat your heart out, J.K. Rowling!' (or some other popular writer).

From ancient times, envy and sorrow were considered bad for the heart. Homer in *The Iliad* repeatedly used the phrase to describe the gnawing despair of the legendary hero Bellerophon who incurs the wrath of the gods. Having seen him through many trials and tribulations, they suddenly turn on him in a fit of jealousy. Ares and Artemis arrange for the deaths of his children Isandros and Laodameia, respectively, and Bellerophon is left to wander the plain of Aleios 'eating his heart out'.

> Lest a mere man should share their glory
> The gods turned against Bellerophon,
> And he wandered evermore through this Aleian field
> Eating his heart out, fleeing the loathed company of men.
> Homer, The Iliad (8th century BC)

By Shakespeare's time it was in common use both as a notion and as a phrase.

Edmund Spenser, *The Faerie Queene* (1596): 'He could not rest; but did his stout heart eat.'

Egg on – *to urge, encourage, incite*

'Egg', in this sense, comes from the Old Norse word *eggja*, referring to the sharp 'edge' of a blade. The link to the modern phrase may be either that one was 'encouraged' by the close proximity of a blade, or the elision of the definitions of the words 'edge', 'sharpness' and 'urgency'.

Anthony Wood, *Athenae Oxoniensis* (1691): 'Mathew Hazard [was] a main Incendiary in the Rebellion, violently egged on by his wife.'

Egg on one's face – *foolish appearance having made a wrong choice*

First used in the USA in the 1960s and in Britain in 1972, this phrase refers to the hustings, where throwing eggs at an opponent is not uncommon. The idea seems to be that a politician with egg on his face is made to look foolish.

Independent (1992): 'The campaign polls made a hash of forecasting the result, and few people are inclined to feel sorry for soothsayers who end up with egg-spattered faces.'

Emperor's new clothes – *an expression suggesting conceit, self-deception, vanity*

Hans Christian Andersen (1805–75) (illustrated) told the story of two rogues who persuaded the Emperor that they had made him a suit of very fine clothes which were, however, invisible to all those who were stupid or incompetent. The clothes, of course, did not exist, but the Emperor was not prepared to admit that he could not see them, and nor were any of his courtiers. When the Emperor paraded in his new 'clothes', it was only an innocent child who was bold enough to tell him and the watching crowd the truth that he was naked.

Essex girl – *a girl not noted for her intelligence or refinement*

There was a craze for jokes on this theme in the autumn of 1991, for example: 'How can you tell when an Essex girl has been using your word processor? By the Tipp-Ex on the screen'; or, 'How does an Essex girl turn on the light afterwards? She kicks open the car door.'

These jokes were a straight lift from the 'blonde jokes' popular in the USA shortly before, and reflected little that was unique to the county of Essex.

Germaine Greer, 'Long Live the Essex Girl', 5 March 2001, in the *Guardian*:

> The Essex girl is becoming more difficult to spot these days. She used to be conspicuous, as she clacked along the pavements in her white plastic stilettos, her bare legs mottled patriotic red, white and blue with cold, and her big bottom barely covered by her denim miniskirt. Essex girls usually come in twos, both behind pushchairs with large infants in them. Sometimes you hear them before you see them, cackling shrilly or yelling to each other from one end of the street to the other, or berating those infants in blood-curdling fashion. Occasionally they are accompanied by the hangdog sire of their child, more often by a mother, who is simply a 16 or 17 years older version of themselves. All parties bar the infants will have a cigarette going.
>
> The Essex girl is tough, loud, vulgar and unashamed. Her hair is badly dyed not because she can't afford a hairdresser, but because she wants it to look brassy. Nobody makes her wear her ankle chain; she likes the message it sends. Nobody laughs harder at an Essex girl joke than she does: she is not ashamed to admit what she puts behind her ears to make her more attractive is her ankles. She is anarchy on stilts; when she and her mates descend upon Southend for a rave, even the bouncers grow pale.

Exception proves the rule – *the existence of an allowed exception to a rule reaffirms the existence of the rule*

This phrase is used colloquially in rather a sweeping way to justify an inconsistency. If an exception is found it somehow reinforces the validity of the rule.

The idea that the rule is proved by a case that does not follow the rule is, however, clearly nonsense. As the old maxim has it, you need only find one white crow to disprove the rule that all crows are black.

The true origin of the phrase is the medieval Latin legal principle *exceptio probat regulum in casibus non exceptis*, which may be translated: 'the exception confirms that the rule holds true for cases not excepted.'

In *Modern English Usage* (1926), Henry Watson Fowler gave an example from his wartime experience: 'Special leave is given for men to be out of barracks tonight till 11 pm', which implies a rule that in other cases men must be back earlier. So, in its strict sense, the principle is arguing that the existence of an allowed exception to a rule reaffirms the existence of the rule. However, it is unlikely that the phrase will ever have its original meaning restored.

F

Face the music – *to face up to the consequences of your actions, put on a bold front in an unpleasant situation*

The expression may derive from the stage, although some authorities take it from the military ceremony in which an officer being cashiered was required to face the drum squad while his charges were read out. Others suggest that it refers to the music of the regimental band when teaching discipline to a cavalry horse.

Cecil Rhodes, *Westminster Gazette* (1897): 'I will not refer to the vulgar colloquialism that I was afraid to face the music.'

Fag-end – *the last, worst bit*

This is not about cigarettes or cigars. The phrase originates in the draper's shop, where the fag-end is that rough, coarse end to a roll of material which is useless and worthless.

Thomas Edlyne Tomlin, *Law Dictionary* (1809): 'The fag-end ... where the weaver ... works up the worst part of his materials.'

Charles Dickens, *Martin Chuzzlewit* (1844): 'To hum ... the fag-end of a song.'

Fair game – *something to be attacked with good reason, legitimately*

'Fair game' were those few animals and birds, mostly vermin, which could be lawfully hunted by commoners after the 1825 legislation giving the ruling classes rights to the countryside and its animals.

Maria Edgeworth, *Belinda* (1801): 'Quiz the doctor ... he's an author – so fair game.'

The opposite, 'forbidden game', was also used, as in William Cowper's *Table Talk* (1780): 'A monarch's errors are forbidden game.' However, only 'fair game' has survived into modern usage.

Fall on deaf ears – *to go unheard, unheeded; to be deliberately ignored*

Although they had been in currency since the 15th century, not until four centuries later were the precise words 'fall on deaf ears' in common use.

The Bible has many references to deafness and a person's wilful refusal to hear. 'He that hath ears to hear, let him hear.' (Mark 4:9, 23)

Another common phrase is 'turn (or give) a deaf ear', as in Edward Hall, *Chronicle of Richard III* (1548): 'She began … to relent and to geve them no deffe are'; or in Bishop Connop Thirlwall, *A History of Greece* (1835): 'She had turned a deaf ear to the persuasions by which they sought to prevail upon her.'

Feather in one's cap – *credit, acknowledgement for one's work, achievement*

It has been the custom among the people of very different cultures to wear a feather on the head for every enemy killed. The American Indians are the best known for this practice.

In England, too, knights wore feathers in their helmets denoting outstanding valour. The origin of the phrase may be traced to Edward, the Black Prince, who, at the age of sixteen, showed such bravery at the Battle of Crécy (1346) that the crest of blind John of Bohemia, one of the mighty knights in the enemy forces, was bestowed on him. The crest, three ostrich plumes, is the emblem of the Princes of Wales to this day.

Thomas Fuller, *Church History* (1655): 'He wore a feather in his cap, and wagg'd it too often.'

Feet of clay – *a fatal flaw, disappointing weaknesses of character in someone hitherto held in high regard*

The prophet Daniel interpreted the dream of the great Babylonian King Nebuchadnezzar. The King had dreamed of a great image of a man whose body was made of precious metals but whose 'feet [were] part of iron and part of clay' (Daniel 2:32–3).

Daniel interpreted it as a vision of a declining kingdom, 'and as the toes of the feet were part of iron and part of clay, so the kingdom shall be partly strong and partly broken' (2:42).

Alfred, Lord Tennyson, *Idylls of the King* (1859): 'They find some stain or blemish in a name of note ... And judge all nature from her feet of clay.'

Fiddle while Rome burns – *to do something unimportant while a crisis remains unaddressed*

This is a reference to Emperor Nero (AD 37–68) who, it is said, played music while the great fire of Rome (AD 64) engulfed the city. He would have actually played a lyre, as the fiddle did not exist in ancient Rome. There are those who believe that he caused the inferno in order to clear the city for his own fabulous villa and pleasure park.

Fernand Braudel Center, Binghamton University, NY, Commentary No. 102 (2002): '*Aciu*! Bush Fiddles While Rome Burns': 'The United States and President Bush are popular in East-Central Europe. This is about the last region of the world, other than Israel, where Pres. Bush can be assured of such a reception today. So Bush bathed in the cheers of this friendly zone. But like Nero, he was fiddling while Rome is burning. The United States is burning, and President Bush seems completely unaware of this.'

Filthy lucre – *money, dishonourable profit*

The Middle English word *lucre* comes from the Latin *lucrum*, gain. This in turn has the root *leu*, to win, to capture as booty. This lends the meaning of profit, booty, loot or value to different words in a number of languages. In

Greek, *apo-lauein* means to enjoy. Old German has *lon* and modern German *Lohn* meaning wages. Modern French *lucre* has the same meaning as in English. It is also, of course, the root of the word 'lucrative', which is similar in German and French.

The word stands by itself to mean dishonourable gain, but is usually found with the reinforcement of 'filthy'.

Titus (1:7): 'For a bishop must be blameless, as the steward of God; not selfwilled, not soon angry, not given to wine, no striker, not given to filthy lucre; But a lover of hospitality, a lover of good men, sober, just, holy, temperate.'

William Ralph Inge, *Lay Thoughts of a Dean* (1926): 'If a Jew wants to be a rich man, he is apt to be keener about his business than a Gentile; but if he has no ambition to make money, and chooses to be a philosopher, or a musician, he will often show a noble indifference to filthy lucre, like Spinoza.'

Finger in the *or* every pie – *to play a part in doing something, to have an interest in every enterprise or activity*

There is an ellipsis in this expression. It is better understood if read 'to have a finger in making the pie', in which case the sense of involvement becomes clear. There is nearly always an implication of meddling in other people's business. This universal human tendency has been reflected in this phrase for at least 400 years.

NORFOLK: All this was order'd by the good discretion
Of the right reverend Cardinal of York.
BUCKINGHAM: The devil speed him! no man's pie is freed
From his ambitious finger.
Shakespeare, Henry VIII (1612)

Country Living (1991): 'Mike Castleton is as local as they come, a King's Lynn man through and through with a finger in numerous pies. Erstwhile trawler owner, market trader, expert on shellfish and a plasterer by trade, he's the kind of chap who gets up at five in the morning and is still going strong at 11 at night, preferably in the pub.'

First-rate – *of the highest class of degree or excellence, the best*

This is a naval expression which refers to a 'ship of the first rate', belonging to the highest, and therefore the most powerful, of the six divisions (rates).

London Gazette (1666): 'Twelve new Ships, all of the first Rate.'

Henry Fielding, *Tom Jones* (1749): 'His natural parts were not of the first rate.'

Fit as a fiddle – *in good health*

The word 'fit' originally meant 'right and proper' (i.e. fitting) and it was only in the 19th century that it came to mean 'in good condition'. Darwin's *On the Origin of Species* (1859) quoted the phrase used by Herbert Spencer (1820–1903), 'survival of the fittest', which is one late example of the word 'fit' used in its old sense. This sense survives today in phrases like 'fit to govern'.

It is difficult to see the relevance of the word 'fiddle' in this context. Fiddles are admired for their sound and sometimes for their symmetrical shape. Indeed, to say 'his face is made of a fiddle' was once a way of describing someone as irresistibly charming.

Sir Walter Scott, *Old Mortality* (1816): 'How could I help it? His face was made of a fiddle.'

It has also been suggested that the phrase is a contraction of 'as fit as a fiddler', which may be a reference to the fact that the instrument involves dextrous playing.

Whatever its provenance, it is certainly one of those many phrases in the English language which have become popular because of alliteration.

Sir Francis Beaumont and John Fletcher, *Women Pleased* (1647): '"Am I come fit, Penurio?" – "As fit as a fiddle."'

Flash Harry – *a self-confident, vulgar person*

The use of the word 'flash' in this context is very long established (*Low Life*, 1764: 'The Jemmies, Brights, Flashes and ... Smarts of the Town').

It conveys the notion of something or someone superficially impressive but with no real substance, as in Admiral William Henry Smyth's *The*

Sailors' Wordbook (1867): 'Flash vessels, all paint outside and no order within.'

'Flash Harry' was coined in the 20th century, as in John Rae, *The Custard Boys* (1960): '"They are just a lot of Smart Alecs" – "Flash Harrys," suggested Peter.'

Jeffrey Miller, *Street Talk: The Language of Coronation Street* (1986) defines Flash Harry as: 'A "greasy" character of extravagant habits, someone who is common, vulgar but self-assured, gangster-like. From "flash" meaning "loud" and in poor taste.'

Flash Harry was also the nickname of Sir Malcolm Sargent (1895–1967), the orchestral conductor. The origin of his nickname, according to Sargent, was that having appeared on the *Brains Trust* radio programme, there followed immediately a concert in Manchester which he was conducting. It was as if he had gone there straight away, in a flash. However, the nickname also encapsulated his extremely debonair looks and manner – smoothed-back hair, buttonhole, gestures and all.

It has also been suggested that Flash Harry was originally the name of the man who would 'flash' the furnaces every morning in Midlands factories.

See also **Smart Alec**.

Flash in the pan – *a brilliant initiative which amounts to nothing, a short-lived success, outright failure after a showy beginning*

This expression comes from a malfunction in the old flintlock rifle. When the trigger was pulled, a flint striking against the hammer produced a spark which fired the priming, a small quantity of gunpowder held in the 'pan'.

This explosion ignited the main charge, forcing the ball to fly from the barrel. Sometimes the priming caught but failed to ignite the main charge, resulting in nothing more than a 'flash in the pan'.

When this happened, the gun was said to be 'hanging fire', giving rise to another idiomatic phrase. See **Hang fire**.

Noël Coward, *Present Indicative* (1937): 'There was little or no surprise that a play of mine should be so appallingly bad, for, in their minds at least, I had never been anything but a flash in the pan, a playboy whose meteoric rise could only result in an equally meteoric fall into swift oblivion.'

Flotsam and jetsam – *rubbish, odds and ends*

'Flotsam' is from the Old French *floter*, to float, and means salvage floating in the water. 'Jetsam' is a shortening of 'jettison', from Old French *getaison*, related to modern French *jeter*, to throw. It means rubbish which has deliberately been thrown overboard.

Flotsam and Jetsam were the names adopted by variety entertainers B.C. Hilliam (1890–1968) and Malcolm McEachern (1884–1945). The names were appropriate, since Flotsam had the high 'floating' voice and Jetsam the low 'sinking' voice.

John Gibson Lockhart, *Memoirs of the Life of Sir Walter Scott* (1837–8): 'The goods and chattles of the inhabitants are all said to savour of Flotsome and Jetsome.'

Fly a kite – *to make a suggestion to gauge opposition or support*

This metaphor comes from the idea of 'seeing how the wind blows' to one particular idea or suggestion.

For example, Lord Palmerston wrote in 1831: 'Charles John [King of Sweden] flew a kite at us for the Garter the other day, but without success.'

In commercial slang, the phrase meant to raise money on credit by a negotiable instrument, an accommodation bill, which did not represent any actual transaction.

John Cordy Jeaffreson, *A Book of Recollections* (1894): 'The wretched piece of paper, with my autograph upon it. But no harm came to me from the little kite.'

From 1880 it came to mean simply 'to raise money'. In the 20th century the phrase acquired doubtful connotations, meaning, for example, to cash a cheque against non-existent funds.

Fly in the ointment – *something trifling that spoils or mars the whole*

The origin of this phrase is probably Biblical, from Ecclesiastes (10:1): 'Dead flies cause the ointment of the apothecary to send forth a stinking savour.'

Others have suggested that its origin is in an earlier phrase, 'a fly in (the) amber'. Insects fossilised in amber were the object of wonderment. Francis

Bacon remarked: 'We see spiders, flies, or ants entombed forever in amber, a more royal tomb.' (*Historia Vitae et Mortis, Sylva Sylvarum*, 1623)

However, this derivation seems improbable. The sense of wonderment is not part of the contemporary phrase, and its origin is more likely to be the apothecary's ointment in Ecclesiastes.

Sydney Smith, in typical fashion, wrote of George Canning (briefly Prime Minister in 1827): 'He is a fly in amber; nobody cares about the fly; the only question is, How the devil did it get there?'

Charles Lamb, *The Last Essays of Elia* (1833): 'A Poor Relation – is the most irrelevant thing in nature – a lion in your path, a frog in your chamber, a fly in your ointment.'

Fly off the handle – *to fly into a fit of rage*

This expression was current among American frontiersmen about 150 years ago. The reference is to an axe-head which, having worked loose on its home-made handle, finally flies off at the next hefty blow.

For an axe to break in this way was dangerous. It also meant that work had to stop until the axe was repaired. It was not therefore surprising that the event was accompanied by a furious outburst of temper, and that angry behaviour became associated with the idea of 'flying off the handle'.

An alternative explanation might be that the person who gets angry is being equated with the axe-head, going violently out of control and possibly doing damage.

Lewis Nkosi, *The Rhythm of Violence* (1964): 'Calm down, for God's sake! Everybody's flying off the handle. What's the matter with everybody?'

Foot the bill – *to pay the bill*

When one adds a list of figures, the total is at the foot of the column. A euphemism for asking a customer to pay was to enquire if he would like to 'foot the bill', meaning to check the arithmetic. In time, this euphemistic sense dropped away.

The phrase dates from about 1844 and was an Americanism until about 1890.

Bishop Lancelot Andrewes, *Sermons* (1629): 'So, it signifies to make the foot of an account. We call it the foot, because we write it below at the foot.'

Footloose and fancy free – *free from care and responsibility*

'Footloose' describes someone who, without responsibilities to restrain him, can wander wherever he wishes. If that person also has no sweetheart to tie him down, he is 'fancy free'. The phrase is appealing because of the alliteration.

Edward Candy, *Words for Murder Perhaps* (1971): 'I'm travelling around you see. Footloose and fancy free, you might call me. I've no special ties anywhere.'

Fork out – *to give up, hand over, pay, contribute one's share*

From the 17th century, 'forks' were the forefinger and middle finger, and to 'fork' was to pickpocket, putting these two fingers into a target's pocket. As time passed, the phrase came to mean handing over, usually money, but not necessarily unwittingly or under duress. It retained, however, a certain sense of reluctance.

'B.E. Gent', *A New Dictionary of the Terms Ancient and Modern of the Canting Crew* (c. 1690–9): 'Let's fork him, Let us Pick that Man's Pocket.'

Ascott R. Hope, *My Schoolboy Friends* (1875): 'I'll tell Vialls if you do not fork out.'

Forty winks – *a very brief sleep, a short nap, a doze*

'Forty winks' is a colloquial phrase dating from the mid-1820s. There is no satisfactory explanation for the choice of 'forty' as opposed to any other number. It is suggested that it derives from Biblical times, when the number indicated a large amount, as in 'forty days and forty nights'. However, the essential meaning of the phrase is that it is a short, not a long, sleep.

The word 'wink' meaning sleep has been common in English since earliest times, as in William Langland, *Piers Plowman* (1362): 'Then Wakede I of my wink.'

'Not to have a wink of sleep' or 'not to sleep a wink' are phrases which date from a similar period.

Punch (1872): 'If a … man, after reading steadily through the Thirty-nine Articles, were to take forty winks …'

Joseph Hatton, *By Order of the Czar* (1890): '"Well, I declare, Dolly, you are going to sleep!" – "I am very tired; only forty winks. Is there time?"'

Fresh as a daisy – *blooming, looking healthy or youthful; strong, active; bright and breezy*

'Daisy' comes from the Old English *dæges eage*, 'day's eye', as in:

> Wele by reson men it call may
> The dayeseye, or ellis the eye of day.
> > Geoffrey Chaucer, 'The Legend
> > of Good Women' (1385)

The name is due to the flower's similarity in appearance to the sun, and the way in which it appears to sleep, regularly closing at sunset, concealing the yellow disc, and opening in the morning. One might think of the daisy having 'slept' and woken refreshed every day.

Eaton Stannard Barrett, *The Heroine* (1815): 'As fresh as a daisy.'

From pillar to post – *badgered and bothered, chased hither and thither from one thing to another without definite purpose*

This is a very old expression and could come from either of two sources.

It may be a reference to the medieval punishment of the pillory (pillar) and the whipping post.

However, it is more likely to relate to the ancient game of real (meaning 'royal') tennis, in which 'pillar' and 'post' were features in the court's architecture.

The original phrase was 'post to pillar', and the order of the words was reversed to facilitate a rhyme with the contemporary pronunciation of 'tost, tossed':

John Lydgate, *The Assembly of Gods* (c. 1420): 'Thus fro post to pylour he was made to daunce.'

Robert Dodsley, *A Select Collection of Old Plays* (1602): 'Every minute tost, / Like to a tennis-ball, from pillar to post.'

From the horse's mouth – *from an original or reputable source, on good authority*

Originally this phrase was racing slang for 'a hot tip'. It alluded to the fact that a horse's age can be discovered by inspecting its teeth. A dealer may be economical with the truth but the evidence in the horse's mouth is absolutely reliable.

After the 1930s the phrase came to mean any kind of evidence given on the best authority.

Aldous Huxley, *Brave New World* (1932): 'Each of them carried a notebook, in which, whenever the great man spoke, he desperately scribbled. Straight from the horse's mouth. It was a rare privilege.'

Full Monty – *the whole thing, the lot, everything; nakedness*

The most likely origin of this phrase (but by no means the only possible one) is that it derives from the first name of Montague Maurice Burton, founder of Burtons, the tailors. Montague Burton opened his first shop in Chesterfield in 1903 and by 1913 he had his headquarters in Sheffield. (By coincidence, the film *The Full Monty*, which gives the phrase its most recent sense of 'nakedness', was set in Sheffield.)

Before the Second World War, Burtons offered a two-piece suit as the basic option, but for a small extra amount one could also have a waistcoat and a spare pair of trousers. Paying the extra meant going the 'full Monty'. Other suggestions are many. It has been said that it is a corruption of 'the full amount'; a reference to bales full of wool imported from Montevideo; gambler's jargon meaning the kitty or pot, deriving from the old US card game called 'monte'; or from the name of the famous London theatrical outfitters, Monty Burmans.

Finally, some cite as the source for the phrase Field Marshal Montgomery, nick-named 'Monty' by his troops during the Second World War. He insisted on a full English breakfast every morning, even when fighting in the desert during the North Africa campaign. Certainly in transport cafés in the 1950s, the phrase 'the full Monty' was used for a full breakfast of bacon, eggs, fried bread, tomato, mushrooms, toast and a cup of tea.

Full of beans – *energetic, lively, in high spirits*

This phrase was originally used of a horse full of energy and in tip-top condition. Beans were supposed to be good for the horse, and 'beany', describing a horse in good fettle, was a word in current use throughout the 19th century.

It was later applied to people; at the end of the 19th century, in a slightly pejorative sense, someone 'too full of beans' was a person whom sudden prosperity had made offensive and conceited.

Robert Smith Surtees, *Handley Cross* (1854): ''Ounds, 'osses and men, are in a glorious state of excitement! Full o' beans and benevolence.'

G

Get down to brass tacks – *to bring the essential facts under discussion, to get to the heart of the matter*

The phrase would seem to be American, probably 19th-century, although its origins are obscure.

Brass tacks in a draper's store were hammered into the counter and used for measuring fabric, suggesting that the customer was about to get down to business and make a purchase. However, this does not convey the idea of removing layers which is implied in the phrase.

Two suggestions are offered. The brass tacks used by an upholsterer would be exposed when a piece of furniture was being radically refurbished or repaired. Alternatively, when a ship's hull was being cleaned of barnacles, the bolts which held the structure together would be revealed. These were made of copper, not brass, nor were they flimsy tacks, but it is conceivable that this was American understatement for humorous effect.

Sinclair Lewis, *Our Mr Wrenn* (1914): 'Highbrow sermons that don't come down to brass tacks.'

Get down to the nitty-gritty – *to get to the real detail, the essentials, the harsh realities*

African-Americans often claim this term is racist. It is said to refer to the noxious debris left in the bottom of slave ships once the slaves who survived the journey had been removed on arrival.

There is a slight link, in that 'nitty-gritty' was indeed originally a black American English expression, and some people guess that it is a rhyming slang euphemism for 'shitty', which also suggests some relevance.

The etymology of the phrase is unknown. Jonathan Lighter, in the *Random House Historical Dictionary of American Slang*, records the first example

from as late as 1956: 'You'll find nobody comes down to the nitty-gritty when it calls for namin' things the way they are.'

Certainly 'nitty-gritty' is found in African-American pop music slang dating from around 1963.

One explanation is that it is a reduplication, using the same mechanism that has given us 'namby-pamby' and 'itsy-bitsy', of the standard English word 'gritty'. This has the literal sense of containing or being covered with grit, but figuratively means showing courage and resolve, so the link is plausible.

American Speech (1974) suggests that 'nits' refers to head lice and 'grits' to the corn cereal. There is no evidence to support the suggestion that the reference is to nits in unclean pubic hair and to grits meaning dried faeces, the interpretation being that 'to get down to the nitty-gritty' means shaving the hair and thoroughly cleaning the infected areas.

The lack of clear origin of the phrase has contributed to such unfounded suggestions and the wide distribution of the slave-ship story.

Time (1963): 'The Negroes present would know perfectly well that the nitty-gritty of a situation is the essentials of it.'

Get hold of the wrong end of the stick – *to misunderstand something entirely, to misinterpret a situation*

The phrase can be traced back to the 1400s in its original form of 'the worse end of the staff' (or lance). The wording changed in the 1800s.

It is also said to date back to the Romans' use of communal toilets. For personal hygiene reasons they used a short staff with a sponge tied to the end, and everybody took great care not to get hold of the wrong end when they used it.

Swell's Night Guide (1846): 'Which of us had hold of the crappy … end of the stick?'

George Orwell, *Coming up for Air* (1939): 'Listen, Hilda. You've got hold of the wrong end of the stick about this business.'

Get on one's wick – *to get on one's nerves, to irritate, to exasperate*

This is rhyming slang, coming from an area of London, Hampton Wick, meaning 'prick'. Other phrases derive from the same source, for example, to dip one's wick.

Kingsley Amis, *I Like it Here* (1958): 'But I wish he wouldn't think he's got the right to knock the English. That's what really gets on my wick.'

Jan Carew, *Black Midas* (1958): '"Come on," Santos bellowed. "If every time you dip your wick, you're going to fall in love, then God help you!" Belle jumped out of bed and pulled on her dress.'

Get out of bed on the wrong side – *be irritable*

It was formerly held to be unlucky to get out of bed on the left side where the evil spirits dwell. The word 'sinister' is from the Latin meaning 'left'. It gives rise to many other phrases, e.g. a 'left-handed compliment' meaning false praise.

Also, when the right ear burns, one is being praised, but if it is the left ear which is burning, there is evil intent (see **Ears are burning**).

G.R. Sims, *Mary Jane's Memoirs* (1887): 'I never lived in a family that so often got out of bed on the wrong side, to use a homely expression.'

Get someone's goat – *to irritate, annoy someone*

The phrase came into use early in the 20th century in America. Its origin is uncertain, but the following theory has been advanced.

It was common for a highly-strung racehorse to have a goat as a stable companion. Goats were thought to have a calming influence on nervy thoroughbreds. It seems that attempts were sometimes made to sabotage a horse's chance of success by stealing the goat the night before a big race, thus reducing the would-be champion to a state of agitation.

This seems rather far-fetched. Another interesting suggestion is that 'goat' refers to a goatee beard, which someone might tug in an annoying way.

Another version is to 'get one's nanny-goat' and the French have a similar expression, *prendre la chèvre*, to take the milch-goat.

Christy Mathewson, *Pitching* (1912): '[He] stopped at third with a mocking smile on his face which would have gotten the late Job's goat.'

Get the bird – *to be rejected*

The phrase originated in the theatre, where the expression meant to be rejected by the audience. Known since the 19th century, the phrase began as 'to get the big bird' and was based on what audiences do when they are dissatisfied – they boo and hiss like a flock of geese.

Peter Kemp, *Mine Were of Trouble* (1957): 'She gave him the bird – finally and for good. So he came to Spain to forget his broken heart.'

Get the sack – *to lose your job*

Labourers and mechanics brought their own tools from job to job in a sack, and when they lost their job their bag or sack was returned to them.

The phrase was current in 17th-century France, as in 'On luy a donné son sac' (They have given him his sack), and also in Middle Dutch, 'den zac krijgen' (to get the sack).

George Orwell, *The Road to Wigan Pier* (1937): 'If they failed to secure a minimum of twenty orders a day, they got the sack.'

Gird up your loins – *to get ready for action*

This is a biblical expression. The Jews wore loose garments, which they girded (belted) about their loins (waist) when travelling or working. Also, tucking the end of their robes into their belts enabled them to run faster.

'He girded up his loins and ran before Ahab.' (1 Kings 18:46)

Eliza Lynn Linton, *The Rebel of the Family* (1880): 'He was standing like the impersonation of masculine punctuality with loins girded.'

Give a tinker's dam *or* damn – *(usually in the negative) therefore not to care about something, to be totally indifferent to something*

At one time itinerant tinkers were familiar figures, roaming the country-side earning their living by mending pots and pans. A hole in a pan would be surrounded by a wall, or dam, of clay or even bread, and solder poured inside. Once the solder had set, the dam would be thrown aside as worthless.

An alternative theory is that tinkers had a reputation for swearing and cursing at every word, so much so that their expletives, their damns and cusses, became meaningless.

Cameron Knight, *Dictionary of Mechanics* (1877): '*Tinker's dam*, a wall of dough raised round a place which a plumber desires to flood with a coat of solder. The material can be but once used; being consequently thrown away as worthless, it has passed into a proverb, usually involving the wrong spelling of the otherwise innocent word "dam".'

Give one a break – *to provide an opportunity*

A break was an interruption in a street performance when the hat could be passed round for a collection. In the 19th century, 'break' was used to describe the collection made by friends for a prisoner's defence or for assistance when he was released from prison.

By itself, 'break', especially in the USA (from 1827), usually meant a piece of good luck. In the UK, 'a bad break' has come to mean an unforeseen stroke of bad luck, or run of misfortunes. This usage may have been influenced by the railwayman's colloquial term 'break' (since 1898), meaning 'a continuous or unbroken run or journey'. It probably also relates to a break in the game of billiards.

Give one the willies – *to give a feeling of nervousness, discomfort, vague fear*

The etymology of the phrase is unknown. Perhaps the origin of 'willies' is 'wiffle-woffles', meaning 'a stomach ache, sorrow, melancholy' (1859), bearing similarities in form and meaning to 'colly-wobbles'.

It has been suggested that the reference is to the willow tree, 'willy' being an ancient form of the word 'willow'. The saying 'she is in her willows' was used of a woman who had lost her lover or spouse. Reference to the willow as a symbol of grief and mourning has, it is argued, extended into meaning apprehension and nervousness.

More than one authority has pointed out that Giselle, the heroine of the 19th-century ballet of that name, is possessed by Wilis, or spirits of beautiful young girls who have died before their wedding day and who dance to express their anger at their death.

Jack London, *The Valley of the Moon* (1913): 'Bert gives me the willies the way he's always lookin' for trouble.'

Give the thumbs up *or* down – *to approve or disapprove*

In Roman gladiatorial contests the audience was asked to decide whether a defeated gladiator should be killed. If they kept their thumbs clenched in their fists he was pardoned: *pollice compresso favor judicabatur*, 'by the clenched thumb the judgement was in favour'.

A medallion from the 2nd or 3rd century AD supports this contention by Anthony Philip Corbeill of the University of Kansas. The medallion shows two warriors who have ceased fighting. A referee stands nearby, pressing a thumb against his closed fist. An inscription above the scene reads: 'Those standing should be released.'

Where did the positive message of the thumbs-up sign come from? Anthropologist Desmond Morris discovered that it arrived in Europe during the Second World War, along with American GIs.

Philemon Holland, *Pliny's Historie of the World, commonly called the Natural*

Historie (translated 1601): 'To bend or bow downe the thumbes when wee give assent unto a thing, or doe favour any person.'

Rudyard Kipling, *Puck of Pook's Hill* (1906): 'We're finished men – thumbs down against both of us.'

Go AWOL – *to leave without permission*

AWOL is an acronym for 'Absent Without Leave' and was used in the First World War for a soldier absent at roll-call but not yet classified as a deserter.

CBS News, 31 March 2004:

> AWOL, From Iraq
> In the year since US-led forces invaded Iraq, hundreds of American soldiers have broken the law and gone AWOL – absent without leave.
>
> Correspondent Dan Rather talks to one soldier, Staff Sgt Camilo Mejia, who abandoned his unit in the middle of the war in one of the most dangerous parts of Iraq.
>
> In his only on-camera interview while still in hiding, Mejia told *60 Minutes II* that he went AWOL because he is morally opposed to a war that has killed or wounded nearly 4,000 US soldiers.

Go bananas – *to go mad with anger, frustration, excitement or the like*

'Going bananas' has its origins in the USA and was adopted in the UK widely by 1976. It had, however, lost its original link with the banana, in the sense 'to go all mushy with emotion, especially excitement' (Harold Wentworth and Stuart Berg Flexner, *Dictionary of American Slang*, 1975).

In the later 1970s the phrase was applied to machines, meaning 'to go wrong, to behave oddly'.

It has been suggested that the phrase may also have been influenced by the instability associated with 'Banana Republics'.

Sunday Sun, Brisbane (1974): 'He just went bananas. My husband tried to take the bottle from him and he wouldn't let go … He jumped on to the television and then on to the china cabinet.'

Both this phrase and 'going pear-shaped' may also reflect the fact that the shape of both fruits deviates from a straight line. (See **Pear-shaped**.)

Go berserk – *to show frenzied action*

The word 'berserk' comes from the Icelandic *berserkr*, made up of two words: *bjorn*, bear and *serkr*, shirt. In Scandinavian mythology a *berserkr* was a fierce Norse warrior, dressed in a bear skin and famed as a furious fighter.

Sir Walter Scott, *The Pirate* (1822): 'The berserkars were so called from fighting without armour.'

Julian Symons, *The End of Solomon Grundy* (1964): 'If you have chaps like old Sol going berserk, it's enough to break up any party.'

Go by the board – *to be lost or abandoned*

'Board' was a nautical term for the side of a ship and therefore, anything that went by the board had been lost or thrown overboard.

Henry Wadsworth Longfellow, 'The Wreck of the Hesperus' (1856):

Her rattling shrouds, all sheathed in ice,
With the masts went by the board.

William D. Whitney, *The Life and Growth of Language* (1875): 'A class of grammatical distinctions which have gone by the board.'

Go for a Burton – *to be killed, ruined, completely spoilt*

During the Second World War, the RAF used this euphemism to speak of colleagues who were killed and missing in action. A 'Burton' is thought to be a reference to strong beer made in Burton-on-Trent. Some even say that the slogan 'Gone for a Burton' featured in advertisements of the period. Friends were not said to have gone to their deaths; they had just gone out for a beer.

Nowadays the phrase has lost its association with death and means anything that is broken or damaged beyond repair.

John Braine, *Room at the Top* (1957): 'We non-coms used to say *got the chopper*. Going for a Burton was journalists' talk.'

Go haywire – *to go wrong, perform erratically, behave in an uncontrolled way, run riot*

Haywire is the wire used in North America for binding bales of hay and straw. When the wire is cut on tightly bound hay bales, it whips back sharply and dangerously. Sudden unpredictable loss of control is the sense of this expression.

Ngaio Marsh, *Surfeit of Lampreys* (1941): 'Some nice homicidal maniac … going all haywire.'

Go on a Cook's tour – *to travel in an organised manner, possibly on a circular tour or one of rather greater extent than originally intended*

Thomas Cook was the founder of the world's original travel agency. A former preacher, he was on his way to a temperance meeting in Leicester when his ideas began to take shape. In 1842, Cook, then 32 years old, believed that social problems were alcohol-related.

When he arrived at the meeting he suggested using a train to transport the temperance supporters of Leicester to a delegate meeting in Loughborough. The suggestion was met with great enthusiasm. The train was arranged with the Midland Railway Company, and on 5 July 1841 around 500 passengers were taken twelve miles and back again for one shilling.

In 1855 Cook began offering trips to Europe. He failed to persuade companies controlling the Channel traffic to allow him concessions, although he managed to acquire one route, Harwich to Antwerp.

Thomas Cook overcame these restrictions by offering a circular tour including Brussels, Cologne, the Rhine, Heidelberg, Baden-Baden, Strasbourg and Paris. It is possibly from this that the figurative use of 'a Cook's tour' derives.

Amelia B. Edwards, *A Thousand Miles Up the Nile* (1877): '[The new-comer in Cairo] distinguishes at first sight between a Cook's tourist and an independent traveller.'

Go the whole hog – *to go all the way, without reservation, completely and thoroughly*

There are many fanciful derivations for this phrase. It could be as simple as a butcher recommending to a customer that it would be cheaper to buy the whole pig, or it could be a cooking expression encouraging the use of the whole animal.

However, it used to be possible to spend a portion of an English shilling simply by breaking off one part of the coin, which was deeply scored with lateral crosses for this purpose. The tail side of a shilling bore the image of a pig, so you could spend only a quarter or indeed you could go the whole hog!

William Cowper says in 'The Love of the World; or Hypocrisy Detected' (1779) that the Muslim divines sought to ascertain which part of the hog was forbidden as food by the Prophet.

> But for one piece they thought it hard
> From the whole hog to be debarred.

Unable to reach a decision, each thought that the portion of meat he wanted was the one to be excepted. As their tastes differed, they decided to eat up the whole hog.

Household Words (1852): 'When a Virginian butcher kills a pig, he is said to ask his customers whether they will "go the whole hog", as, in such case, he sells at a lower price than if they pick out the prime joints only.'

An early example in its figurative sense comes from *The Beaver*, the Hudson Bay Company's magazine: '2 June 1840 … The Govr dropt in upon us last night at five, dined with the Sheriff and me at Joe's and "went the whole hog" after, by discussing some first rate port.'

Go to the wall – *to be ruined, to fail in business; to succumb in a conflict or struggle*

The origin of the phrase probably relates to funerals and the practice of placing the dead next to the churchyard wall, prior to the body's interment in the graveyard.

An alternative suggestion is that in medieval chapels, for example at Dover Castle, stone seating was provided around the walls to support the elderly and the infirm. The weak went to the wall while the stronger members of the congregation stood.

The Nineteenth Century, a monthly review (1891): 'In Berlin a newspaper would very soon go to the wall if it did not present its subscribers with light entertainment.'

Anthony Trollope, *The Last Chronicle of Barset* (1867): 'In all these struggles, Crosbie had had the best of it, and Butterwell had gone to the wall.'

Go with the flow – *to follow the majority, have no strong opinion*

Thought to be a recent American expression, the phrase actually originates many centuries earlier with Marcus Aurelius who was crowned Emperor of Rome in the year AD 161. Marcus Aurelius Antoninus was a great military leader but he also had a sincere desire for peace that manifested itself in his philosophical writings.

In a reign characterised by war and disaster, it was through Stoic philosophy that Marcus found the strength to deal with his many problems. These beliefs were expressed in his *Meditations*, in which he exhibits the tensions he felt between his position as Emperor and his prevailing feeling of inadequacy. He believed that 'all things flow naturally' and that it was better to 'go with the flow' than to try to change the course of events.

A variation of the phrase is 'to go with the tide', as in John Donne, *Letters* (1631): 'I had the same desires when I went with the tide.'

Gone to pot – *ruined, destroyed*

In 16th-century literature there are numerous references to this expression, and it probably suggests cutting up those bits of meat which were of little use or left over and thrown into the cooking pot.

Another explanation is that it refers to a pot into which broken metal objects, or perhaps stolen articles, were thrown to be melted down.

John Galsworthy, *In Chancery* (1920): 'I shouldn't wonder if the Empire split up and went to pot. And this vision of the Empire going to pot filled a quarter of an hour with qualms of the most serious character.'

Gone west – *lost, finished, destroyed*

The context is usually that of a plan, project or business deal which has gone disastrously wrong. The origin may be the sun setting in the west.

Alternatively, the site of the Tyburn gibbet was in central London near where Marble Arch is presently located. London's main prisons, Newgate and The Clink, were on the east side of the city. A condemned man would be loaded on to a cart and taken west, never to return.

Robert Greene, *The Art of Conny-Catching* (1592): 'So long the foists [thieves] put their villanie into practice, that West-ward they go, and there solemnly make a rehearsal sermon at tiborne.'

G.D.H. and Margaret Cole, *Death of a Millionaire* (1925): '"There's valuable evidence gone west," he said. "It may be hard to pick up the trail now."'

Good egg – *a dependable person*

It is impossible to tell from simply looking at the shell whether an egg is fresh or not. Once the egg is broken it may reveal an unpleasant surprise, but a good egg will be found completely sound to its centre. So it is with people; the outward appearance will not reveal a person's true character.

Athenaeum (1864): 'A "bad egg" … a fellow who has not proved to be as good as his promise.'

Observer headline (1992): 'Is Red Ken a good egg on Labour's new menu?'

Good health! – *a toast usually accompanying an alcoholic drink*

In 19th-century England cholera was rife, and a particularly deadly outbreak occurred in 1848, reaching epidemic proportions in August 1849 in the Broadwick Street area of Soho. The prevailing view at the time was that cholera was spread by 'miasma', bad air arising from decayed organic matter.

It was a local physician, Dr John Snow, who suggested that cholera was linked to polluted water, and he proved this when he found that 87 of the 89 victims he examined were known to have drunk from the Broadwick Street well.

Snow called for the authorities to take the handle off the pump, and almost immediately the outbreak was halted. For a long while afterwards, the locals would drink ale and wine and avoid water, toasting each other's good health, knowing they were safe from the disease.

Appropriately enough, there is a pub called the John Snow on Broadwick Street today.

Goody Two-Shoes – *a smug person*

The History of Goody Two-Shoes (1765) was written, probably by Oliver Goldsmith, for John Newbery (1713–67), a notable publisher of children's books. It featured a girl called Goody who was so pleased with her new shoes that she showed them off to everyone with excessive pride. The character's real name was Marjorie Meanwell. 'Goody', short for 'good wife', was a common name for a married woman.

'The Pleasure she took in her two shoes ... by that Meanes [she] obtained the name of Goody Two-Shoes.'

Gordon Bennett – *an exclamation*

'Gordon' may well just be an evasion of 'Gawd', and 'Bennett' a random addition. A euphemism therefore, for 'Gawd A'mighty!'

The use of the name Bennett is, however, unlikely to be random. Some have suggested that the exclamation refers to James Gordon Bennett (1795–1892), the founder and editor of the *New York Herald*. It is more likely to refer to his son, a colourful character of the same name, who was famed for sending Henry Stanley in search of David Livingstone in central Africa.

James Gordon Bennett (1841–1918) took over from his father the management of the *Herald* in 1867. In 1869–71 he financed Stanley's expedition into Africa to find Livingstone, and from 1879 to 1881 he supported the ill-fated expedition of G.W. De Long to the Arctic region.

Born with a silver spoon in his mouth, he took every opportunity to live life as a playboy; his wild lifestyle and extravagant spending gained him notoriety in high society. On one occasion, at a New Year's party in 1877 held by his fiancée's father, he got so drunk that he mistook the fireplace for a toilet and proceeded to urinate in front of his prospective in-laws and their guests. Other tales include the occasion when, annoyed by the bulky roll of money in his back pocket, he burnt it in an impetuous fit.

Got my dander up – *made me angry*

'Dander' is conjectured by some to be a figurative use of an alternative word for dandruff, but it is possibly connected to 'dander' meaning ferment. Dander in the latter sense is a word of West Indian or American origin.

The phrase 'to get one's dander up' was idiomatic American before being absorbed into the English language.

Sir J. Dalrymple, *Observations on his Yeast-cake* (c. 1796): 'The season for working molasses lasts five months, of which three weeks are lost in making up the dander, that is, the ferment.'

It may also derive from the Dutch *donde* meaning thunder, as in Seba Smith, *Letters of Major Jack Downing* (1830): 'He was as spunky as thunder, and when a Quaker gets his dander up, it's like a Northwester.'

Grasp the nettle – *to face a problem with determination*

The nettle, which causes so much discomfort when lightly touched, will not sting if grasped firmly.

> Tender-handed stroke a nettle
> And it stings you for your pains
> Grasp it like a man of mettle
> And it soft as silk remains.
> Aaron Hill, 'The Nettle's Lesson' (1743)

Grass widow – *a woman whose husband is temporarily away, for example on business*

Some writers have suggested that this is a corruption of 'grace-widow', but etymologists are quite sure that the phrase has always been recorded as 'grass widow'. In support, the German equivalent *Strohwitwe* may be translated 'straw widow'.

The phrase is ancient, but in its first recorded use in Thomas More's *Dialogue Concerning Heresyes* (1528) it meant an abandoned mistress or unmarried woman who had cohabited with several men: 'Tyndall wolde by thys waye make saynt Poule to say thus. Take & chese [choose] in but such a widow as hath but one husbande at onys … I thynke saynt Poule ment not so. For then had wyuys [wives] ben in his time lytel better than grasse wydowes be now. For they be yet as severall as a barbour's chayre and never take but one at onys.'

Perhaps this sense of promiscuity suggests that the grass in 'grass widow' refers to surreptitious love-making in fields or in the straw of a barn.

One theory cites the period of the British Raj in India when wives were sent away during the hot summer to cooler (and greener) hill stations. There were the opportunities then for infidelity or sexual peccadilloes, which were famously recorded by Rudyard Kipling. The Anglo-Indian dictionary *Hobson-Jobson* (1886) said that the term was applied 'with a shade of malignancy'.

Lady Dufferin, *Viceregal Life* (1884): 'Expectant husbands come out to meet the "grass widows" who have travelled with us.'

Great Scott! – *an exclamation of surprise, wonder, admiration or the like*

This exclamation seems to have originated in America in the late 1860s, perhaps referring to General Winfield Scott (1786–1866), a popular figure after his victorious Mexican campaign.

General Scott proposed a bold plan, an amphibious attack on the coastal Mexican town of Vera Cruz. It was the largest amphibious landing of any nation up to that date.

Scott landed about three miles south of Vera Cruz on 10 March 1847, and laid siege. By the end of the month the city had surrendered. It was the first in a series of successes that would make General Scott an American hero.

Winfield Scott so impressed the people of Mexico that a delegation visited his camp to find out what he would require to lead the new government. Scott refused politely. His eye was on a bigger prize (President of the United States).

Green with envy – *extremely envious or jealous*

Through Shakespeare's references in *Othello* to 'the green-ey'd monster', green is associated with envy.

A greenish complexion was formerly held to be indicative of jealousy, and as all the green-eyed cat family 'mock the meat they feed on', so jealousy mocks its victim by loving and loathing it at the same time.

> IAGO: O! beware, my lord, of jealousy;
> It is the green-ey'd monster which doth mock
> The meat it feeds on.
>
> Shakespeare, *Othello* (1604)

Grin like a Cheshire cat – *to smile constantly and foolishly*

The mysterious Cheshire cat makes an unforgettable appearance and disappearance in Lewis Carroll's *Alice's Adventures in Wonderland* (1872): '"I wish you wouldn't keep appearing and vanishing so suddenly; you make one quite giddy!" – "All right," said the Cat; and this time it vanished quite slowly, beginning with the end of the tail, and ending with the grin, which remained some time after the rest of it had gone. – "Well! I've often seen a cat without a grin," thought Alice; "but a grin without a cat! It's the most curious thing I ever saw in all my life!".'

The Cheshire cat existed long before Lewis Carroll, and stories abound as to its origin.

Cheshire is famous for its cheeses, and some say that long ago the cheeses were either made in the shape of a grinning cat or had the head of a cat stamped on them.

Alternatively, the cat may have been the unsuccessful attempt of a sign painter to represent the lion rampant on the coat of arms of an influential Cheshire family.

Julian Huxley, *Man in the Modern World* (1947): 'A faint trace of God, half metaphysical and half magic, still broods over this world, like the smile of a cosmic Cheshire Cat. But the growth of psychological knowledge will rub even that from the universe.'

Groggy – *dizzy and unsteady*

In 1740, Admiral Edward Vernon started the custom of issuing rum diluted with water to sailors, substituting it for the neat spirit then issued to both officers and men. He was known as 'Old Grog' because he wore a cloak made of grogram – a mixture of silk and mohair. The issue of rum or 'grog' was named after him.

Admiral Vernon is best known for his success in what became known as the 'War of Jenkins' Ear'. In 1738, a sea-captain by the name of Robert Jenkins accused the Spanish of illegally boarding his ship and cutting off his ear when he resisted. In one account, he threw the ear on a table in the presence of Parliament.

'Written on Board the Berwick' from Thomas Trotter, *Notes and Queries* (1781):

> A mighty bowl on deck he drew,
> And filled it to the brink;
> Such drank the Burford's gallant crew,
> And such the gods shall drink,
> The sacred robe which Vernon wore
> Was drenched within the same;
> And hence his virtues guard our shore,
> And Grog derives its name.

Guinea pig – *a human being used for medical experiments, someone testing something for the first time*

The guinea pig is not a pig and does not come from Guinea in Africa. It is a central South American rodent. This would seem to invalidate the suggestion that the guinea pig was brought to England in 'Guineamen', vessels that made the triangular voyage to Guinea and the New World as part of the slave trade.

Also, the story that they were sold for a guinea (£1.05) seems unlikely at a time when a household servant earned £5 per year.

'Guinea pig' was first used by George Bernard Shaw in 1913 to refer to a human who was being experimented upon. The guinea pig had been used for medical experimentation in the 19th century, but the laboratory rat was by far the more common.

It may have been the experiments conducted by Louis Pasteur (illustrated) in Paris on infectious diseases, rabies in particular, in the 1880s and 90s that brought the guinea pig to wide general attention in this context.

George Bernard Shaw, 'Quintessence of Ibsenism Now Completed' (1913): 'The ... folly which sees in the child nothing more than the vivisector sees in a guinea pig: something to experiment on with a view to rearranging the world.'

Gung-ho – *excessively zealous*

'Gung-ho' is associated with tough adventurism. It means 'work together', from the Chinese *kung* (work) and *ho* (together). During the Second World War the term was adopted as a motto by a US Marine division under General E. Carlson (1896–1947).

Ian Kemp, *British GI in Vietnam* (1969): 'He ... was one of the most "gung-ho" (exceptionally keen to be personally involved in combat) characters I ever met.'

Gutter press – *scandal sheets*

Albert Barrère and C.G. Leland, *A Dictionary of Slang, Jargon and Cant* (1889) have suggested that this is a reference to a term used in printing. The inside margins or blank space between two facing pages is called the gutter, and the gutter space is that extra space allowance used to accommodate the binding in books and magazines.

It is more likely that it means appropriate to the gutter, of a low or disreputable character.

Patrick Quentin, *Suspicious Circumstances* (1957): 'One of those ... terrible gutter magazines which make fortunes unearthing people's private lives.'

H

Had one's chips – *out of luck, failed; dying*

The most common interpretation is that this phrase refers to a gambler who has risked and lost all his stake money, his 'chips'.

An earlier suggestion is a naval story in which workers in a dockyard were allowed to take home off-cuts of timber, known as chips, as a perk of the job. If a man fell out of favour with the foreman, perhaps for trying to take too many, he was told that he had had his chips.

Missouri Republican (1879): 'If you wish to express the demise of a friend … in Southern Colorado … it would be more elegant to say that "he'd passed in his chips".'

Gerald Durrell, *A Zoo in My Luggage* (1960): '"Cor!" said the constable, in a voice of deep emotion, "I thought I'd 'ad me chips that time."'

Hail from – *come from*

Until the 18th century, in the days of sailing ships, the custom was to 'hail' or attract the attention of passing ships to ascertain their port of departure. Gradually the nautical jargon 'hailed from' transferred to people and their home towns.

Muirhead Robertson, *A Lombard Street Mystery* (1888): 'Most of the pupils hailed from France.'

Hair of the dog – *alcohol as an antidote to a hangover*

For many years it was believed that the bite of a mad dog could be healed by placing its hair on the open wound.

The allusion is to the old notion that the burnt hair of a dog is an antidote to its bite. The general principle is that 'like cures like', as for example in homeopathy.

Charles Dickens, *Barnaby Rudge* (1840): 'Drink again. Another hair of the dog that bit you, captain.'

Halcyon days – *times of peace and tranquillity*

The word 'halcyon' comes from the Greek for kingfisher and is made up of two words, *hals*, the sea and *kuo*, to brood. It reflects the ancient Greek belief that kingfishers built nests for rearing their young which floated on the sea.

Greek mythology tells of the goddess Halcyone who, beside herself with grief when her husband drowned in a shipwreck, cast herself into the sea. The gods, moved by her devotion, brought him back to life, changing both Halcyone and her husband into kingfishers. Further, the gods said that, from that time, whenever kingfishers were brooding on their nests in the sea, the water would be kept calm and no storm would arise.

According to legend, kingfishers bred on the seven days before and the seven days after the winter solstice. These were halcyon days, guaranteed to be calm and fair.

And wars have that respect for his repose
As winds for halcyons when they breed at sea.
  John Dryden, 'Stanzas on Oliver Cromwell' (1658)

Isaac Disraeli, *Amenities of Literature* (1841): 'Peace and policy had diffused a halcyon calmness over the land.'

Ham actor – *a poor actor with an exaggerated, unnatural style*

Speculation, all of it quite plausible, abounds over this phrase. A favourite theory is that the term is an abbreviation of 'hamfatter', an American word dating from about 1875 which described seedy, second-rate actors who, through lack of money, were forced to use ham fat to clean off their make-up.

A variation of this is that the ham fat was used as a base for burnt cork by touring minstrels wishing to black their faces. There was also a well-known song from the George Christie Minstrels days called 'Ham Fat', about an amateurish actor.

Another theory refers to Hamish McCulloch, nicknamed Ham and leader of a troupe known as Ham's Actors, who toured Illinois around the 1880s. No one really knows if their performances deserved to be described as 'ham'.

Like a strutting player, whose conceit
Lies in his hamstring, and doth think it rich
To hear the wooden dialogue and sound
'Twixt his stretch'd footing and the scaffoldage.
    Shakespeare, *Troilus and Cressida* (1601)

S.B. Charters, *Country Blues* (1959): 'The singing of these little "hamfat" bands never reached the artistic intensity of men like Blind Lemon.'

Listener (1957): 'Nor does he purvey anything of Wales as it is – rather the hammed up version of Wales that the stupider sort of Englishman prefers.'

Hang fire – *to be pending, delayed*

This is an expression from the use of firearms. When the main charge in a gun was slow to ignite, the gun was said to be hanging fire.

Usually the phrase refers to a decision or event that is delayed, but it may be used of someone slow to take decisive action. Sir Walter Scott, 'Letter to G. Ellis' (1801): 'Leyden's Indian journey … seems to hang fire.'

See also **Flash in the pan**.

Hangdog look – *a shamefaced guilty expression*

In medieval times, animals which had caused harm or death were put on trial and, if found guilty, sentenced to death. The practice was common throughout Europe.

In Savoy in eastern France in 1487, beetles were formally charged with the destruction of a vineyard, and in the same year in Switzerland it was claimed that a cock had laid an egg and should therefore answer charges of sorcery.

In an age when unhygienic conditions were widespread, it was only to be expected that dog bites would quite often prove fatal, thus bringing about a charge of murder.

A 'hangdog look' originally described the expression of someone considered fit to hang, like a dog, for his crimes, but it has weakened to mean little more than shamefaced.

Charles Dickens, *Nicholas Nickleby* (1838–9): '"He, he!" tittered his friend, "you are so very funny!" – "I need be," remarked Ralph dryly, "for this is rather dull and chilling. Look a little brisker, man, and not so hangdog like."'

Hanged, drawn and quartered – *a particularly cruel form of execution*

A prisoner sentenced to death was drawn behind a cart on a hurdle or tied to a horse's tail, then hung by the neck and quartered.

John Capgrave, *The Chronicle of England* (1460): '[Serle was] condempned to be drawe thoro oute the good townes of Ynglond, and aftir to be hanged and quartered at London.'

Later, drawing (in the sense of disembowelling) and decapitation was added to the punishment, after the hanging and before the quartering.

William Wallace in August 1305 was therefore sentenced to be drawn, *detrahatur*, to the Tower of London, hanged, *suspendatur*, disembowelled or drawn, *devaletur*, and then beheaded and quartered, *decapitetur et decolletur*.

Lord Chief Justice Ellenborough (1750–1818) would say to those condemned: 'You are drawn on hurdles to the place of execution, where you are to be hanged, but *not* till you are dead; for while you are still living, your body is to be taken down, your bowels torn out and burnt before your face; your head is then cut off, and your body is divided into four quarters.' (*Gentleman's Magazine*, 1803)

Hanky-panky – *mild trickery; something improper; minor sexual impropriety*

The phrase is thought to come from 'hocus pocus', although the path is not entirely clear. (See **Hocus pocus**.)

Weekend Telegraph (1991): 'We've heard the tales of holiday hanky-panky. Your average male ski instructor is a preening, mirror-shaded hunk with a professional status one step up from a gigolo. Yet whatever their reputation, many skiers are happy to entertain the possibility of a holiday fling with their instructor.'

Happy as a clam – *perfectly content*

One may wonder why this American phrase, dating from the 1830s, singles out the clam as the epitome of happiness. The answer is in the full version of the original phrase, which was 'happy as a clam at high tide' or, sometimes, 'happy as a clam at high water'.

Clam digging was done at low tide, when one has more chance of finding and extracting them. At high water, clams are comfortably covered in water and so able to feed safely.

> Inglorious friend! Most confident I am
> Thy life is one of very little ease;
> Albeit men mock thee with their smiles,

And prate of being 'happy as a clam!' …
What though thy shell protects thy fragile head
Though thou art tender, yet thy humble bard
Declares, O clam! thy case is shocking hard!
John G. Saxe, 'Sonnet to a Clam' (?1847)

Joseph Lincoln, *Cap'n Warren's Wards* (1912): 'So, when I went to sea as a cabin boy, a tow-headed snub-nosed little chap of fourteen, I was as happy as a clam at high water 'cause I was goin' in the ship he was mate of.'

Happy as a sand-boy – *very happy*

In Charles Dickens' *The Old Curiosity Shop* (1840) there is an inn called the Jolly Sand Boys, which suggests that the phrase 'jolly as a sand boy' was already common currency. These boys sold sand to the owners of shops and taverns to absorb the mud on customers' boots.

John Bee, *Slang – A Dictionary of the Turf* (1823): '*Sand-boy*, all rags and happiness; the urchins who drive the sand-laden neddies through our streets, are envied by the capon-eating, turtle-loving epicures of these cities. "As jolly as a sand-boy", designates a merry fellow who has tasted a drop.'

Happy as Larry – *extremely happy*

This probably comes from the English dialect word 'larrie', meaning to joke, or the Cornish word 'larrikin', which means a 'larker'. The 'larrikin' in Australia or New Zealand was a gypsy, a traveller or a young hooligan. Both of these may have influenced this phrase.

The Australian usage of 'larrikin' seems to have originated in Melbourne not long before 1870, but the story that it evolved by a reporter quoting an Irish policeman's pronunciation of 'larking' seems to be a figment. Equally fantastic is the suggestion that it derives from two slang words, 'leary kinchen', meaning clever child pickpocket – an Australian Artful Dodger!

The expression may also come from the Australian boxer Larry Foley (1847–1917), but it is hard to see, first, why he was so happy and, second, how the phrase could then have originated in New Zealand as well as Australia.

Tom Collins, *Barrier Truth* (1905): 'Now that the adventure was drawing to an end, I found a peace of mind that all the old fogies on the river couldn't disturb. I was as happy as Larry.'

Hat trick – *three successes one after another*

In cricket, when a bowler dismisses three batsmen with three successive balls, it is called a hat trick. Some say that this was because the hat was passed around for a collection, or that sometimes as a result he was awarded his club cap. Others say that this feat entitled him to be presented by his club with a new hat or some equivalent.

'Unusual Hat-tricks. All stumped: by W.H. Brain off C.L. Townsend, Gloucestershire v. Somerset at Cheltenham 1893.' (*Wisden*)

Haul somebody over the coals – *to reprimand severely*

One of the penalties for those who failed to pay taxes was to be drawn very slowly across a bed of hot coals. It was also used by the Church to deter heretics. This explains the phrase 'give someone a roasting'.

William Fulke, *A Confutation of a Treatise made by William Allen* (1565): 'St Augustine, that knew best how to fetch an heretike ouer the coles.'

Frederick Marryat, *Newton Forster* (1832): 'Lest he should be "hauled over the coals" by the Admiralty …'

Have a beef – *to have something to complain about*

To 'cry beef' in the early 19th century meant to set up a hue and cry. It may have been a very early example of rhyming slang, meaning 'Stop, thief!' It was also known before that time that the cry of 'Stop, thief' was mocked and drowned out by fellow criminals shouting 'Hot beef' in an attempt to confuse law-abiding citizens and aid the thief's getaway.

The slang term, to 'beef' or 'have a beef', seems to be originally American, adopted in the UK around 1942, probably from usage in the services.

The Road, Denver (1889): 'He will be coming down town again soon on crutches, "beefing" about cancer of the stomach.'

J.B. Priestley, *Let the People Sing* (1939): 'Too much arguin' an' beefin', majority an' minority nonsense, talking shop stuff.'

Have a dekko – *have a look*

This is sometimes thought to be Cockney rhyming slang, like 'have a butcher's' (butcher's hook = look). The phrase actually comes from the Hindustani word *dekho*, the imperative of *dekhna*, meaning 'to look' or 'to see'. It was introduced into the English language by troops returning from India in the late 1800s.

F.B. Young, *Portrait of Clare* (1927): 'He's promised to look in this evening, just to have a "dekko" as he calls it, and see that you're all right.'

Have one's work cut out – *to have to do more than one easily can*

An assistant cuts the cloth from which the tailor makes his garments. Sometimes there is more cut cloth prepared than the tailor can reasonably handle.

R. Austin Freeman, *The Magic Casket* (1927): "'You will have your work cut out,' I remarked, 'to trace that man. The potter's description was pretty vague.'"

Heath Robinson – *complicated, ingenious, amateur, makeshift*

W. Heath Robinson's father, uncle and grandfather were all employed either drawing or engraving images for publication. As Robinson grew up, new process methods developed, like the photographic transfer of an artist's drawing to an engraved printing plate.

Robinson (1872–1944) was famous for his series of drawings poking fun at various facets of modern living. A typical Heath Robinson involved a panoramic view of a complex and convoluted contraption.

The device, usually dilapidated from intense use, is designed to perform some very basic operation in the most complicated way.

It is usually run by a large group of attendants, each executing a simple task like ringing a bell or cutting a string. The device derives its humour as much from the cleverness and complexity of the contraption as from the serious attention and implied effort of the operators.

Heath Robinson applied his special touch to topics like Golfers (an easy and frequent target), The War, Flat Life (post-war housing space was at a premium), Gardening, Motoring, Husbands, Flying and many others.

Robinson enjoyed the impression he made on people, and was quoted as saying: 'I really have a secret satisfaction in being considered rather mad.'

Hide one's light under a bushel – *to conceal one's talents, to be self-effacing and modest about one's abilities*

This is a reference to the Sermon on the Mount, in which Jesus says, 'Neither do men light a candle and put it under a bushel, but on a candlestick' (Matthew 5:15). A bushel was a solid container of pottery or wood holding a fixed eight-gallon measure. A candle or any light placed under the bushel would, of course, be invisible and shed no light at all.

Bishop Robert Sanderson, *Sermons* (1627): 'The light of God's word, hid from them under two bushels for sureness: under the bushel of a tyrannous clergy ... and under the bushel of an unknown tongue.'

High jinks – *excited, high-spirited behaviour*

This phrase, of Scottish origin, goes back to the early 19th century and refers to pranks and frolics indulged in at drinking parties. One game was to throw dice to see who should drink a large bowl of liquor and who should pay for it.

The following passage suggests that 'high jinks' was a game of forfeits.

Sir Walter Scott, *Guy Mannering* (1815): 'The frolicsome company had begun to practise the ancient and now forgotten pastime of high jinks. This game was played in several different ways. Most frequently the dice were thrown by the company and those upon whom the lot fell were obliged to assume and maintain for a certain time, a certain fictitious character, or to repeat a number of fescennine [i.e. obscene, scurrilous] verses in a particular order. If they departed from the characters assigned, or if their memory proved treacherous in the repetition, they incurred forfeits, which were compounded for by swallowing an additional bumper, or by paying a small sum toward the reckoning.'

Hobson's choice – *no choice*

A Cambridge carrier who hired out horses, Thomas (Tobias) Hobson (c. 1544–1631) compelled his customers either to take the next horse in line or take no horse at all. This strict rule ensured that everyone had an equal chance of getting a good horse and none was overworked.

Roger North, *Life of Lord Guildford* (1734): 'They wanted a competition to make the money fly; and they said, Hobson's choice was no choice.'

Hobson's choice is also rhyming slang for 'voice', as in *New Statesman* (1961): 'The landlady, Queenie Watts, throws her Hobson's so hard that on a clear night you could hear it in Canning Town.'

Hocus-pocus – *a juggler's trick, conjuring, sleight of hand, trickery, deception*

A ridiculous string of mock Latin was the meaningless formula used by conjurors and jugglers in the 17th century (*Hocus pocus, toutous talontus, vade celerita jubes*). The first two words are possibly a parody of the words of consecration in the Mass (*Hoc est Corpus Meum*, This is My Body) while the rest was reeled off to occupy the attention of the audience.

An alternative etymology, which has some merit, is proposed by Henry J. Todd in his late-18th-century edition of Dr Johnson's monumental *Dictionary of the English Language* (1755). A famous Italian juggler, Ochus Bochus, gained such a reputation that other jugglers, and then conjurers, repeated his name over their tricks – perhaps for luck or to impress a gullible public. Early uses of the phrase are, indeed, often in the context of jugglers rather than conjurers.

It could be, however, that the conjurers were invoking a much older power. In James Fitzgerald, *Britain's Historical Drama* (1832), Ochus Bochus was a magician and demon among the Saxons, dwelling in forests and caves.

The modern word 'hoax' is probably a contraction of hocus pocus, which also supplied the now rare verb 'to hocus' meaning to cheat. It is thought that **Hanky-panky** comes from the same root.

> Here Hocas lyes with his tricks and his knocks,
> Whom death hath made sure as a jugler's box;
> Who many hath cozen'd by his leigerdemain,
> Is presto convey'd and here underlain.

Thus Hocas he's here, and here he is not
While death plaid the Hocas, and brought him to th' pot.
Sir J. Mennes and J. Smith, Witts Recreations,
with a Thousand Outlandish Proverbs (1654)

Hoi polloi – *the masses*

This is a direct translation of the Greek, meaning 'the many', generally used in a slighting sense.

John Dryden, 'Essay of Dramatic Poesy' (1688): 'If by the people you understand the multitude, the *hoi polloi*, 'tis no matter what they think; they are sometimes in the right, sometimes in the wrong; their judgment is a mere lottery.'

Hoist with one's own petard – *to be defeated by one's own argument or actions, caught in one's own trap, ensnared in the danger intended for others*

A petard was a piece of medieval siege machinery in which a vast barrel was filled with gunpowder and fixed to a fortification, and then a gunpowder trail was lit. Unfortunately, gunpowder was very unstable and sometimes the retreating officer did not get out of the way in time.

Shakespeare, *Hamlet* (1604): 'For 'tis the sport to have the enginer / Hoist with his own petar.'

Hold the fort – *to maintain normality, to keep things running in the absence of others*

During the American Civil War (1861–5), General Sherman immortalised the phrase at the battle of Allatoona (1864). When gathering his army on top of Mount Kennesaw, near Atlanta, Georgia, Sherman signalled down to General Corse that reinforcements were arriving and he must 'hold the fort' until he had gathered enough men to mount an attack on the siege soldiers.

The phrase made its way to Britain in 1873 via the American evangelists Dwight Lyman Moody (1837–99) and Ira David Sankey (1840–1908), who introduced a poem written by Philip Bliss.

> 'Hold the fort, for I am coming,' Jesus signals still;
> Wave the answer back to heaven, 'By Thy grace we will.'
> > P.P. Bliss, 'Sacred Songs and Solos sung by
> > Ira D. Sankey' (c. 1870)

John Stroud, *The Shorn Lamb* (1960): 'I'm going out for an hour or so, can you hold the fort?'

Holy Grail – *uniquely prized object*

'Grail' comes from the Old French word *graal*, which in turn comes from the Latin *gradalis*, meaning bowl. The Holy Grail was Christ's cup or platter at the Last Supper.

According to one account, it was used by Joseph of Arimathea to catch Christ's blood at the crucifixion. He later brought it to North Wales where it disappeared.

Other sources say that it was brought by angels from heaven and entrusted to a body of knights who guarded it on top of a mountain. When approached by anyone not of perfect purity, it vanished, and the quest for it became the source of most of the adventures of the Knights of the Round Table.

There is a mass of literature concerning the Grail Cycle, from the *Mabinogion* and Robert de Boron's *Joseph d'Arimathie* (12th century) to Sir

Thomas Malory's *Le Morte d'Arthur* (1485), to Alfred, Lord Tennyson's 'Morte d'Arthur' (1842) and *Idylls of the King* (1855–85). Fascination with the story continues today with the huge success of Dan Brown's *The Da Vinci Code* (2003).

William T. Stead, *If Christ Came to Chicago* (1894): 'The quest of the almighty dollar is their Holy Grail.'

Hook, line and sinker – *completely, totally*

This phrase is often prefixed by 'to swallow', and refers to a person's extreme gullibility. The allusion is to the fish who, not crafty enough to recognise the bait on the hook, swallows it trustingly, and goes on to take in the line and sinker (weight).

Len Deighton appropriately chose 'Hook, Line and Sinker' as the title of his trilogy of novels exploring the treachery and deceit of the world of the spy.

Erle Stanley Gardner, *The Case of the Stuttering Bishop* (1936): 'A couple of private dicks that you don't know anything about show up with a cock-and-bull story, and you swallow it hook, line and sinker.'

How the other half lives – *a light-hearted expression used by the less fortunate to describe the rich*

This is one of those phrases that for some strange reason has come to mean the opposite of its original sense. Originally it was used by the well-to-do to describe the poor.

Jacob A. Riis entitled his studies among the tenements of New York in 1890 *How the Other Half Lives*. It was an account of desperate poverty and hardship. The tenements were houses occupied by three, four or more families, living independently and doing their cooking on the premises. A set of rooms consisted of one or two dark closets, used as bedrooms, with a living room twelve feet by ten. The staircase was often a dark well in the centre of the house, and no direct through ventilation was possible, each family being separated from the other by a partition.

François Rabelais, *Pantagruel* (1532): 'Et la commencay a penser qu'il est bien vray ce que l'on dit, que la moitie du monde ne scait comment l'aultre vit.' (And there I began to think that it is very true, what is said, that half the world does not know how the other half lives.)

Hunch – *an intuitive feeling*

According to gambling superstition, touching a hunchback's hump brought good luck, and this became an American gamester's idiom from the beginning of the 20th century.

Hartley Howard, *Highway to Murder* (1973): 'My sixth sense told me I'd got myself an extra shadow. That hunch was all I had to go on.'

I

If the cap fits – *if it is appropriate*

The full phrase is 'If the cap fits, wear it', meaning if the remark applies to you, apply it to yourself. Hats and caps vary only slightly in size but everyone knows their own when putting it on. The phrase is to be found in Nicholas Breton, *Pasquil's Fooles-cappe* (1600), where it refers to a dunce's cap.

In America the phrase is 'if the shoe fits' or even 'if the slipper fits'.

The Memoirs of Captain Peter Drake (1755): 'Mr Miller, to show the Cap fitted him, made a Stroke with his Cane … at me.'

If the mountain will not come to Mohammed – *to swallow one's pride to make something happen; if unable to have one's way, bow to the inevitable*

In 'On Boldness', an essay written in 1625, Francis Bacon explains that when people asked Mohammed to give miraculous proof of his teaching he ordered Mount Safa to move towards him.

When it failed to do so, he said: 'God is merciful. Had it obeyed my words, it would have fallen on us to our destruction. I will therefore go to the mountain and thank God that He has had mercy on a stiff-necked generation.'

Francis Bacon, *On Boldness* (1625): 'If the Hill will not come to Mahomet, Mahomet will go to the hil.'

Illegitimi non carborundum – *Don't let the bastards grind you down*

This cod-Latin phrase was used by US General 'Vinegar Joe' Stilwell as his motto during the Second World War, though it is not suggested that he devised it. Similar usage by British army intelligence has been noted early in the war, and something like the phrase existed in 1929. Carborundum is a trademark for silicon carbide, a leading commercial grinding substance. In politics, the motto was popularised by 1964 Republican Presidential nominee Senator Barry Goldwater, who hung the sign in his office.

The same meaning is also conveyed by the phrase *nil carborundum* (as in the title of a play by Henry Livings, 1962). This is a pun on the genuine Latin phrase *nil desperandum*, which means 'never say die', or, literally, 'there is nought to be despaired of', from Horace, *Odes*, 1.7.27: 'Nil desperandum est Teucro duce et auspice.' (Nothing is to be despaired of with Teucer as leader and protector.)

In a cleft stick – *in a difficult situation, in a dilemma; in a situation in which one can go neither forwards nor backwards*

The phrase may derive from the way in which snakes were trapped by pinning them down behind the head with a forked stick.

Alternatively, it may be the form of torture inflicted on Ariel by the witch Sycorax in Shakespeare's *The Tempest* (1611), which was to confine him in the trunk of a cleft pine tree.

PROSPERO:
This blue-eyed hag was hither brought with child
And here was left by the sailors. Thou, my slave,
As thou report'st thyself, wast then her servant;
And, for thou wast a spirit too delicate
To act her earthy and abhorr'd commands,
Refusing her grand hests, she did confine thee,
By help of her more potent ministers
And in her most unmitigable rage,
Into a cloven pine; within which rift
Imprison'd thou didst painfully remain
A dozen years; within which space she died
And left thee there; where thou didst vent thy groans
As fast as mill-wheels strike.

General P. Thompson, *The Corn Laws* (1829): 'The other side are in a cleft stick; they cannot go on long as they are, and they cannot stir into any new path without demolishing the Corn Laws.'

In a jiffy – *extremely quickly*

The word 'jiffy', with its ordinary meaning of an instant or a very brief time, appeared in English during the 18th century. Its origin is unknown.

It has, however, been suggested that the phrase derives from the unit of time used in computer engineering, but it long pre-dates the computer age.

A jiffy is the length of one cycle, or tick, of the computer's system clock. In the past, this was often equal to one period of the alternating current powering the computer, i.e. 1/60th of a second in the US and Canada, usually 1/50th of a second elsewhere. More recently the jiffy has become standardised, more or less, as 0.01 second (10 milliseconds).

It is also a unit of time used in chemistry and physics, equal to a 'light centimetre', the time required for light to travel a distance of one centimetre. This is a very brief interval indeed, about 33.3564 picoseconds. This definition of the jiffy was proposed by the American physical chemist Gilbert N. Lewis (1875–1946), who was one of the first to apply principles of quantum physics in chemistry.

Frederick Marryat, *Peter Simple* (1833): 'We were ordered to South America; and the trade winds took us there in a jiffey.'

In a pickle – *in a mess; in a sorry plight; in a state of disorder*

A Dutch 16th-century idiom, the words are *in de pekel zitten*, 'to sit in the pickle'. *Pekel* is brine or vinegar in which food is preserved.

Erskine Caldwell, *Georgia Boy* (1943): 'I've got that marriage ceremony to perform in less than half an hour. It's too late for me to hunt up anybody else to ring the bell, and if you don't ring it for me, I'll be in a pretty pickle.'

In a shambles – *in a state of complete disarray*

The word 'shambles' derives from the Old English word *sceamul*, pronounced 'shamell', which meant stool or table.

The origin of The Shambles, in the city of York, is *fleshammels*, meaning meat stalls, for it was here that the city's butcher's market was located. The Shambles is often called Europe's best-preserved medieval street. Mentioned in the Domesday Book, it has been in continuous existence for over 900 years. One can still see the wide window sills of the houses, where the meat was displayed for sale.

The mess of blood and animal parts made 'shambles' a metaphor for general disorder and chaos.

Henry Cogan, *The Voyages and Adventures of F.M. Pinto* (translated 1653): 'This City hath an hundred and three score Butchers shambles, and in each of them an hundred stalls.'

Daily Telegraph (1979): 'Haiti remains a dictatorship, its economy in a shambles.'

In cahoots – *in league, in partnership, having a secret understanding*

This is an American term possibly deriving from the French word *cahute*, meaning a cabin or small hut which housed French settlers during the 17th century. The phrase came to be used by native Americans to describe groups of people colluding secretly.

Others suggest that the word may derive from *cohort*, Spanish and

French, defined in the old French and English Dictionary of Claudius Hollyband (1593) as 'a company, a band'.

John Russell Bartlett, *Dictionary of Americanisms* (1848): 'Pete Hopkins ain't no better than he should be, and I wouldn't swar he wasn't in cahoot with the devil.'

In clink – *in prison*

Dating from the 12th century, the Clink was a prison in Southwark, London, which had a colourful history, being both a debtors' prison and the local gaol. It was destroyed in the Gordon Riots of 1780. There is now a prison museum on the site.

'Clink' comes from the Middle English word *clenchen* which also gives us 'clinch' and 'clench', the underlying sense being secure fastening.

Rudyard Kipling, 'Barrack-room Ballads' (1892):

And I'm here in the Clink
For a thundering drink
And blacking the Corporal's eye.

In limbo – *lost and uncertain*

'Limbo' acquired its modern meaning as a region on the borders of hell – neither in hell nor in heaven – from the Latin *limbus*, meaning border or edge.

This is the area for departed spirits to whom the benefits of redemption do not apply, through no fault of their own. *Limbus infantium* is therefore the limbo for children who die before baptism or before they are responsible for their actions. *Limbus partrum* is the halfway house between earth and heaven where the patriarchs and prophets who died before Christ's crucifixion await the last day.

Thomas Carlyle, *The Life of John Sterling* (1851): 'As yet my books are lying as ghost books, in a limbo on the banks of a certain Bristolian Styx.'

In one's black books – *out of favour*

'Black books' have long been official or legal documents, for example *The Black Book of the Admiralty*, a 14th-century collection of maritime law, or *The Black Book of the Exchequer*, an official account of royal revenues, payments, perquisites and the like, in the reign of Henry II.

It was only in the 16th century, during the reign of Henry VIII, that black books became officially associated with punishment or censure, specifically being an official return containing the reports of visitors upon the abuses in the monasteries.

Nicholas Amherst in his *Terrae Filius, or the Secret History of the University of Oxford* (1726) speaks of the proctor's black book and says that no person whose name is found there can proceed to a degree.

James Payn, *From Exile* (1881): 'This unfortunate youth is so deep in your black books.'

See also **Blacklist**.

In the bag – *virtually certain*

This is probably a reference to the bag in which game is carried after it has been successfully hunted.

It is suggested that it may also be the bag behind the Speaker's Chair in the House of Commons, for petitions to Parliament. This seems unlikely, because at that stage a bill can rarely be considered virtually certain to be enacted.

P.G. Wodehouse, *Hot Water* (1932): 'We're sitting pretty. The thing's in the bag.'

Sidney Baker, *The Australian Language* (1945): 'A horse set to lose a race [because it has been 'nobbled'] is said to be *in the bag*.'

In the cart – *in an awkward, false or losing position; in trouble, in difficulty*

The cart in question is probably the cart in which convicts were taken to execution. (See **Hanged, drawn and quartered**.)

J.B. Hobbs, *Cricket Memoirs* (1924): 'We made 238, which was enough practically to put South Africa hopelessly in the cart.'

In the dog-house – *in disgrace*

This phrase, most commonly applied to a husband who is out of favour with his wife, originated from J.M. Barrie's *Peter Pan* (1904). Mr Darling, who has ill-treated Nana the Dog, believes that this is why his children have flown to Never Never Land. Until they return he will, as a punishment, sleep in Nana's kennel.

J.B. Priestley and Jacquetta Hawkes, *Journey Down a Rainbow* (1955): 'And the men, so often "in the dog house" … are baffled and miserable, telling one another that women have always been like this, not knowing what they want, the crazy creatures.'

In the doldrums – *depressed, low spirited, dull, drowsy*

This idiom is probably rooted in the Old English word *dol*, meaning dull. It may also be influenced by 'tantrum'.

The doldrums are also an area of difficult sailing conditions around the Equator where the north-east and south-east trade winds converge. In the 19th century, when sailors became very demoralised through inactivity, they gave the name 'doldrums' to that area.

The Times (1883): 'The ship of State has escaped the tornado, but seems becalmed in a kind of political and financial doldrums.'

In the nick of time – *at the very last minute, only just in time*

A tally, or a nick-stick, was used to keep track of time, of points in sporting events, of commercial transactions, and (as late as 1826) of official government book-keeping records. With the widespread use of the tally, it is not surprising that reference to it should enter popular parlance. 'To nick it down', for instance, meant to record something, and 'to nick the nick' meant to hit the right time for something.

'In the nick of time' is the only extant expression. It probably has sporting origins. Team scores were notched up on nick-sticks, and when a winning point was scored just before the end of a contest it was in the nick of time.

Archibald Lovell, *The Travels of Monsieur J. de Thevenot into the Levant* (translated 1687): 'If he had not gone down at the very nick of time, the Ship could not have failed of being very quickly blown up.'

In the offing – *likely to happen, possibly imminently*

The origin of this saying is nautical, from the 17th century. 'Offing' was slang for offshore. A ship approaching a port or coastline, close enough to be seen from the shore, was said to be 'in the offing'.

Captain John Smith, *The Seaman's Grammar and Dictionary* (1627): 'The Offing ... is the open Sea from the shore, or the middest of any great stream is called the Offing.'

Nancy Mitford, *Love in a Cold Climate* (1949): 'That look of concentration which comes over French faces when a meal is in the offing.'

In the pink – *in excellent health*

Shakespeare was first to use this popular garden flower as a metaphor for the perfect embodiment of a particular quality.

This image was often copied and it spread to include, most notably, 'the pink of good condition'.

> MERCUTIO: Nay I am the very pincke of curtesie.
> ROMEO: Pink for flower.
> > Shakespeare, *Romeo and Juliet* (1592)

J.B. Priestley, *The Good Companions* (1929): 'I am writing these lines to say I am still in the pink and hoping you are the same'.

In two shakes of a lamb's tail – *very quickly, in no time at all*

Known since 1840, the phrase is possibly an elaboration of the simpler 'in two shakes' (of the dice), and it is abbreviated to that even now.

Author unknown, *A Norfolk Vet* (2000): 'The reference is to lamb's tails which they shake very rapidly while sucking from their mother's teat or from a bottle, as any shepherd will have observed. Quite why lambs shake their tails while sucking is another question – foals, calves and piglets certainly don't. I reckon the speed of shaking to be about 300 wags per minute.'

Quentin Tarantino, *Pulp Fiction* (US, 1994): 'I'll be with you in two shakes of a lamb's tail.'

Indian giver – *a person who gives a gift only to demand its return*

This American expression of the late 18th century refers to early American Indians who did not give a gift without expecting one of equivalent value in return. If this was not forthcoming, the original gift had to be refused or returned.

H.C. Bolton, *Journal of American Folk-Lore* (1892): 'If an American child, who has made a small gift to a playmate is indiscreet enough to ask that the gift be returned, he (or she) is immediately accused of being an Indian-giver, or, as is commonly pronounced Injun-giver.'

Indian summer – *a period of calm, dry, mild weather, with a hazy atmosphere, occurring in the autumn*

This phrase is generally thought to have originated in America, where the meteorological phenomenon prevalent in the west of the country was originally noticed when the region was still occupied by the Indians.

Similar phrases originate elsewhere: 'All-Hallown summer', of English origin but now obsolete; 'St Luke's little summer', also English; and 'St Martin's summer' from France. 'All Hallown summer' was also used figuratively to mean brightness or beauty lingering or reappearing in old age.

Others suggest that 'Indian summer' means a false summer. This is supported by 'St Martin's summer', which refers to the market for cheap jewellery on the site of St Martin de Grand in Paris after it was torn down in the 16th century.

J. Freeman, *Sermons* (1812): 'Two or three weeks of fair weather, in which the air is perfectly transparent, and the clouds, which float in a sky of purest azure, are adorned with brilliant colours … This charming season is called the Indian Summer, a name which is derived from the natives, who believe that it is caused by a wind which comes immediately from the court of their great and benevolent God Cautantowwit, or the south-western God.'

Irons in the fire – *enterprises, projects in hand, undertakings to be attended to*

Two derivations are proposed. Some say that the efficient blacksmith had several irons in the fire ready for when he needed them. Others suggest that it alludes to the industrious laundress who would keep two or three flat irons heating for when the one she was using cooled.

Aldous Huxley, *Antic Hay* (1923): 'He was always busy, always had twenty different irons in the fire at once, was always fresh, clear-headed, never tired. He was always unpunctual, always untidy.'

It just growed like Topsy – *it has come out of nowhere and developed without encouragement*

Topsy was a little slave girl in *Uncle Tom's Cabin* by Harriet Beecher Stowe. When Aunt Ophelia asks Topsy about her family, she denies that she has one or that she was ever even born.

'Have you ever heard anything about God, Topsy? … Do you know who made you?' – 'Nobody, as I knows on,' said the child … 'I spect I grow'd. Don't think nobody ever made me.'

Clive Rouse, *The Old Towns of England* (1936): 'The planning of towns in mediaeval England can be said to have followed no given rule – they were like Topsy who "just growed".'

It's not *or* it ain't over until the fat lady sings – *a caution against over-confidence*

Dan Cook in 1976 wrote in the San Antonio *News-Express*: 'the opera ain't over until the fat lady sings'. He was encouraging people to remember that sports games are never finished until the final whistle is blown.

The reference is to the final act of the opera, in which the heroine often appears. Opera singers are often endowed with a figure as full as their voice.

The comparatively recent sports associations disguise the fact that it is actually a rather older expression, which occurs in several forms: 'It ain't over till the fat lady sings'; 'The opera isn't over until the fat lady sings'.

Ralph Keyes wrote a book with the title *Nice Guys Finish Seventh* in which he says that several informants recalled hearing the expression for decades before it suddenly became nationally known in 1978.

'Church ain't out 'till the fat lady sings' appears in a 1976 booklet entitled *Southern Words and Sayings,* suggesting that its origin wasn't linked with opera but with church-going.

Ivory tower – *a sheltered existence away from the problems and realities of life*

The French Romantic poet, playwright and novelist Alfred de Vigny led a life of disappointment and frustration. In his later years he withdrew from society and became very solitary, although he continued to write.

In a poem, 'Pensées d'Août' (1837), the critic Sainte-Beuve called Vigny's existence his *tour d'ivoire*, ivory tower.

Nicholas Blake, *The Whisper in the Gloom* (1954): 'I'm going to plunge you into reality, my little Ivory-Towerist.'

J

Jerry-built – *very poorly built; of very low quality*

The phrase long pre-dates the Second World War and has nothing to do with the slang expression 'Jerry' as a synonym for German.

There have been several suggestions for the origin of the word 'Jerry'. The term has been linked with Jericho, the walls of which came tumbling down, and a jury mast, which was a mast or rigging which had been patched up after a storm.

However, it probably comes from the personal name Jerry, which is found in similar phrases denoting an inferior person or thing, such as 'jerrymumble', to tumble about, 'Jerry Sneak', a mean sneaking fellow, and 'jerry-shop', a cheap beer house. These all existed before jerry-built was first recorded in 1869.

John Ruskin, *Fors Clavigera: Letters to the Workmen and Labourers of Great Britain* (1875): 'Rows of jerry-built cottages are creeping up.'

Jot and tittle – *the very smallest amount*

The jot is 'i', the Greek letter *iota*, the smallest of the Greek alphabet. Hence the phrase 'I don't care a jot'.

The tittle is from medieval Latin *titulus*, meaning 'label', which is the mark or dot over the i.

'Till heaven and earth pass, one jot or one tittle shall in no wise pass from the law, til all be fulfilled.' (Matthew 5:18)

K

Kangaroo court – *illegal court of justice*

There is no clear provenance for this term. First recorded in Texas in 1853, it seems to have nothing to do with Australia. Dictionaries assume it to be an Americanism.

However, there is evidence linking it with the 1849 California gold rush, which many Australian prospectors joined.

The most plausible explanation suggests that informal courts were held in the gold diggings to control illegal prospectors, who were called 'claim-jumpers', and that the association of ideas between jumping and kangaroos was too strong to resist. However, this might just be a popular etymology.

It may refer to the courts set up in American prisons in the 19th century to regulate the distribution of money and tobacco and to judge prisoners who had 'jumped over' the rules.

One authority suggests that the kangaroo court defies the law in the same way as the kangaroo defies the laws of nature.

None of these explanations seems entirely satisfactory.

The phrase obtained wide currency in UK in 1966 when it was applied to the irregular punitive measures taken by certain trade unions against members who were regarded as strike-breakers.

The Times (1966): 'Shop stewards at Theale are to meet tomorrow to consider paying back the sums levied by a kangaroo court.'

Keep at bay – *hold at a safe distance*

Abai is an Old French word meaning 'barking of hounds in a pack', from which the English word 'baying' is derived.

However, some suggest that this phrase may refer to the legendary protective powers of the bay tree and the bay laurel.

Early references indicate that *abai* is the origin, as in Lord Berners, *The Boke of Duke Huon of Burdeux* (1532): 'As the wyld bore doth kepe a baye against the mastyues [mastiffs] and bayynge houndes.'

Keep mum – *keep your mouth shut, keep silent, keep a secret*

The key here is an old dice game called 'mumchance' which had to be played in absolute silence.

The word 'mum' is connected with 'mumble' (German *mummeln*, Danish *mumle*). It also represents the sound made with closed lips.

Shakespeare, *Henry VI Part II* (1590): 'Seal up your lips, and give no words but – mum.'

Keep one's pecker up – *be in good spirits, keep one's chin up, never say die*

'Pecker' means beak. If a bird holds its beak and therefore its head up, it gives the appearance of confidence and courage.

James Joyce, *Ulysses* (1922): 'Keep your pecker up, says Joe. She'd have won the money only for the other dog.'

'Pecker' is also US slang for 'penis'. Hence the good advice from Norman Moss in *What's the Difference?* (1973): 'The Englishman in North America should beware of the phrase "keep your pecker up".'

Keep the wolf from the door – *to ward off hunger*

The wolf here is hunger. Since ancient times, the wolf has been a symbol of poverty and want. Fables depict the wolf as ravenously hungry. The French say 'manger comme un loup', to eat like a wolf, and the Germans have the expression 'Wolfshunger'. In English, someone who eats ravenously is said to 'wolf' their food.

John Goodman, *The Penitent Pardoned* (1679): 'That hungry Wolf, want and necessity, which now stands at his door.'

Keep up with the Joneses – *to maintain one's social level, keep up appearances*

This was the title of a cartoon strip by the artist Arthur Momand ('Pop') in the *New York Globe*. It commented on social aspirations. Originally based on the artist's own attempts to keep up with his neighbours, it started in 1913 and ran for 28 years.

More about conspicuous consumption than mere survival, the phrase became common currency in an increasingly affluent and status-conscious age, as in Lee Gibb's book entitled *The Joneses: How to Keep Up with Them* (1959).

Keep your shirt on – *don't lose your temper*

The phrase originates in the USA. Taking one's shirt off was a sign that one was ready to fight. 'Keep your shirt on' therefore meant 'stay calm'.

New York Spirit of the Times (1854): 'I say, you durned ash cats, just keep yer shirts on, will ye?'

Kick the bucket – *to die*

One explanation is that suicides, having fixed the noose around their necks, would stand on a bucket and then kick it away. However, a bucket, from the Old French *buquet*, meaning balance, was also a beam from which things could be hung, including slaughtered pigs. As they struggled they too would kick the bucket.

A third suggestion is that it is an allusion to the bucket that was formerly put out to collect for the widow of a workmate. Some of those passing by kicked the bucket instead of throwing in a coin.

John Wolcot ('Peter Pindar'), *Works* (1806): 'Pitt has kicked the bucket.'

Kill the goose which lays the golden eggs – *to destroy a source of profit through greed*

In 1484 William Caxton translated into English a fable by Aesop which tells the tale of a peasant who had the good fortune to own a goose that laid golden eggs. In his hurry to become rich, he cut the goose open to have all the eggs at once, thus butchering his source of future wealth.

Aesop's moral was that one should be content with one's fortune and guard against greed.

The Times (1992): 'For the communist city government, which owns a half share, McDonald's will be like the goose that laid golden eggs.'

Kilroy was here – *a catchphrase which appeared early in the Second World War, written on walls as if by magic*

No satisfactory explanation has been given, although hundreds have been suggested, for this piece of graffiti which appeared everywhere that British or American soldiers fought or were stationed in the Second World War.

Kilroy became the US super-GI who always got there first, wherever GIs went. It became a challenge to place the logo in the most unlikely places.

Stories abound. It was said to be on top of Mount Everest and the Statue of Liberty, on the underside of the Arc de Triomphe, and scrawled in the dust on the moon.

An outhouse was built for the exclusive use of Truman, Stalin and Churchill when they attended the Potsdam conference. The first person to use it was Stalin. He emerged and asked his aide (in Russian): 'Who is Kilroy?'

The puzzle may have been solved in 1962 by the *San Francisco Chronicle*, which proposed a credible origin:

> Two days before the Japanese attack on Pearl Harbor, an unimposing, bespectacled 39-year-old man took a job with a Bethlehem Steel Company shipyard in Quincy, Massachusetts.

As an inspector, James J. Kilroy began making his mark on equipment to show test gangs he had checked the job. The mark: 'Kilroy was here'. Soon the words caught on at the shipyard, and Kilroy began finding the slogan written all over the installation.

Before long, the phrase spread far beyond the bounds of the yard, and Kilroy – coupled with the sketch of a man or at least his nose peering over a wall – became one of the most famous names of the Second World War.

When the war ended, a nationwide contest to discover the real Kilroy found him still employed at the shipyard.

And last week, James Kilroy … died in Boston's Peter Bent Brigham Hospital, at the age of 60.

Knock into a cocked hat   *to beat in a contest by a wide margin, to defeat easily*

In a game of nine-pins, the inner three were placed in a triangle in the shape of a cocked hat. If after one bowl the three in the centre remained intact, the pins would be considered 'knocked into a cocked hat'.

The idea is that of a hat being knocked out of shape. The reason for the choice of hat is probably that a naval officer's cocked hat could be doubled up and carried flat.

Listener (1965): 'The splendid earthworks and engineering structures of the railways today … knock the M1 into a cocked hat.'

Knock off work – *to finish work for the day*

It has been suggested that the phrase dates from the days of slave galleys. The man who beat time to keep the oarsmen pulling in unison would give a special knock to indicate when there was to be a change of shift.

'Knock off' has meant to cease, to desist at least since the 17th century. The specific sense applying to work dates from the 18th century.

George Daniel, 'Trinarchodia, Henry V' (1649): 'The Sun (who quafft French blood to Harrie's health) knock's of / And can noe more.'

Andrew Barton, *The Disappointment* (1767): 'As for McSnip, he intends to knock off business, home to England and purchase a title.'

Knock seven bells out of – *to beat severely, if not actually to knock* *someone out*

A nautical phrase, known by 1929, it is not clear why it refers to only seven out of the eight bells available aboard ship. Perhaps it is one bell short of a fatal beating?

People (1995): 'If they [louts] misbehave, the players leave the pitch and kick seven bells out of them.'

Knock the gilt off the gingerbread – *to spoil the best part of* *something, rob something of its attraction*

The gilded and painted carvings at the bow and stern of sailing ships were known as gingerbread work, from the custom of sprinkling gilt on gingerbread biscuits to make them more attractive. To knock the gilt off the gingerbread incurred the displeasure of the ship's captain and also damaged the most visible part of the vessel.

Naval Chronicle (1804): 'As the sailors term it, there is an abundance of gingerbread work.'

Knuckle down *or* under – *to give in or give way, to yield*

The phrase comes from placing one's knuckles on the ground in shooting or playing marbles.

Known since 1740, to 'knuckle down' and to 'knuckle under' were used synonymously in the sense of giving in to someone else. The phrase may derive from the submissive posture suggested.

Independent (1995): 'Protestors denounced the ban on travel to jobs in

Israel and the expansion of Jewish settlements on the West Bank. "No to starvation, no to settlements. We are a people who won't knuckle under."'

The sense of knuckle down, meaning to apply oneself earnestly, came later (*Webster's Dictionary*, 1864).

Colin Beveridge, 'Behind closed doors: time to knuckle down', *IT Management: Project Management* (2001): 'In the fourth of a series of six articles, one of the UK's most experienced IT managers argues that it's time for a stronger work ethic and a more conventional approach to tracking progress in the IT department.'

Kowtow to – *to show deference, behave obsequiously to*

This entered the English language in the early 19th century, and is an approximation of the Chinese words *k'o t'ou*, literally 'knock head', for the custom of touching the ground with the forehead as a sign of worship, respect and submission.

The Times (1972): 'Peking has referred officially to Hong Kong's shameful colonial status only once since President Nixon's dignified *kowtow* and the belated entry of the People's Republic into the United Nations.'

L

La-di-da, Lah-di-dah – *affectedly refined of costume, voice, manners*

This is possibly an imitation of 18th-century foppish pronunciation of 'Lord', spoken as a mild oath.

Its great vogue was due to a music-hall song from 1880: 'He wears a penny flower in his coat, La-di-da!'

Westminster Gazette (1895): 'I may tell you we are all homely girls. We don't want any la-di-da members.'

Lame duck – *person unable to succeed*

The phrase originated from mid-18th-century Stock Exchange slang for someone unable to meet his financial obligations.

It has since been applied more generally. In US politics, it means an office-holder who is not or cannot be re-elected, and in politics in the UK, any office-holder whose authority has been undermined.

In nautical slang, a lame duck was a damaged ship, particularly one left without a means of propulsion.

In industry, it is used of a commercial firm that cannot survive without financial help, especially by means of government subsidy.

William Makepeace Thackeray, *Vanity Fair* (1847–8): 'I'll have no lame duck's daughter in my family.'

P.A. Eaddy, *Hull Down* (1933): 'Our old "lame duck" hadn't done so badly after all.'

Lark about – *have fun, play tricks, frolic*

The origin is somewhat uncertain. It may come from a Yorkshire dialect word, 'lake', meaning 'play', which in turn originates from Scandinavian languages, for example *leka* in Swedish.

On the other hand, it is quite as likely that the word may have originated in some allusion to the lark, just as 'skylarking' has a similar meaning.

The word 'lark' also specifically means riding across country, as in Thackeray's *Vanity Fair* (1847–8): 'Jumping the widest brooks and larking over the newest gates in the country.'

Harrington O'Reilly, *Fifty Years on the Trail* (1889): 'I was always larking about and playing pranks on my schoolfellows.'

Last *or* final straw – *an insignificant event which brings about a final catastrophe*

'The last straw' is an abbreviation of the proverb 'It's the last straw that breaks the (laden) camel's back', and both are current. It is not the original proverb, however. As recorded in Thomas Fuller's *Gnomologia* in the 17th and 18th centuries, people spoke of 'the last feather that broke the horse's back'.

A number of languages, for example French, Spanish and Arabic, have similar proverbs. The French say: 'C'est la goutte (d'eau) qui fait déborder le vase', 'It is the drop (of water) which makes the vase overflow.'

The first appearance of the phrase in its modern usage is in Charles Dickens, *Dombey and Son* (1848): '"I won't detain you any longer then," returned Mr Dombey disappointed. "Where have you worked all your life?" – "Mostly underground, Sir, 'till I got married. I come to the level then. I'm a going on one of these here railroads when they comes into full play." – As the last straw breaks the laden camel's back, this piece of underground information crushed the sinking spirits of Mr Dombey. He motioned his child's foster-father to the door who departed by no means unwillingly … He said, with an emotion of which he would not, for the world, have had a witness, "Poor little fellow!"'

Laughing up one's sleeve –
deceiving somebody, hiding one's true feelings

The extravagant large sleeves worn by Elizabethans were so huge that it was possible for just a moment to hide one's face behind them and, therefore, one's true feelings. John Daus, *Sleidane's Commentaries* (1560): 'If I coveted nowe to avenge the injuries that you have done me, I myghte laughe in my slyve.'

Lead someone up *or* down the garden (-path) – *to mislead*

The phrase may refer to the place where in Victorian times promises of matrimony were made, and not always fulfilled, or where a seduction might be attempted safely.

Alfred, Lord Tennyson, 'Come Into the Garden, Maud' (1858):

Come into the garden, Maud,
For the black bat, Night, has flown,
Come into the garden, Maud,
I am here at the gate alone;
And the woodbine spices are wafted abroad,
And the musk of the roses blown.

Noël Coward revised the words, delightfully recorded by Joyce Grenfell, reflecting how sceptical Maud should be about the innocence of the invitation.

Alternatively, the origin may be in the days when people kept one or two domestic pigs. When the time came for slaughter, the pig would be led, away from the eyes of children, up the garden path to an outhouse to meet its fate.

Ethel Mannin, *Sounding Brass* (1925): 'They're cheats that's wot women are! Lead you up the garden and then go snivellin' around 'cos wot's natcheral 'as 'appened to 'em.'

G.D.H. and Margaret Cole, *Murder at Crome House* (1927): 'To lead Flint up the garden-path and relieve him of his cash.'

Leave in the lurch – *to leave somebody in a vulnerable state, desert someone in difficulty*

'Lurch', from the French *lourche*, was an old game similar to backgammon. It is also the loser's score when his opponent is very far ahead.

In cribbage, for example, one was said to be 'in the lurch' if the winner scored the full 61 before the other player had even turned the corner of the board and scored 31. The connection between the saying and the history is obscure.

Philemon Holland, *Livy's Roman Historie* (translated 1600): 'The Volscians seeing themselves abandoned and left in the lurch by them … quit the campe and field.'

Let the cat out of the bag – *to reveal a secret*

First recorded in the 18th century, this probably refers to a dishonest farmer substituting a cat or some other valueless animal, in a tied bag, claiming it was a young pig. When the bag was opened, the truth, in the form of a cat, jumped out.

William Makepeace Thackeray, *Vanity Fair* (1847–8): 'Letting the cat of selfishness out of the bag of secrecy.'

Lick into shape – *to make something into good condition, make presentable*

From earliest times, people believed that bear cubs were born shapeless and had to be licked into shape by their parents. The story gained currency apparently from the Arab physician Avicenna (979–1037), who tells it in his encyclopedia.

Robert Burton, *The Anatomy of Melancholy* (1621): 'Enforced, as a Bear doth her Whelps, to bring forth this confused lump, I had not time to lick it into form.'

Life is just a bowl of cherries – *everything is wonderful*

'Life is just a bowl of cherries' is a modern proverbial expression originating apparently in the song by Lew Brown (music by Ray Henderson), first heard in the American musical *Scandals* by George White (1931).

Like Billy-o *or* Billio *or* Billyoh – *doing something very vigorously*

This probably refers to George Stephenson's famous steam locomotive *Puffing Billy* (1813) which by the standards of the day was a miracle of mechanical engineering. 'Puffing like Billy-o' and 'running like Billy-o' were common phrases.

However, the phrase has also been associated with Joseph Billio, rector of Wickham Bishops, Essex, ejected from his church by reason of his non-conformity. He was noted for his energy and enthusiasm.

Another possibility is that it refers to Nino Biglio, an officer in Garibaldi's army, who would dash enthusiastically into battle shouting: 'I am Biglio! Follow me, you rascals, and fight like Biglio!'

Further, it has been suggested that it is a polite alternative to 'like the devil'.

Lion's share – *the largest portion of anything*

Recorded by 1790, the phrase accurately reflects the fact that the lion is given the largest share of the food obtained for him by the lionesses in his pride.

It probably also derives from Aesop's fable of the lion, the fox and the ass:

> The Lion, the Fox and the Ass entered into an agreement to assist each other in the chase. Having secured a large booty, the Lion on their return from the forest asked the Ass to allot his due portion to each of the three partners in the treaty.
>
> The Ass carefully divided the spoil into three equal shares and modestly requested the two others to make the first choice. The Lion, bursting out into a great rage, devoured the Ass.
>
> Then he requested the Fox to do him the favour to make a division. The Fox accumulated all that they had killed into one large heap and left to himself the smallest possible morsel. The Lion said:
>
> 'Who has taught you, my very excellent fellow, the art of division? You are perfect to a fraction.' He replied, 'I learned it from the Ass, by witnessing his fate.'

Punch (1872): 'The art of finding a rich friend to make a tour with you in autumn, and of leaving him to bear the lion's share of the expenses.'

Live the life of Riley – *live a carefree existence*

Some have suggested that this is a reference to a popular song of the Victorian era:

> Is that Mr Reilly? Is that Mr Reilly that owns the hotel?
> Well if that's Mr Reilly they speak of so highly
> Upon my soul Reilly you are doing quite well!

The earliest recorded reference to the phrase is, however, 1919, in Harry Pease's 'My Name is Kelly':

> Faith and my name is Kelly, Michael Kelly,
> But I'm living the life of Reilly just the same.

Load of cobblers – *complete rubbish*

Cobblers' awls are pointed tools for making holes. 'Cobblers' awls' is rhyming slang for 'balls'. (See also **Codswallop**.)

Melody Maker (1968): 'Geno Washington says Grapefruit's recent attack on the Maryland Club, Glasgow was a "load of cobblers". They are one of the best audiences in Britain, says Geno.'

Lock, stock and barrel – *completely, in its entirety*

The lock, stock and barrel are the main parts of a gun. The lock is the device which sparks the charge; the stock is the handle and framework holding the other parts in place; the barrel is the metal tube through which the shot is propelled.

George Whyte-Melville, *Digby Grand* (1853): 'When a woman is a trump there is nothing like her; but when she goes to the bad, she goes altogether, "stock, lock and barrel".'

Look a gift horse in the mouth – *to find fault with a gift, to spoil an offer by inquiring too closely into it*

Known by 1546 (as 'given horse'), the proverb alludes to the fact that the age of a horse is commonly assessed by the length of its teeth. If offered a gift of a horse, one would be ill-advised to look in its mouth for fear of discovering unwelcome information.

Samuel Butler, 'Hudibras' (1663):

> He ne'er consider'd it, as loth
> To look a Gift-Horse in the mouth.

Loose cannon – *someone out of control who could cause damage*

Cannons on a ship's deck needed to be secure. Otherwise when fired or in a storm they would cause damage or injury.

In 1988 Colonel Oliver North was convicted of lying to Congress, destroying an official document, and accepting an illegal gratuity. Those anxious to distance President Ronald Reagan's administration from implication in the same charge called North a 'loose cannon', accusing him of acting without authority in the illegal sale of arms to Iran.

Observer (1987): 'Gung-ho, loose cannon, cowboy, Jesus freak – there is already a cottage industry in manufacturing Ollie epithets. Lynching [Oliver] North is quickly becoming a national sport.'

Lose one's marbles – *to lose one's mental faculties*

Almost certainly of American origin, the expression was first recorded in the journal *American Speech* in 1927.

It is suggested that marbles means 'furniture, movables' derived from the French *meubles*, and dating from 1864. To lose one's marbles would therefore mean to lose the mind's furniture.

Local expressions seem to support this. In Cheshire, 'he's got all his chairs at home' was used to mean 'he's all there, alert', and in Yorkshire, if someone is a bit lacking in the head, they say 'he hasn't got all his furniture at home.'

Among other suggestions is the idea that the phrase refers to the famous marbles that Lord Elgin brought back from the Parthenon. They were exhibited in the British Museum in 1816, incurring, to this day, the wrath of the Greeks.

Another explanation is that it derives from an earlier phrase, 'let his marbles go with the monkey', from a story about a boy whose marbles were carried off by a monkey.

Or again, that its origin is the Old French *marbre* from Latin *marmor*, Greek *marmoros*, from *marmarein*, to sparkle. The suggestion is that the sparkle goes out of life when one loses one's marbles.

English Dialect Society, *West Cornwall Words* (1880): 'Those that have marbles may play, but those that have none must look on.'

Margaret Millar, *The Soft Talkers* (1957): 'She's a fattish little *hausfrau* with some of her marbles missing.'

Lynch law – *law administered by private individuals and followed by summary execution; mob rule*

In its original definition, a lynching simply meant punishment by an un-authorised self-constituted body. Only later did it come to mean summary execution, usually by hanging, and most commonly in the 20th century the killing of black Americans in the south by whites.

In Virginia in the 1780s, during the American Revolution, two officers, Captain William Lynch and Colonel James Lynch, were trying to bring order and justice to this lawless area. Vigilantes organised judicial tribunals in which the law was defined by an unconstitutional court.

Though it is now taken to involve execution, William Lynch, the more likely of the two officers to be the origin of 'lynch law', wrote in 1780: 'If [these lawless men] will not desist from their evil practices, we will inflict such corporeal punishment on him or them, as to us shall seem adequate to the crime committed or the damage sustained.'

The first appearance in print appears to be a humorous article in the *New-England Magazine* (1835) entitled 'The Inconveniences of Being Lynched'. Again, punishment was harsh but fell short of execution.

There is one other candidate, Charles Lynch, a magistrate who presided over extra-legal trials of Tories during the War of Independence.

M

Mad as a hatter – *completely mad, crazy*

This phrase will always be associated with *Alice in Wonderland* by Lewis Carroll, but it was in currency well before 1865 when the famous children's book was published.

There is no single undisputed derivation. Some say the use of mercury in hat-making meant that hatters developed the shakes and twitching.

It has been suggested that the original 'mad hatter' was Robert Crab, a 17th-century eccentric living at Chesham, who gave all his goods to the poor and lived on dock leaves and grass.

Carroll himself is said to have based his character on one Theophilus Carter, a furniture dealer who was known locally as 'the Mad Hatter', partly because he wore a top hat and partly because of his eccentric notions. An example of the latter was his invention of an 'alarm clock bed' that woke the sleeper by tipping him on to the floor. (Hence comes, perhaps, the Mad Hatter's obsession with time and his keenness to stir the sleepy dormouse.)

Others have suggested that the word is not 'hatter' but 'atter', which means venom or poison and is therefore a reference to the effects of poisoning.

Make a bee line – *to use the shortest route between two places*

In days gone by, it was thought that bees were single-minded in their work and always flew in a straight line back to the hive. This piece of country lore has since proved untrue.

There is a similar snippet of country wisdom about crows, who are supposed to fly directly to their intended destination. Hence the expression **As the crow flies**.

Sally Line brochure (1991): 'You can make a bee-line for the South of France, or slip into the Low Countries within minutes.'

Make a hash of something – *to mess something up*

A hash is a mess of food made up of a mixture of meat and vegetables.

Lord Houghton, *Life, Letters and Friendships* (1847): 'Lord Grey has made somewhat of a hash of New Zealand and its constitution.'

Make a mountain out of a molehill – *to get something out of all proportion, to make a difficulty of trifles*

This appears to be an original phrase by Nicholas Udall in his work *Paraphrase of Erasmus* (1548–9).

Latin has *Arcem e cloaca facere*, to make a stronghold out of a sewer, and the French have *Faire d'une mouche un elephant*, to make an elephant out of a fly.

Thomas Hutchinson, *Diary and Letters* (1778): 'I told him his nerves were affected; every molehill was a mountain.'

Make a pig's ear – *to make a mistake, botch or bungle something*

The ear of a slaughtered pig is its most worthless part, no good for anything. The full idiom from the 16th century reads: 'You cannot make a silk purse out of a sow's ear' – that is, you cannot make something useful and beautiful out of something useless and ugly.

Elisabeth Hargreaves, *Handful of Silver* (1954): '"I've made a real pig's ear of it, haven't I?" said Basil, with an attempt at lightness.'

Make bricks without straw – *to try to do something without the appropriate resources*

While the Israelites were in Egypt (Exodus 5), the Pharaoh ordered that they should no longer be given straw to make bricks. They had to find it themselves. The Israelites were not being told literally to make bricks without straw. Straw was an indispensable binding material for sun-dried bricks. However, they were expected both to produce the same number of bricks and collect the straw from which they were made.

Modern archaeology has made numerous discoveries which confirm events recorded in the Bible, including bricks without straw at Pithon. Lower levels had good quality straw, middle levels had less (including much which was torn up by the roots, as someone in a rush to meet a quota would be inclined to do), and the top levels had no straw at all.

Miss M. Betham-Edwards, *Disarmed* (1883): 'The fact is, you are fast being spoiled. But your task from today will be to make bricks without straw. No appeal shall induce me to have pity on you.'

Make ends meet – *to live within one's means*

The complete phrase is 'make both ends of the year meet'. 'Ends' is a reference to the beginning and end of the (financial) year, and 'meet' means tally or add up.

Tobias Smollett, *Roderick Random* (1748): 'He made shift to make the two ends of the year meet.'

Make no bones about – *to say so without a fuss, without hesitation; make no scruple*

In the 15th century, the phrase was more usually 'find no bones (in the matter)'. This, together with the phrase 'without more bones' (late-16th–19th centuries), meaning without further obstacle, delay or discussion, would indicate that the reference is to bones in soup or stew.

Nicholas Udall, *Erasmus Upon the New Testament* (1548): 'He made no manier of bones ne stycking, but went in hand to offer up his only son Isaac.'

Make the grade – *to reach the standard, be able to do something*

This is a reference to the railroad-building programme in America in the 19th century, where locomotives had to be able to make the gradient – 'grade' for short – if they were to cross the continent.

Sewell Ford, *Inez and Trilby May* (1921): 'It's Gwendolyn that's got to do the hustling. Three days! I doubt if she can make the grade.'

Male chauvinist (pig) *or* MCP – *a man who holds stereotypically male views and prejudices*

'Male chauvinism' was a phrase in the 1950s. The word 'pig' was added later, probably as result of the strong feelings aroused on both sides by the women's liberation movement in the 1970s.

Chauvinism originally referred to excessive patriotism, after Nicolas Chauvin, a French general during Napoleon's campaigns who became famous for his unquestioning devotion to his leader.

Time (1970): 'European women have accepted their lot much more readily than their American counterparts. Recently, however, growing numbers ... have launched their attack on male chauvinism.'

New Yorker (1970): 'Hello, you male chauvinist racist pig.'

Man in a grey *or* dark suit – *a colourless administrator or technocrat*

When The Beatles set up the Apple organisation in the 1960s, John Lennon said it was an attempt 'to wrest control from the men in suits'. Sometimes such people are simply called 'suits'.

The 'men in grey suits' were the senior members of the Tory party, whose responsibility it was to tell Prime Minister Margaret Thatcher when it was time for her to leave office. The reference is again to faceless, shadowy figures.

Broadcast (1987): 'With this latest career move can we expect to see the *wunderkind* [John Birt] transformed into the proverbial Man In A Grey Suit?'

Man on the Clapham omnibus – *the ordinary or average person, the man in the street*

According to a 1903 law report, Lord Bowen, hearing a case of negligence, first made reference to this person: 'We must ask ourselves what the man on the Clapham omnibus would think.'

This particular bus route may have been chosen because it sounds suitably prosaic, or because the route passes from Clapham Junction through Whitehall and Westminster, providing a link between governors and governed.

There is evidence that the 'Clapham omnibus' was a figure of speech as early as the mid-19th century. In 1857, reference was made in a journal to 'the occupant of the knife-board of a Clapham omnibus'. (The knife-board was a bench on the upper deck.)

Listener (1965): 'The class character of our education will remain until … the scions of Lord Snow and the man on the Clapham omnibus attend the same comprehensive school.'

Mata Hari – *an alluring and seductive woman*

Mata Hari was the assumed name of the Dutch dancer and courtesan Margaretha MacLeod, née Zelle. The name is said to be a Malay expression for the sun, meaning 'eye of the day'.

In the First World War, Mata Hari was employed by the Germans to seduce Allied officers and pass on their secrets. The precise details of her espionage activities remain obscure. She was captured by the French and sentenced to death in 1917. Her defence was that she had agreed to act as a French spy without telling the French authorities about her agreement with the Germans. It is said that in a last-minute, but unsuccessful, attempt to divert the attention of the firing squad, she opened her dress, revealing her nakedness.

Adam Hall, *Tango Briefing* (1973): 'You wouldn't have to frisk this pint-sized Mata Hari; you could see she was armed half a mile away.'

Mealy mouthed – *unwilling to speak plainly for fear of causing offence*

The origin of the phrase is Greek, *melimuthos*, which means, literally, 'honey speak'.

Tom Ticklefoot, *Some Observations upon the Late Tryals of Sir George Wakeman* (1679): 'He was not mealy mouth'd but would … have talked his mind to Knights, or any Body.'

Mickey Finn – *a drink that has been drugged, usually to render a person helpless so that a crime can be committed*

There is a story that the phrase derives from a certain Mickey Finn, the owner of the Palm Garden Restaurant and the Lone Star Saloon on Whiskey Row, Chicago. These establishments were havens for pick-pockets and petty thieves, mostly trained by Finn himself.

One of Finn's common methods was to lace drinks with chloral hydrate (knock-out drops) and then rob his victims before dumping them.

The two bars were closed down in 1903, although Finn escaped jail and found work as a barman, selling his recipe to other unscrupulous vagabonds.

Other authorities say, more mundanely, that the phrase was probably originally a trade name. It was first used around 1930, and applied to a laxative pill made for horses.

Its current meaning was adopted in the UK around 1943, and the phrase appeared in Margery Allingham's *More Work for the Undertaker* (1947).

Later, a Mickey Finn was used to describe an ostensibly harmless drink 'spiked' with hard liquor, usually as a practical joke.

Kylie Tennant, *The Battlers* (1941): 'In the show world a "gee-man" [market trader's stooge] or "micky finn" was socially on the level of a duck's feet.'

Might as well be hanged for a sheep as a lamb – *if the result is going to be the same, one might as well take the greater, rather than the more trivial risk*

Up to 1841, the penalty for sheep-stealing was hanging. So why steal a lamb, with less meat and wool and, therefore, less saleable value, when one could steal a sheep? If caught, the punishment would be the same.

D.H. Lawrence, *Sons and Lovers* (1913): 'It seemed as if she did not like being found in her home circumstances ... but she might as well be hung for a sheep as a lamb. She invited him out of the mausoleum of a parlour into the kitchen.'

Mind one's P's and Q's – *to watch one's manners, be careful*

This is probably a reference to teachers encouraging schoolchildren to note the difference between the letter 'p' and the letter 'q', both of which have tails in the lower case and which are next to each other in the alphabet. It could also have been an instruction to printers' apprentices in the handling of type.

However, some argue that 'P's and Q's' stood for 'pints and quarts', to which the publican referred on his bill. The customer needed to mind his P's and Q's when the reckoning came after a night's drinking.

Another suggestion is that in France during the reign of Louis XIV (1643–1715), when huge wigs were fashionable, dancing masters would warn their pupils to 'mind your P's (*pieds*, feet) and Q's (*queues*, wigs)', lest the latter fall off when bending low to make a formal bow.

In whatever case, it is easy to see how this phrase came to be used as an invocation for good, responsible behaviour.

Miss the bus – *to miss an opportunity, be too late to participate in something*

John Henry Newman, the famous Oxford theologian, caused great upset when he became a Roman Catholic. One of his followers, Mark Pattison, set off to visit the great man to discuss the reasons for this step, but missed the bus. Some say that he lost his nerve and missed it on purpose. Whether he did or not, it was a missed opportunity.

John Morley, *Critical Miscellanies* (1886): 'Though he [Mark Pattison] appeared ... as much a Catholic at heart as Newman ... it was probably his constitutional incapacity for heroic and decisive courses that made him, according to the Oxford legend, miss the omnibus.'

Manchester Guardian Weekly (1940): 'He [Neville Chamberlain] boasted that Hitler had "missed the bus".'

Moaning Minnie – *a complaining person*

The German trench-mortar of the First World War was a devastating weapon, nicknamed 'Minnie' from its German name *Minenwerfer*, literally 'mine thrower'. Although it did not moan, in its larger forms the shell made a woofing sound as it turned in the air.

The civilian slang phrase current in the Second World War was the nick-name for the air-raid warning sirens, which were called 'wailing Winnie' or 'moaning Minnie'.

The army may have used the nickname Moaning Minnie to refer, after the Blitz, to the German multi-barrelled field mortar and its shell.

New Zealand News (1972): 'I don't want to give the impression of being a moaning Minnie but may I ... make a special plea to the railmen to ... get back to work.'

Molly-coddle – *to pamper, fuss over*

'Molly' is probably from the woman's name, perhaps influenced by the French *molle*, soft.

It has been variously conjectured that 'coddle' here is the same word as 'coddle', meaning to parboil, to boil gently, or to caress or coax (a dialect form of 'cuddle'), or 'caddle', meaning to trouble or worry.

It is more likely to come from 'caudle' (Latin, *calidum*). A caudle was a warm drink consisting of thin gruel mixed with wine or ale, sweetened and spiced, given chiefly to sick people.

The word has been listed in no dictionary before 1818. By the early 19th century, the verb 'to caudle' meant to treat someone as an invalid or to pamper.

'Rita', *My Lady Coquette* (1881): 'Fresh air is a thousand times better for her than mollycoddling and medicines.'

Moot point – *an issue open to various interpretations*

The word 'moot' can be traced back to an Anglo-Saxon word, *gemot*, meaning 'meeting'. So, a *wardmote* was a ward meeting, a *burgmote* a town meeting and a *witengemote* a meeting of wise men. In a few towns, for example Aldeburgh in Suffolk, the town hall is still called the Moot Hall.

By the 16th century, young law students had the opportunity to test their skills at 'mootings' or 'moot courts', which were hypothetical trials held at the Inns of Court in London.

Sir Charles Wogan, *Swift's Works* (1732–3): '"My lords and gentlemen," says he, "It is a very moot point to which of those causes we may ascribe the universal dulness of the Irish."'

More … than you can shake a stick at – *plenty*

There are several shades of metaphorical meaning to this expression which is found in mid-19th-century literature, particularly in the USA.

It probably refers to a farmer counting his animals by pointing with his stick, and therefore shaking his stick at each one. If he had so many animals that he could not count them all in this way, it would suggest that he had a great number.

'Nothing worth shaking a stick at' means nothing of value. The sense of defiance and aggression suggests that there may be a connection with a soldier in battle shaking a stick at a vanquished enemy.

Lancaster Journal of Pennsylvania (1818): 'We have in Lancaster as many taverns as you can shake a stick at.'

James K. Paulding, *A Book of Vagaries* (1868): 'The roistering barbecue fellow swore he was equal to any man you could shake a stick at.'

Mount a boycott – *to ostracise someone, to refuse to use or buy something*

The phrase comes from Captain Charles Boycott, and 'to boycott' or 'mount a boycott' describes what was done to him rather than what was done by him.

Boycott was an ex-British soldier who acted as an agent for absentee landlords in County Mayo, Ireland during the late 19th century. He was a hard man, dispossessing tenants if they fell into rent arrears. The tenants retaliated by isolating him and refusing to have any dealings with him or his family.

They were encouraged by Charles Parnell of the Irish Land League, who said that those who grabbed land from people evicted for non-payment of rent should be treated like 'the leper of old'.

Eventually the tenants brought about Boycott's own downfall by leaving his harvest to rot, and he fled back to England where he died in 1897.

Interestingly, the word has been adopted by other languages: French *boycotter*, German *boycottiren* and Russian *boycottirovat*.

William Gladstone, in *The Standard* (1881): 'The neighbours of the Boycotted man refuse to hold any intercourse with him and his family; they will not eat with him, drink with him, buy from him or sell to him.'

'Conscientious Consuming' website: 'The Rainforest Action Network initiated a boycott against Burger King for purchasing beef that was raised in destroyed rainforests. According to the Rainforest Action Network, the protests conducted at the restaurants and the associated negative publicity were particularly effective in changing Burger King's use of "rainforest beef."'

Mumbo-jumbo – *meaningless ritual*

First recorded in English in the early 18th century, it meant an object of foolish veneration. This gives the key to its origin, the anglicised approximation of a Mandingo term, probably *Mama Dyumbo*, said to mean 'venerable ancestor with pompon', a grotesque idol or god venerated by certain West African tribes.

Mungo Park, a Scottish physician, set off in 1795 in search of the Niger and the fabled city of Tellem. In his *Travels in the Interior of Africa* (1795–7), Mumbo Jumbo 'is a strange bugbear, common to all Mandingo towns and much employed by the Pagan natives in keeping their wives in subjection'. When the ladies of the house become too quarrelsome, Mumbo Jumbo is called in. He may be the husband or his agent suitably disguised, who comes at nightfall making hideous noises.

When the women have been assembled and songs and dances performed, 'Mumbo fixes on the offender'. She is 'stripped naked, tied to a post, and severely scourged with Mumbo's rod, amidst the shouts and derision of the whole assembly'.

Murphy's law – *if anything can go wrong, it will*

Some claim that Murphy was Captain Ed Murphy, a development engineer who worked with Colonel J.P. Stapp on US Air Force Project MX981 which studied the effects of high acceleration on human beings. In 1949, Murphy found that a piece of equipment had been incorrectly wired and said of the technician involved: 'If there is any way to do things wrong, he will.'

At a press conference at which the safety record of his project was being considered, Colonel Stapp put its success down to planning for what he called 'Murphy's law'. It was intended, according to some, as a prescription for avoiding mistakes in the design of a valve for an aircraft's hydraulic system. If a part could be fitted in more than one way, it was only a matter of time before it would be fitted the wrong way. The answer was to design it so that there was only one way to fit it.

Others, for example the astronaut John Glenn in *Into Orbit* (1962), say that Murphy was fictitious: 'We blamed human errors like this on what aviation engineers call "Murphy's Law". "Murphy" was a fictitious character who appeared in a series of educational cartoons put out by the US Navy ... Murphy was a careless, all-thumbs mechanic who was prone to making such mistakes as installing a propeller backwards.'

N

Namby-pamby – *wishy-washy, insipid or weakly sentimental; babyish or childish*

This is the nickname of Ambrose Philips (1674–1749), whose pastoral poetry and poems for children led the dramatist Henry Carey (c. 1687–1743) to develop this sobriquet around his Christian name.

The following is a typical example of Philips's artless art, 'Ode to Mistress Charlotte Pulteney' (1727):

> Timely blossom, infant fair,
> Fondling of a happy pair,
> Every morn and every night
> Their solicitous delight,
> Sleeping, waking, still at ease,
> Pleasing without skill to please,
> Little gossip, blithe and hale,
> Tattling many a broken tale.

Name is mud – *discredited, in disgrace*

Some associate this with Samuel Mudd, the doctor who treated President Abraham Lincoln's assassin. On 14 April 1865, John Wilkes Booth shot Lincoln at Ford's Theatre in Washington DC and escaped by jumping on to the stage, breaking his leg in the process. (See **Break a leg**.)

The son of a wealthy plantation owner, Samuel Mudd set up his medical practice on a farm five miles from Bryantown, Maryland. Mudd, an advocate of slavery, supported the Confederacy during the Civil War and often expressed his dislike, even hatred, for Lincoln and his policies.

About four o'clock on the morning following Lincoln's assassination, two men on horseback arrived at the Mudd farm. They were John Wilkes

Booth, in severe pain, and David Herold. Mudd welcomed them into his house, carrying Booth upstairs to a bed where he dressed his badly fractured leg. The following day, Mudd made arrangements with a nearby carpenter to construct a pair of crutches.

When a military investigator tracking Booth's escape route reached Mudd's home three days later, Mudd claimed that the man whose leg he had treated 'was a stranger to him'.

A Military Commission convicted Mudd and sentenced him to life in prison. He was pardoned in 1869 by President Andrew Johnson and returned to Maryland, where in 1876 he was elected to the state legislature. Mudd died in 1883.

Although the association may have popularised the phrase, its usage pre-dates Dr Mudd. The word 'mud' is defined as something worthless or polluting, the lowest part of anything, the lowest stratum, the dregs. It had been used in this sense for many years.

'J. Bee', *Slang* (1823): '*Mud* – a stupid twaddling fellow. "And his name is mud!" ejaculated upon the conclusion of a silly oration, or of a *leader* in the Courier.'

Neck and crop – *entirely, violently, all of a heap*

The crop is the throat of a horse. The reference is to a rider falling forwards headlong from the saddle and desperately grasping for the neck and crop to save himself. (See also **Come a cropper**.)

A variant of the phrase is 'neck and heels', as in: 'I bundled him out neck and heels.'

Michael Scott, *Tom Cringle's Log* (1833): 'Chuck them neck and crop … down a dark staircase.'

Alan Ross, *Australia 63* (1963): 'Titmus … trying to force an in-swinger away, was bowled neck and crop.'

Neck of the woods – *a person's neighbourhood*

The phrase originates in America, although the word 'neck' had been used in England since the 1500s to describe a narrow strip of land surrounded by water. Settlers in the US used it to describe narrow strips of woodland in the new country. Native Indian settlements, often located in forests, were identified by which 'neck of the woods' they could be found in.

'Grey Owl', *Men of the Last Frontier* (1931): 'A man may be soaking wet, half-frozen, hungry and tired, landed on some inhospitable neck of the woods, vowing that a man is a fool to so abuse himself'.

John Wainwright, *The Devil You Don't* (1973): 'In this neck, I say what. I also say when.'

Nine days' wonder – *something which arouses great interest that quickly fades*

The nature of this wonder is open to speculation. One theory is that the phrase originates from the Catholic 'Novena', festivals of nine days' duration, in which the statue of the saint being honoured is carried through the streets.

The Latin root, *novenus*, meaning 'nine each', may have been confused with *novus*, meaning 'new, wonderful'.

A more mundane interpretation is that the festival focuses attention for nine days but is soon forgotten in the anticipation and preparation for the next.

Finally, the phrase may refer to kittens and puppies, whose eyes remain closed for about nine days after birth, during which time they experience a wondrous existence before coming into the world of reality.

Geoffrey Chaucer, *Troylus and Criseyde* (1374): 'Ek wonder last but nine nyght nevere in toune.'

Bishop Hall, *Meditations and Vows* (1606): 'So those things … shall be wonders to me; and that not for nine dayes, but for ever.'

Thomas Hughes, *Tom Brown at Oxford* (1861): 'His escape on the night of the riot had been a nine-days' wonder.'

Nineteen to the dozen – *very quickly*

Meaning, generally, to talk very quickly; earlier variants were to talk 'nine words at once' or to talk 'thirteen to the dozen'.

It has been said that the phrase is from copper and tin mines in 18th-century Cornwall. Often struck by flooding, they used coal-powered

pumps which cleared 19,000 gallons of water for every twelve bushels of coal. This was significantly faster than the earlier hand-powered pumps, hence 'nineteen to the dozen'.

Other authorities are not so sure. V.H. Collins in his *Book of English Idioms* (1956) asks: 'Why "nineteen"? The obvious numeral would be the round number "twenty". Possibly "nineteen" was chosen just because, not being what might have been expected, it seemed to give a more striking effect.'

Elizabeth Sheridan, *Betsy Sheridan's Journal* (1785): 'The Mother was good humour'd and Civil but talks nineteen to the dozen.'

No flies on (someone) – *to be quick-witted, alert, active*

First used in the ranches of America and Australia in the mid-1800s, the phrase refers to the lively, active cattle and horses which attracted fewer flies than the slow, sluggish animals which would stay still for longer periods of time.

Observer (1961): 'There are no flies on Benaud. If England start bowling their overs slowly, no one will have to draw his attention to it.'

No great shakes – *not very good, nothing remarkable or unusually able or clever*

A shake of the dice which reveals a low score is not much use to anyone.

The origin is almost certainly dicing, and considering its first recorded use, the expression must have been known as early as the 17th century.

Lord Broughton, recalling an 1816 art show in *Recollections of a Long Life* (1865), wrote: 'W. said that a piece of sculpture was '*nullae magnae quassationes*' (Latin, literally, for no great shakes) and the others laughed heartily.'

Another suggestion (Robert Hendrikson, *Encyclopaedia of Word and Phrase Origins*, 1997) is that the expression derives from the provincial word 'shake', meaning to brag. According to this improbable theory, someone who is no great shakes would be nothing to brag about.

No man's land – *an area of unclaimed land*

In the First World War this described the dangerous area between opposing trenches, contested by both sides and belonging to neither. Its width along the Western Front could vary a great deal. The average distance in most sectors was about 250 yards. However, at Guillemont it was only 50 yards, whereas at Cambrai it was over 500 yards. The narrowest gap was at Zonnebeke, where British and German soldiers were only seven yards apart.

The phrase was also used in the 14th century to describe an area outside the walls of London used for execution, 'No-man's land' meaning it was not owned by anyone. In the old manorial open-field system, the name was used for any scraps of land without ownership.

The Rolls Series, *Chronicles of Edward I and II* (1320): 'Quaedam domina nomine Juliana ... fuit combusta apud Nonesmanneslond extra Londonius.' (A mistress by the name of Juliana was burnt in No-man's land outside London.)

George Ewart Evans, *The Pattern under the Plough* (1966): 'The belief that a piece of land in the parish should be left untilled. In English villages this is sometimes called *Jack's Land* or *No-man's Land*.'

No names, no pack-drill – *no names mentioned, refusal to betray a confidence*

The reference is to a one-time British army punishment in which soldiers were made to march up and down carrying a heavy pack. The meaning is that if one mentions no names, no one will be punished.

Rudyard Kipling, *Soldiers Three* (1890): 'Mulvaney was doing pack-drill – was compelled that is to say, to walk up and down in full marching order, with rifle, bayonet, ammunition, knapsack and overcoat.'

'Bruce Graeme', *The Undetective* (1962): '"It's a lie, mister. Who told you?" – "No names, no pack-drill."'

No stone unturned – *every possible expedient tried in order to bring about a result*

To 'leave no stone unturned' was also found formerly as 'to move, roll *or* turn every stone *or* all the stones'. It is thought to be a very old idiom traceable to ancient Greece.

After the Greeks defeated the Persians at the battle of Plataea in 477 BC, Polycrates set about finding the treasure which he thought had been left in the tent of the Persian general Mardonius. After searching everywhere he turned to the oracle at Delphi, who advised him to 'move every stone' in his search. Polycrates took that advice and subsequently found the treasure. The phrase soon became popular, and only a few years later, in 410 BC, Aristophanes called it 'that old proverb'. At nearly 2,500 years old, 'no stone unturned' may even be the oldest English idiom.

Gilbert Walker, *A Manifest Detection of the Most Vyle and Detestable Use of Dice-Play* (c. 1550): 'He will refuse no labour nor leave no stone unturned, to pick up a penny.'

Nose to the grindstone – *working very hard; working someone else very hard*

A grindstone (used for sharpening tools and knives) was also a form of punishment in medieval times. This sense continues particularly in the original form of the phrase, 'to hold (*or* keep) someone's nose to the grindstone', which means to treat them harshly or, figuratively, to grind them down.

A famous cartoon of 1650 shows the future Charles II's nose being held to the grindstone by the Scots.

The first example of the phrase recorded is in John Frith's *A mirrour or glasse to know thyself* (1533): 'This Text holdeth their noses so hard to the grindstone, that it clean disfigureth their faces.'

These references cast doubt on a curious explanation of the phrase which comes from California. It is claimed that the grindstone was not for sharpening tools, but was a traditional water-powered grist mill. The grindstones had to be set exactly the right distance apart. If the gap was too big, the corn didn't grind properly, too small and the grain overheated and began to burn. The miller could not see the gap, and so had to use his nose to detect the first signs of any burning.

Nosey parker – *someone who pokes their nose into other people's business, the personification of inquisitiveness*

'Nosey' clearly gives the impression of someone with a long pointed nose which he would use to pry into the affairs of others.

It is suggested that the name Parker was added either arbitrarily, or from the dialect word 'pawk', meaning inquisitive, or perhaps from 'parker', an old name for a park-keeper.

It may be an allusion to Matthew Parker, Archbishop of Canterbury (1504–75). He was noted for the detailed articles of inquiry concerning ecclesiastical affairs generally and the conduct of the clergy, which he issued for the visitations of his province and diocese.

It is more likely that the phrase dates from the 19th century. The Duke of Wellington was described as 'Old Nosey' (1851) and a 'parker' was a rabbit living in a park (1846). Ramsay Spencer shrewdly comments: 'The Great Exhibition took place in 1851, in Hyde Park, drawing huge crowds of enquiring visitors of all classes, so it may also have provided unusually ample opportunities for Peeping Toms and eavesdroppers in the purlieus.'

This seems to supply a more probable origin than the various alternative folk-lore theories. Whatever the source, by the 1900s there was a character on comic postcards called 'Nosey Parker'.

Jilly Cooper, *Women and Super Women* (1974): 'The social security ladies come nosy-parkering around.'

Not a sausage – *nothing at all (particularly money)*

The expression is said to derive from Cockney rhyming slang, in which 'bangers and mash' (i.e. sausages and mash) means 'cash'. 'Not a sausage' therefore means *no* cash.

An RAF usage since 1940 is equivalent to: 'Not a plane in the sky; no luck.' In the mid-20th century, the phrase became more general and meant 'nothing at all', as in 'not a dicky-bird'.

The Times (1981): 'Mr Healey said the press did not print Labour's actual policies. "Not a sausage."'

Not enough room to swing a cat – *cramped conditions*

In the 16th century, cats were sometimes put into bags, strung up and used for moving archery practice. Shakespeare refers to this in *Much Ado About Nothing*.

A century or so later, 'cat' being an abbreviation for the cat-o'-nine-tails, the phrase may have been used to describe the lack of space in the old sailing ships where the cat was often administered.

However, it is believed that the expression was already well known before its suggested nautical use.

Tobias Smollett, *The Expedition of Humphry Clinker* (1771): 'At London, I am pent up in frouzy [i.e. smelly] lodgings where there is not room to swing a cat.'

Not fit to hold a candle – *a much inferior person, not to be compared with*

This is said to be a reference to the humble linkboys who held candles in theatres and other places of evening entertainment, or to a servant lighting his master's way around the house or up to bed.

W.E. Norris, *No New Thing* (1883): 'Edith is pretty, very pretty; but she can't hold a candle to Nellie.'

Not on your Nellie *or* Nelly – *not likely, not on any account, no way*

From Cockney rhyming slang, Nellie is 'Nellie Duff', which rhymes with 'puff'. Puff is slang for breath and therefore life itself. The phrase literally means 'not on your life'.

'Cockney' is the term used to describe any person born within the sound of Bow Bells, the bells of St Mary-le-Bow church in Cheapside, east London. Rhyming slang is a code of speaking in which a common word can be replaced by the whole or an abbreviated form of a well-known phrase which rhymes with that word.

Cockney rhyming slang has been evolving in the East End since the 16th century. It is thought to have originated from the seamen and soldiers who used the London docks, from the ethnic minorities which have made up the population of the city, principally Irish and Jewish, and from gypsies who arrived in the 16th century.

Eric Partridge, *Adventuring Among Words* (1961): 'The trouble [with Cockney rhyming slang] begins when part, usually the latter part, of the rhyming phrase is omitted, as so often it is, as in ... "not on your Nellie" for "... Nellie Duff" = not on your "puff" = "not on your life" or "most certainly not" or less politely, "like hell, I will!"'

Not to mince words *or* matters – *to speak bluntly*

This refers to meat being minced to make it more digestible, and therefore to words or matters being 'minced' to make them more palatable, more acceptable.

Thomas Carlyle, *On Heroes, Hero-Worship and the Heroic in History* (1841): 'A candid ferocity, if the case calls for it, is in him; he does not mince matters.'

Not worth his salt – *not deserving of his pay*

Soldiers in Roman times received the necessities of life, including salt, as part of their wage. The Latin for salt is *sal*, and *salarium* is the ration of salt given. This eventually became the English word 'salary'.

Andrew Jackson (US President, 1767–1845): 'Any man worth his salt will stick up for what he believes right, but it takes a slightly better man to acknowledge instantly and without reservation that he is in error.'

Robert Louis Stevenson, *Treasure Island* (1883): 'It was plain from every line of his body that our new hand was worth his salt.'

Nutty as a fruitcake – *mad*

The nut has for some reason long been associated with the brain and, by extension, mental problems ('nutcase', 'nuthouse', etc.).

It may have arisen because of the nut's hard shell and soft kernel which compare with the human skull and a brain that has gone soft, as in the phrase 'soft in the head'.

The phrase 'nutty as a fruitcake' has been common in the USA since the 1930s and in England since about 1943, partly through the influence of US servicemen.

P.G. Wodehouse, *Company for Henry* (1967): '"He doesn't strike me as unbalanced." – "On his special subject he's as nutty as a fruit cake."'

O

Of the first water – *without equal, of the highest type, superlative*

This phrase has its roots in the jewellery trade. The quality of diamonds and pearls has been categorised for hundreds of years as first, second, third water and so on. This also features in some other European languages, but it probably has its origins in the Arabic word for water, *ma*, referring to the absolute clarity of perfectly clear water.

Chambers' Cyclopaedia (1753): 'The first water in diamonds means the greatest purity and perfection of their complexion, which ought to be that of the clearest drop of water.'

W.B. Boulton, *Gainsborough* (1905): 'He ... assumed the airs of a beau and lady-killer of the first water.'

Off the cuff – *ad lib, extemporised*

Speakers at dinners could write notes on their cuffs, particularly when men's formal cuffs were made of celluloid. This made it appear that they were speaking from memory.

Josephine Tey, *The Singing Sands* (1952): 'If you're not too busy could you do something off the cuff for me?'

Old Bill *or* the Bill – *the police*

The etymology of 'Old Bill' is uncertain. Originally, around 1915, the phrase meant a veteran of the First World War, or any old soldier, especially with heavy, drooping whiskers.

Old Bill was a disillusioned old soldier portrayed by the artist and journalist Captain Bruce Bairnsfather (1887–1959) in his publications *Old*

Bill and *The Better 'Ole*. In the trenches, cowering in a wet and muddy shell hole in the midst of a withering bombardment, he says to his grousing pal Bert: 'If you know of a better 'ole, go to it.'

'Old Bill' meant a taxi driver (from 1917) and a rank outsider in a horse race (1920s). From the 1950s or earlier, it meant a policeman.

Many ex-servicemen took employment with the Metropolitan Police after the war, and were recruited by posters showing Bairnsfather's Old Bill in a Special Constable's uniform.

Another possible etymology is a blend of the popular song 'Won't You Come Home, Bill Bailey?' with 'The Old Bailey'. It may also be a reference to a halberd or 'bill', an axe or blade attached to a handle and carried by constables and watchmen.

Zachary Scott, *Paper Money* (1977): 'The Old Bill knew about him.'

Old chestnut – *a tired old joke; any over-familiar topic*

Although its origins are in an English melodrama, it was an American actor who coined its usage. The actor, William Warren, found occasion to quote from *The Broken Sword* (1816), a rather mediocre play by William Dillon.

One of the characters has an irritating habit of telling and re-telling stories. He is embarking on one such tale about a cork tree when his companion, Pablo, interrupts, crying: 'A chestnut. I should know as well as you, having heard you tell the tale these twenty-seven times, and I am sure it was a chestnut.'

Warren, who played the part of Pablo in the melodrama, was at a dinner one evening when a fellow guest started to recount a well-worn and rather elderly anecdote, whereupon Warren murmured: 'A chestnut. I have heard you tell the tale these twenty-seven times.' This appropriate quoting of the play delighted the company and the phrase spread.

Mid Sussex Times (1991): 'The problem concerns that old chestnut, the professional foul, and the new guide lines issued by FIFA in July that affect not only British football but the game the world over.'

On cloud nine – *extremely happy, elated*

Originating in America in the 1930s, the usual explanation of the phrase's origin is the terminology used by the US Weather Bureau. Cloud nine is cumulo-nimbus, a cumulus cloud of great vertical extent, topped with shapes of mountains or towers. When it reaches 30,000 or 40,000 feet it is 'cloud nine'. The closeness to heaven suggests happiness.

There is some doubt about this explanation, because the phrase also appears as 'on cloud seven', 'eight' and even 'thirty-nine'.

Other phrases like 'in seventh heaven (of happiness)' and 'over the moon' are related.

Gerald Green, *The Hostage Heart* (1976): 'Dr Motskin will pump you so full of pain-killers you'll be on cloud nine.'

On one's beam-ends – *utterly exhausted, down on one's luck, desperate, broke*

The beams of a ship are the timbers which stretch across it and hold it together. If the ship is on its beam-ends, it is in danger of capsizing, the horizontal beams having become vertical.

Since the early 19th century, 'beam-ends' has been naval slang for buttocks.

Frederick Marryat, *The King's Own* (1830): 'Our first lieutenant was ... on his beam-ends with the rheumatiz.'

On one's hobby-horse – *in full flow on one's pet subject*

A hobby is a light horse. A hobby horse is either a construction like a horse worn by morris dancers under their skirts to make it appear that they are riding a horse, or a stick with an imitation horse's head. The implication is that this is a favourite pursuit.

For centuries, hobby horses, Jacks-in-the-Green, straw men and other similar characters brought life and colour to civic processions in towns and cities across the country. Many of them can be seen in carvings in local churches. Four hundred years ago, the Puritans rid the streets of these practices, along with morris dancing and other ungodly festivities such as Christmas and football.

John Wesley, *Sermons* (1791): 'Every one has (to use the cant term of the day ...) *his hobby-horse*! Something that pleases the great boy for a few hours.'

On one's tod – *alone*

This expression is Cockney rhyming slang: 'on one's tod' = on one's Tod Sloan = on one's own. Variants are 'Jack Jones' and 'Pat Malone'.

Tod Sloan (1874–1933) was a popular American jockey who first rode in England in 1897 before being banned by the Jockey Club in 1901. He was memorable in the history of thoroughbred racing, both for his contributions to the sport and his flamboyant manner.

Sloan gained his name from the nickname 'Toad' which fellow jockeys gave him due to his short legs. Soon Toad gave way to 'Tod' and later to 'Todhunter'.

Sloan popularised the 'monkey-on-a-stick' style of riding, the universal style today. His abnormally short legs led to shortening the stirrup leathers so that his knees nearly touched his chin. He rode above the horse's withers, giving him the advantages of a better balanced horse, less wind-resistance, and the use of the whip instead of the spurs. Soon all jockeys adopted Sloan's winning style.

Sloan is also remembered as the first jockey to demand a percentage of the winnings rather than a fee per ride. At the height of his career, Sloan cavorted with the likes of Diamond Jim Brady and Lillian Russell. He travelled with a valet and trunks of clothes. Tod Sloan squandered his money and died in obscurity.

T.E.B. Clarke, *The Wide Open Door* (1966): 'I'm on me Tod 'cept for the baby.'

(For rhyming slang, see also **Not on one's Nellie**.)

On tenterhooks – *tense and nervous*

From the Latin *tendere*, a 'tenter' was a wooden frame used to stretch newly woven cloth to allow it to dry and stretch evenly. The cloth was attached to the frame by 'tenterhooks'. Today's meaning is therefore to be in a state of tension.

Thomas More, *The Confutation of Barnes* (1532): 'The churche … is stretched out in the stretcher or tenter hookes of the crosse, as a churche well washed and cleansed.'

William King, *Transactioneer* (1700): 'The poor People have set their Wits, as if it were on the Tenter-hooks, to make Turnep-Bread in Essex.'

On the cards – *something that could happen*

In the novels of Charles Dickens, 'on the cards' means liable to turn up, in the same way as the situation is revealed when playing cards are turned up.

Instead of playing cards, it is more likely to refer to fortune-telling with tarot cards. The modern tarot deck has been traced back to 15th-century

Italy, and to a trick-taking game called 'triumphs' (*tarots* in French). The traditional tarot deck consists of two sets of cards, one having 22 pictures (the major arcana), such as the Fool, the Devil, Temperance, the Hermit, the Sun, the Lovers, the Hanged Man, and Death. The other set (the minor arcana) has 56 cards with kings (or lords), queens (or ladies), knights, knaves (pages or servants), sticks (or wands, cudgels or batons), swords, cups and coins.

Finally, the phrase may be an allusion to a horse-racing programme, or 'card'.

Charles Dickens, *David Copperfield* (1849): 'By way of going in for anything on the cards, I call to mind that Mr Micawber … composed a petition to the House of Commons.'

On the grape-vine – *heard as unsubstantiated information*

During the American Civil War, telegraph lines were slung between trees, but as the wind blew, they sagged and looked increasingly like the Californian grape-vine.

A shortened version of 'a despatch by grape-vine telegraph', the 'grape-vine' was a secret means employed by the chiefs of the underworld to ensure rapid and trustworthy transmission of important news. It was adopted into England from the USA in the 1920s and became military slang for a mysterious source of rumours. It has a similar meaning to the 'bush telegraph', a phrase from Australia, current since about 1890.

J.T. Farrell, *Studs Lonigan* (1934): 'Down there at that express company, they find out about everything a guy does. They got the best grape-vine in the world.'

On the horns of a dilemma – *having to choose between equally unacceptable, undesirable or distasteful alternatives*

'Dilemma' is a term from logic, from the Greek *lemma*, meaning assumption or proposition, itself from *lambanein*, to grasp.

A dilemma is a double *lemma*, and it describes the attempt to drive one's opponent to face unacceptable alternatives. The Romans called this *argumentum cornutum*, an argument with horns.

The allusion is to a bull tossing its victim whichever horn is grasped, as in Nicholas Udall, *Erasmus upon the New Testament* (1548): 'Thys forked questyon; which the sophisters call an horned question, because that to whether of both parties a bodye shall make a direct aunswere, he shall renne on the sharpe poyncte of the horne.'

Francis Bacon, *The History of the Raigne of King Henry VII* (1622): 'A dilemma that bishop Morton ... used, to raise up the benevolence to higher rates; and some called it his fork, and some his crotch ... "That if they met any that were sparing, they should tell them that they must needs have, because they laid up: and if they were spenders, they must needs have, because it was seen in their port and manner of living."'

On the treadmill – *subjected to exhausting, never-ending work, usually without acknowledgement*

This is a reference to the machine used in Victorian prisons for those sentenced to hard labour. The treadmill was a row of evenly spaced wooden planks joined at each end by a large cog. This formed an endless

staircase which the unfortunate prisoner was forced to climb for hours on end.

In April 1895, Oscar Wilde, the playwright, was convicted of gross indecency with Lord Alfred 'Bosie' Douglas, the third son of the Marquis of Queensberry. He was sentenced to two years' hard labour at Reading Gaol and wrote of the treadmill: 'If this is the way the Queen treats her prisoners, she doesn't deserve to have any.'

Sydney Smith, *Works* (1824): 'The labour of the treadmill is irksome, dull, monotonous and disgusting to the last degree.'

Sir Alfred Lyall, *Life of Marquess Dufferin* (1905): 'He found himself again on the official treadmill.'

On the wagon – *teetotal*

Common in the USA from around 1904, the original phrase was 'on the water-wagon'. It referred to the wagons which were used for spraying dusty streets and providing communal water. Anglicised by 1908, it was shortened to 'on the wagon'.

Len Deighton, *Twinkle, Twinkle, Little Spy* (1976): 'They dug him out of a bar ..., stoned out of his mind ... He stayed on the wagon for years.'

Once in a blue moon – *very rarely, hardly at all*

In the 18th century, 'blue' appears to have been added for emphasis to an established phrase, 'once in a moon'. There may even have been a factual link to the moon being blue when volcanoes erupted or during dust storms.

According to the popular definition, it is the second full moon to occur in a single calendar month.

The average interval between full moons is about 29.5 days, while the length of an average month is roughly 30.5 days. This makes it very unlikely that any given month will contain two full moons, though it does sometimes happen.

On average, there will be 41 months that have two full moons in every century. Once in a blue moon literally means therefore once every two-and-a-half years.

National Skat and Sheepshead Questionnaire (1976): 'How many of you readers "blow" the big hand – the one that appears once in a blue moon?'

One over the eight – *one drink too many, slightly drunk*

From about 1914 this was in common usage in the services, based on soldiers' belief that it was quite safe for a man to drink eight glasses of beer. It was in common parlance by around 1925, and a slightly later variant was 'one over the odds'.

Edward Fraser and John Gibbons, *Soldier and Sailor Words* (1925): '*One over the eight*, one drink too many.'

One swallow does not make a summer *or* a summer make – *one piece of good news does not put everything right; a single example is not necessarily proof of a generality*

'Mia kelidon ear ou poiei', one swallow does not make a spring, was a Greek proverb recorded by Aristotle (384–322 BC) in *Nicomachaean Ethics*.

The English version was not common until the 16th century. It refers to the annual migration of swallows from the warm south to Europe as winter draws to a close.

Richard Taverner, *Proverbes of Erasmus* (1552): 'It is not one swalowe that bryngeth in somer. It is not one good qualitie that maketh a man good.'

Open Sesame – *a means of getting to an inaccessible place, the key to a mystery or anything that acts like magic in obtaining favour, admission, recognition or the like*

This was the phrase used by the 40 thieves to open a rock door in the story of Ali Baba in *Arabian Nights Entertainments* or *The Thousand and One Nights*. Derived from an Egyptian text probably of 14th- or 15th-century origin, the story was first translated into English by R. Heron and W. Beloe in the 18th century.

'He observed that they were forty in number. Ali Baba saw the robbers, as soon as they came under the tree, each unbridle his horse and hobble it.

Then all took off their saddlebags, which proved to be full of gold and silver. The man who seemed to be the captain presently pushed forward, load on shoulder, through thorns and thickets, till he came up to a certain spot, where he uttered these strange words: "Open, Sesame!" And forthwith appeared a wide doorway in the face of the rock. The robbers went in, and last of all their chief, and then the portal shut of itself.' (From Sir Richard Burton's translation of 1888.)

The basis of the tales is that they were told nightly by Sheherezade, bride of Sultan Schahriah, to stave off her execution.

Sesame (*Sesamum indicum*) is an East Indian herb used in Egypt for the flavouring of cakes and bread.

Charles S. Calverley, *Verses and Translations* (1894): 'Thy name shall be a Sesame, at which the doors of the great shall fly open.'

Over a barrel – *helpless to act, at the mercy of others*

At one time, a person who had almost drowned would be draped face down over a barrel, which would then be gently rocked back and forth until the water had drained from the victim's lungs. The person was of course helpless to act for himself and totally dependent on his rescuers. In the same way, someone experiencing business difficulties might find himself powerless to act and forced to accept another's terms.

Raymond Chandler, *The Big Sleep* (1939): 'We keep a file on unidentified bullets nowadays. You might use that gun again. Then you'd be over a barrel.'

Over the moon – *highly excited, extremely delighted, ecstatic*

Although 'to jump over the moon (for delight)' was known previously, the earliest recorded use of 'over the moon' is 1857. Lady Cavendish wrote in her diary about how she broke the news of her youngest brother's birth to the rest of her family: 'I had told the little ones who were first utterly incredulous and then over the moon.'

It was also part of the rather precious slang of a group of arts-loving Victorians and Edwardians called 'The Souls', who used a semi-secret language to communicate to each other exclusively.

Margaret Kennedy, *Together and Apart* (1936): 'She didn't know she had a brother and she's over the moon.'

Over the top *or* OTT – *exaggerated, overstated, an affected or theatrical way of speaking or acting*

The expression 'to go over the top' originated in the trenches of the First World War. It meant to charge over the parapet and out of the trenches on the attack.

A letter from the trenches, 20 July 1918: 'We are going over the top this afternoon and only God in Heaven knows who will come out of it alive.'

Strangely, the phrase came to mean some action, speech or writing which, like an unrestrained theatrical performance, comes across as unconvincing, exaggerated and embarrassing.

'The State of Play' (1989) quoted in the *Independent*:

Look at sport – I'm sure you'll agree
It's much more fun when it's OTT.

P

Paddle one's own canoe – *to be self-reliant, do one's own thing without help from anyone else*

A favourite expression of Abraham Lincoln, it was first written in 1828 but gained real popularity after a poem by Sarah Bolton in *Harper's Magazine* (May 1854):

> Voyage upon life's sea,
> To yourself be true,
> And, whatever your lot may be,
> Paddle your own canoe.

The poem became the basis of a popular song.

Noël Coward, *Design for Living* (1932): 'Even if I can't quite achieve such – such splendour, there are other lessons for me. There's the lesson of paddling my own canoe, for instance – not just weighing down someone else's and imagining I'm steering it!'

Paint the town red – *to go on a spree, have a riotously good time*

On the night of 5–6 April 1837, an Irish nobleman, the Marquis of Waterford, and some drunken friends indulged in 'mad pranks', including literally painting part of a town red near Melton Mowbray in Leicestershire.

The Marquis was renowned for his sadistic taste in practical jokes. Masquerading as 'Spring Heeled Jack', he leapt huge hedgerows, breathing flames from his mouth and attacking passers-by, mostly young women. Friends who studied applied mechanics helped him invent boots with powerful springs in the heels and he learned the technique of 'fire-eating' in order to complete the terrifying image.

Chicago Advance (1897): 'The boys painted the town [New York City] red with firecrackers [on Independence Day].'

Palm off – *to impose (a thing) fraudulently on someone, pass off by trickery or fraud*

This derives from conjuring tricks and 'palming' a card.

New York Law Journal (1973): 'A claim that Borden attempted to "palm off" its dried soup package as that of Lipton's.'

Pandora's box – *a present that seems valuable but in reality is a curse; a seemingly straightforward situation but with trouble in store*

In Greek legend and according to Hesiod, Pandora was the first mortal woman. To punish Prometheus (who had stolen fire to give to man) Zeus ordered Hephaestus to fashion a beautiful woman who was named Pandora, meaning 'all-gifted'.

She was so called because each of the gods gave her some power or attribute, such as beauty, grace and intelligence, but these gifts were to bring about the ruin of man, for Hephaestus also gave her the power to lie and deceive.

She brought with her a great vase (Pandora's box) which she opened, and all the evils flew forth. They have ever since continued to afflict the world. Hope alone remained at the bottom of the urn.

J.E.T. Rogers, *Economic Interpretations of History* (1888): 'The favours of Government are like the box of Pandora, with this important difference, that they rarely leave hope at the bottom.'

Pardon my *or* the French – *excuse the strong or bad language*

The Anglo-French relationship has always been strained, particularly as many British people have a certain prejudice against the French. 'Pardon my French' is therefore to say that one is about to behave as a Frenchman.

Michael Harrison, *All the Trees Were Green* (1936): 'A bloody sight better (pardon the French!) than most.'

Pass the buck – *to evade blame and shift responsibility to someone else*

An American phrase, coming from the game of poker, it is said to refer to a knife with a buckhorn handle that was placed in front of a player to indicate that he was the next dealer. The buck was passed on with the responsibility for dealing and/or holding the jackpot.

The earliest recorded use of the phrase is by Mark Twain in 1872.

Will Irwin, *The Red Button* (1912): 'The Big Commissioner will get roasted by the papers and hand it down to the Deputy Comish, and the deputy will pass the buck down to me, and I'll have to report how it happened.'

In his famous allusion to this phrase, President Harry S. Truman wrote in *Public Papers* (1952): 'When the decision is up before you – and on my desk I have a motto which says "The buck stops here" – the decision has to be made.'

Pay on the nail – *to pay promptly*

The original derivation of the phrase is unknown. It is not even certain which sense of the word 'nail' it refers to. Though different in meaning, it may correspond to the French *sur l'ongle*, literally meaning 'on the fingernail' and therefore precisely, exactly. Dutch has *op den nagel* and German *auf den nagel*, in the same sense.

In medieval days, nails were pillar-like counters and when deals were struck, payment was publicly placed 'on the nail'.

Outside the Corn Exchange at Bristol such 'nails' can still be seen in the form of four bronze pillars, and it is said that if a buyer was satisfied with the sample of grain shown 'on the nail', he paid on the spot. The market pillars probably took their name from the expression rather than the other way around.

George Bernard Shaw, *The Intelligent Woman's Guide to Socialism and Capitalism* (1928): 'The cost of the materials the gunners used up in a single day was prodigious. If they had had to pay on the nail, out of their wages, for the cannons they wore out and the shells they fired, there would have been no war.'

Pay through the nose – *to be overcharged*

This has the sense of being fooled into paying more than one should for a product or service. Its root may lie in the notion of being led by the nose like an animal.

However, this seems inadequate and several other suggestions have been made.

It is said that in the 9th century the Danes imposed a poll tax in Ireland and that it was called the 'Nose Tax' because non-payers had their noses slit.

'Rhino' has been a slang word for money since the 17th century, and this may be linked with the Greek *rhinos* (nose). The origin of this may be the value of the Malay rhinoceros, 'worth its weight in gold' to the opportunists who converted every part of the animal into aphrodisiacs for sale to Chinese mandarins.

The idea of one being bled for money may be linked with a nosebleed. The fact that the expression came into written English no earlier than the end of the 17th century makes these last theories more likely than a derivation from the Nose Tax.

Mme Frances D'Arblay (Fanny Burney), *Cecilia* (1782): 'She knows nothing of business, and is made to pay for everything through the nose.'

Pear-shaped – *something that has gone drastically wrong*

There is no really satisfactory derivation for this 1960s expression, but it has been suggested that it refers to pilots trying to do a complicated manoeuvre such as a loop-the-loop, and, when it goes wrong, the perfect circle turning out to be pear-shaped.

It is also an all-too-apt description of the consequences of middle-aged spread, when the lower portions of the human torso start to be bigger than the upper.

From the BBC *Top Gear* website: 'Greg Parry sent in this snap but doesn't confess to being behind the wheel when things started to go pear-shaped. We'll give him the benefit of the doubt ...'

(See also **Go bananas.**)

Pecking order – *status based on rank*

This was first used in 20th-century studies of animal behaviour and was extended, in popular language, to humans. The studies revealed that hens attacked others by pecking them, often without revenge, and therefore established their own social position.

Times Literary Supplement (1974): 'The term "pecking order" has become part of common parlance ... After a brief trial of strength, every animal in the flock or the herd learns to know its place.'

Jeremy Potter, *Foul Play* (1967): 'The inspector had a pretty low rating in the CID's pecking order ... His office overlooked an unbroken expanse of sooty wall.'

Peeping tom – *a voyeur*

In 1040, according to legend, Lady Godiva begged her husband Leofric, Earl of Mercia and Lord of Coventry, to remove certain onerous taxes which he had imposed on his tenants. He said he would do so if she rode naked through the city of Coventry. Lady Godiva did so, her modesty preserved by her long hair, and the Earl kept his promise.

This legend is recorded by Roger of Wendover (d. 1236) in his *Flores Historiarum*, and it was adapted by Paul de Rapin in his *History of England* (1723–7) into the story commonly known.

Over subsequent centuries this story has been embellished. A 17th-century addition was that the people of Coventry stayed indoors as a sign of respect for Lady Godiva's modesty. A tailor named Tom could not resist the temptation, peeped through his curtains and was blinded as a result.

Pell-mell – *confusion and haste, disorderly mingling*

From Old French *pesle mesle* (12th century), the word was variously presented as *pelle-melle* (14th century) and also *mesle-pesle*, *melle-pelle*, *mesle-mesle* and *brelle-mesle* (12th century). The element *mesle* comes from *mesler* or *mêler*, to mix.

The origin of *pele* is uncertain. It has been suggested that it comes from *pelle*, a shovel, or *paele*, a pan, so that the phrase would mean mixed together with a shovel or in a pan. It is more likely to be merely one of the many rhyming combinations in English, for example, **Namby-pamby**, **Shilly-shally**, Nitty-gritty (see **Get down to the nitty-gritty**).

Another suggestion is that it comes from the game *paille maille*, which was played in France by peasants in the 14th century before being introduced to England, via Ireland, where it became the modern game of croquet.

'Pell-mell', it is said, is a corruption of the Anglicised version of this game, Pall Mall, which involved striking a wooden ball down a long alley with hoops at both ends. Sometimes the balls got into a terrible muddle, hence the phrase.

Thomas Kyd, *Cornelia* (1594): 'The murdring Enemie Pesle-Mesle pursued them like a storme of hayle.'

Penny has dropped – *a remark is suddenly understood*

This refers to slot machines which are inactive until the penny is put into the slot. The earliest machines date back to the 1880s, but their popularity increased until there were more than 200 models in the 1930s. Scenes on early cinematograph machines hinted at the macabre or the titillating; to find out what the butler saw, be part of the crowd at an execution or admire the charms of 'The Tiger Lady', all one needed to do was drop a penny in the slot.

Sunday Times (1991): 'Attitudes were changing in both countries. "The penny has slowly dropped that far from it being an advantage to be associated with hostages, it is a positive millstone," said a British diplomat.'

Phoenix from the ashes – *something that is born again*

According to Greek legend, the phoenix, a fabulous Arabian bird, the only one of its kind, lived 500 to 600 years, at the end of which it made a nest of spices, sang a melodious dirge, flapped its wings to set fire to the pile, burnt itself to ashes and came forth with new life.

> My ashes as the Phoenix, may bring forth
> A Bird, that will revenge upon you all.
> Shakespeare, *Henry VI Part III* (1593)

Hugh Macmillan, *Bible Teachings in Nature* (1870): 'The phoenix of new institutions can only arise out of the conflagration and ashes of the old.'

Pidgin English – *grammatically incorrect English spoken by foreigners*

This 'language', often known as 'business English', developed during the 19th century with the emergence of British trade with China. It was an amalgam of English and Chinese, with some Chinese pronunciation and grammatical form. The word 'business' produced some difficulties and was pronounced 'bidgin' or 'pidgin'.

An example of pidgin English is a letter purportedly from a Chinese wet nurse, disappointed that the colours were not trooped as usual on the Queen's birthday: 'Sir, Long time my have stop Hongkong side, any year Queen's bursday have got that soldier man play-pidgin City Hall overside. My chin-chin you tluly talkee my what for this year no got – no have got largee lain! How fashion? Some flen talkee my that soldier man b'long alla same olo man – two time one day he no can – some man talkee that soldier man taipan he more likee walkee that horse go topside sleep!' (Naai Ma, Hong Kong, 27 May 1878).

Pie in the sky – *a foolish hope based on little evidence; a prospect, often illusory, of future happiness, especially as a reward in heaven for virtue or suffering on earth*

A militant trade union song-book, *Songs of the Workers* (1911), included 'The Preacher and the Slave' by Joe Hill:

> You will eat, bye and bye,
> In that glorious land above the sky;
> Work and pray, live on hay,
> You'll get pie in the sky when you die.

It may be that Joe Hill did not invent the phrase but that it was simply an existing ironical slogan of the time.

Sunday Express (1959): 'With the election moving remorselessly nearer, pie-in-the-sky days are here again. Everything our hearts could desire is promised us by politicians.'

Piece of cake – *something that can be easily done*

An RAF expression since 1938, it means that something is as easy as enjoying a piece of cake. It is similar to the RAF expression 'a cake-walk', meaning a raid or an attack that turns out to be easy.

At the time of the Berlin airlift in 1948, a cartoon appeared depicting a Transport Command pilot saying: 'Oh, it's a piece of Gatow, old boy!' A clever play on the French word *gâteau*, cake, Gatow was one of the Berlin airfields vital to the supply operation.

Terry McLean, *Kings of Rugby* (1960): 'They took the field against Canterbury as if the match were a "piece of cake".'

Pie-eyed – *drunk*

Originally a slang American expression, the phrase means to be intoxicated to such an extent that one's vision is affected.

The only rather far-fetched notion for the derivation of this 20th-century expression is that the eyes of the drunk are watery red and he struggles to keep them open. It seems that this resembled a pie, and the phrase has stuck for the last century.

S.E. White, *The Rules of the Game* (1910): "'Oh *he's* in town …" – "Drunk, eh?" – "Spifflicated, pie-eyed, loaded, sloshed.'"

Pig in a poke – *a purchase that was not properly examined before it was made*

It was the custom in old country fairs to sell suckling pigs. The trader would have one pig on show and the rest would be neatly tied in sacks, or 'pokes', ready to take away. A dishonest trader would put cats in the pokes and the unwary customer would pay for his pig, only to discover the deception later.

The Middle English word *poke* is the root of the present-day word 'pocket', meaning 'little poke'.

See also **Let the cat out of the bag**.

David Christie Murray, *John Vale's Guardian* (1890): 'I can't buy a pig in a poke … Let me know what you've got to sell, and then maybe I'll make a bid for it.'

Pigeon-hole – *to classify*

From earliest times, the English ate pigeons as part of their diet. The birds nested either in holes set in walls or in openings on a dovecote. By 1789, the slots on desks for filing papers were known as pigeon-holes. By the mid-19th century the noun had also become a verb, to pigeon-hole, which means to classify information or to come back to it later.

David Emery Gascoyne, *A Vagrant and Other Poems* (1950): 'Keep your labels for people who need them; I cannot be pigeon-holed neatly.'

Pin money – *pocket money, a woman's allowance of money for her own personal expenditure*

In the 14th and 15th centuries, pins and needles were scarce because their manufacture was controlled by a Crown monopoly. A husband would make an allowance for his wife to meet the bills for dressmaking and similar tasks. It was also quite usual for wills to contain special bequests for the purpose of buying pins. When they became cheap, women spent their allowances on other fancies, but the term 'pin money' remained in vogue.

Thomas Vanbrugh, *The Relapse* (1696):

> MISS HOYDEN: Now, nurse, if he gives me two hundred a year to buy pins, what do you think he'll give me to buy fine petticoats?
> NURSE: Ah, my dearest, he deceives thee foully, and he's no better than a rogue for his pains! These Londoners have got a gibberage with 'em would confound a gipsy. That which they call pin-money is to buy their wives everything in the versal world, down to their very shoe-ties.

Pipe down – *to keep quiet, stop being aggressive or noisy*

This is a nautical expression from the days when a boatswain would pipe his command for silence and lights out on board ship.

Penguin New Writing (1942): 'I didn't see him again until pipe-down.'

Sean O'Faolain, *Midsummer Night Madness* (1932): '"Shut up, you" said the Tan angrily and the little fellow piped down miserably.'

Pipe dream – *a fanciful plan with little hope of realisation, a 'castle in the air'*

The pipe is a reference to an opium pipe and the dream to the fantasies induced by smoking opium.

Bettina Von Hutten, *Pam* (1904): 'Look at the sea and tell me if, in your wildest pipe-dream, you ever saw anything lovelier.'

Daily Telegraph (1959): 'In that event, the Channel project would cease to be an engineer's pipe-dream'.

Piping hot – *very hot*

This very old expression dates back to Chaucer. It refers to the fact that food can be so hot that it sizzles and whistles as it comes off the stove.

It later became used in the sense of fresh, quite new, just come out.

Geoffrey Chaucer, *The Miller's Tale* (c. 1386): 'Wafres piping hoot out of the gleede.'

Thomas Middleton, *Your Five Gallants* (1607): '"Whence comes he, sir?" – "Piping hot from the university."'

Pissed as a newt – *very drunk*

There are many suggestions for the origin of the phrase.

The newt, being an amphibious reptile, can submerge itself in liquid as a drunk might do.

The original expression is thought to have been 'as tight as a newt'. Perhaps the reference is to its tight-fitting skin reflecting the state of being 'tight' with alcohol.

Paul Beale (reviser of Eric Partridge's *Dictionary of Slang*), 1987: 'The great thing about newts is the characteristic they share with fishes' arse'oles: they are watertight. And you can't get tighter than that!'

Richard Lakin Mason, *The World of Suzie Wong* (1957): 'Christ, I'm pissed. I'm pissed as a newt.'

Plain as a pikestaff – *totally obvious, evident; easy to understand*

Some authorities believe that the phrase refers to the pike, a weapon used by the infantry. The pike was rather like a spear but its shaft was so long that it was easily visible to all around.

This explanation fits neatly with the modern meaning. However, another theory, supported by 16th-century references, suggests that the expression has changed in form and meaning over the years.

Pedlars shouldered a sturdy staff, known as a packstaff, on to which they tied their bundle. Constant use wore the wood plain, and so we find the phrase 'plain as a packstaff'.

Bishop Joseph Hall, *Satires* (1597): 'Pack-staffe plaine, uttring the thing they ment.'

'Plain as a pikestaff' was a later 16th-century variant and refers to a stout stick with a metal tip, used for support by those travelling on foot. The pikestaff was a simple, utilitarian affair and so the original phrase meant 'basic, unelaborate' rather than its modern sense of 'obvious'.

Thus Charles Cotton, *Scarronides* (1664), has 'plain as a pike-staff without gilding', and when Trollope writes in *The Last Chronicle of Barset* (1867), 'The evidence against him was plain as a pikestaff', he means not that the evidence was obvious but that it was simple and to the point, even blunt.

John Galsworthy, *The Man of Property* (1906): 'He would not give way till he saw young Bosinney with an income of his own. That June would have trouble with the fellow was as plain as a pikestaff; he had no more idea of money than a cow.'

Plain sailing – *easy progress, perfectly straightforward, no need for hesitation about the course of action*

The phrase was originally 'plane sailing', navigation by plane charts which showed the earth as flat. These were much simpler, obviously, than later navigation systems which assumed the earth was spherical.

Nicholas Owen, *Journal of a Slave Dealer* (1756): 'If he can take an observation and is acquainted with that part of navigation call'd plain sailing, without any of the practical part of seamanship.'

George Bernard Shaw, *Androcles and the Lion* (1916): 'Without the proper clues the gospels are, to a modern educated person, nonsensical and incredible … But with the clues they are fairly plain sailing. Jesus becomes an intelligible and consistent person.'

Play ducks and drakes – *to throw away idly or carelessly; to play idly with; to handle or use recklessly; to squander*

'Ducks and drakes' is a game played by skimming a flat stone over the surface of the water. It is a game of idle amusement and this leads to the use of the phrase as meaning irresponsible behaviour.

A.H. Bullen, *A Collection of Old English Plays: Dick of Devon* (1626): 'The poorest ship-boy / Might on the Thames make duckes and drakes with pieces / Of eight fetched out of Spayne.'

> Ye ... grew
> So witty that ye play'd at ducks and drakes
> With Arthur's vows.
>
> Alfred, Lord Tennyson,
> 'The Last Tournament' (1872)

Play fast and loose – *to behave in a cavalier fashion, to blow both hot and cold, to say one thing and do another*

'Fast and loose' was a rigged betting game played at fairgrounds. A visitor was invited to fix a skewer-like stick into a table with a coiled string or belt attached. When he claimed to have it 'fast', the operator would show that it was in fact 'loose'. As he had arranged the stick and the string in advance, this was hardly surprising!

Shakespeare, *Love's Labour's Lost* (1594): 'To sell a bargain well is as cunning as fast and loose.'

John Lothrop Motley, *The Rise of the Dutch Republic* (1855): 'The English Queen ... had ... almost distracted the provinces by her fast-and-loose policies.'

Play havoc – *to cause destruction, damage, distress, disruption or the like*

'Havoc' is an English word derived from the Old French *havot*, meaning plunder. 'Crier havot', to shout havoc, was an invocation to plunder and destroy.

Shakespeare, *Julius Caesar* (1601): 'Caesar's spirit ... / Shall ... with a monarch's voice / Cry "Havoc", and let slip the dogs of war.'

G.D. Abraham, *Mountain Adventures* (1910): 'The hot sun, reflected off the snow, played havoc with his complexion.'

The Times (1969): 'The noise and clatter of high-revving engines can play havoc with a driver's nerves.'

Pleased as Punch – *greatly delighted*

Mr Punch, in Punch and Judy, always gloats with self-satisfaction at the success of his evil actions.

The story, roughly in its present form, is attributed to an Italian comedian, Silvio Fiorillo, who flourished around 1600. Punch, in a fit of jealousy, strangles his infant child, whereupon his wife Judy belabours him with a bludgeon until he retaliates and beats her to death. He flings both bodies into the street, but is arrested and shut in prison, whence he escapes by means of a golden key.

The rest is an allegory showing how the light-hearted Punch triumphs over: (1) Ennui, in the shape of a dog; (2) Disease, in the disguise of a doctor; (3) Death, who is beaten to death; and (4) the Devil himself, who is outwitted.

J.R. Lowell, *Letters* (1873): 'I am as pleased as Punch at the thought of having a kind of denizenship, if nothing more, at Oxford.'

Ploughman's lunch – *bread and a piece of cheese*

This has a remarkably recent provenance, being the invention of Richard Trehane, Chairman of the English Country Cheese Council. He coined the phrase to encourage more pubs to sell cheese. It was an enormous marketing success.

R. Trehane in B.H. Axler, *The Cheese Handbook* (1970): 'English cheese and beer have for centuries formed a perfect combination enjoyed as the Ploughman's Lunch.'

The Times (1975): 'The pubs specialise in lunchtime catering ... and you can get a decent "ploughman's" for between 20p and 30p.'

Plug a song *or* book – *to promote a song* or *book*

The phrase is said to originate from Captain Leonard Plugge, the founder and main broadcaster of one of the first commercial radio stations, Radio Normandie, which transmitted to England during the 1930s.

One of the station's sources of income was to receive payments to play records and to promote them throughout the country.

However, the word 'plug' appears in this sense as early as 1902, and an alternative etymology is that it comes from 'to plug away with', meaning to persevere with something.

The origin may also be 'plug', meaning a book which does not sell well and becomes bad stock. American Dialect Society, *Dialect Notes* (1901) has '*Plug*, a book left on an author's or publisher's hands.' It is possible that this kind of plug was obviously in need of a plug in the modern sense, and the older meaning dropped away.

George Ade, *The Girl Proposition* (1902): 'They were friendly to the prosperous Bachelor and each one determined to put in a few quiet plugs for Sis.'

Clive James, 'The Fate of Felicity Fark in the Land of Media' (1975):

> She found the concentration of rehearsal
> More challenging by far than plugging *Persil*.

Plumb the depths – *to sink low*

A plumb line is a piece of lead attached to a line which enables a mariner to see how deep the water is at an inlet or port to avoid running aground.

Jonathan Swift, *Gulliver's Travels* (1726): 'I consulted the most experienced seamen upon the depth of the channel, which they had often plummed.'

Arthur Hugh Clough, 'Amours de Voyage' (1849): 'So I plumb the deeps of depression.'

Point-blank – *pointing or aiming straight at the mark; at very close range; level, direct, straight; straightforward, blunt*

It has been suggested the phrase comes from the French *point blanc*, meaning 'white point', as on a target. However, no such use is found in French or in any Romance language.

'Blank' in English has long been used to mean the white point at the centre of a target. 'Point' therefore refers to the pointing of an arrow or gun at the blank. The hyphenated combination of point-blank is of the same class of words as 'break-neck', 'cut-throat' or 'stop-gap'.

> As level as the cannon to his blank
> Transports his poisoned shot.
> Shakespeare, *Hamlet* (1602)

Mme Frances d'Arblay (Fanny Burney), *Diary* (1779): 'What a point-blank question! Who but Sir Joshua would have ventured it!'

Possession is nine points of the law – *in a dispute over property, the law favours the current owner*

This means nine points out of a possible ten. Alternatives are 'nine-tenths of the law' or 'nine parts of the law' and an earlier version, 'possession is eleven points of the law' (i.e. out of a possible twelve).

The original nine points of the law were said to be: (1) money; (2) patience; (3) a good cause; (4) a good lawyer; (5) a good counsel; (6) good witnesses; (7) a good jury; (8) a good judge; (9) good luck.

John Arbuthnot, *The History of John Bull* (1712): 'Possession … would make it much surer. They say "it is eleven points of the Law!"'

Post-haste – *immediately, with urgency*

In the 16th century, letters were delivered by a relay system of postal messengers on horseback. The horses would be ridden hard and would need to be changed every twenty miles or so. Fresh horses were kept ready at various post-houses or inns along the way, available to ordinary travellers as well as to the post-boys. To gain prompt attention and priority choice of horse, a messenger with a packet to deliver would cry 'Post haste!' when he entered the stable yard.

'By return of post', the phrase now used to request an immediate answer to a letter, had a much more literal meaning when the service was in its infancy. It meant that the reply should be carried back by the same messenger, or 'post', that had delivered the message.

Shakespeare, *Othello* (1604): 'The Duke ... requires your haste, post-haste appearance, / Even on the instant.'

Today (1991): 'End to monopolies, post haste.'

Pour cold water on – *to curb enthusiasm, discourage*

Although the expression goes back to 200 BC, it was used in its current sense, meaning to discourage, only in the 19th century.

Herman Melville, *Moby-Dick* (1851): 'Iceland Sailor, I don't like your floor, maty; it's too springy to my taste. I'm used to ice-floors. I'm sorry to throw cold water on the subject; but excuse me.'

Pour oil on troubled waters – *to smooth over a dispute, to soothe by gentle words, to use tact and diplomacy to restore calm after a quarrel*

The violence of waves is much decreased when oil is poured on them. Pliny in the 1st century AD referred to seamen using oil to calm turbulent waters.

Its currency in England may owe more to Bede's *Ecclesiastical History* (AD 731). There the story is told of St Aidan, an Irish monk from a monastery on the island of Iona. A young priest was to escort a maiden destined to be the bride of Oswy, King of Northumbria. Concerned that she might encounter stormy weather, Aidan gave the priest a jar of holy oil to pour on the sea. The priest did this when a storm arose and the waters became calm.

W.B. Baring, *The Croker Papers* (1884): 'Lord G. [Bentinck] ... spoke angrily. D'Israeli poured oil and calmed the waves.'

Pretty *or* fine *or* rare kettle of fish – *a right muddle*

A 'kettle of fish' is an old name, originating from the Scottish borders, for a kind of *fête champêtre* or riverside picnic, at which a newly caught salmon is boiled in a fish kettle and eaten. The discomfort of this sort of party may have led to the ironic phrase 'a pretty kettle of fish', meaning an awkward state of affairs, a mess or a muddle.

Sir Walter Scott, *St Ronan's Well* (1823): 'As the whole company go to the water-side today to eat a kettle of fish, there will be no risk of interruption.'

Duke of Wellington, *Dispatches, compiled by Lt. Col. Gurwood* (1837): 'If so, we shall have a fine kettle of fish at Scringapatam.'

Henry Fielding, *Tom Jones* (1749): 'Fine doings at my house! A rare kettle of fish I have discovered at last.'

A more recent variation is the use of the phrase 'a different' or 'another kettle of fish', meaning a different state of affairs, a different matter altogether.

Evelyn Waugh, *Put Out More Flags* (1942): 'Until now the word "Colonel" for Basil had connoted an elderly rock-gardener on Barbara's GPO list. This formidable man of his own age was another kettle of fish.'

Pull one's finger out – *to get on with it, get a move on, get cracking*

One suggestion for the phrase's derivation is that it comes from military history. In order to keep gunpowder secure in the ignition hole near the base of the cannon, a crewman was instructed to put his finger into the hole. When the powder was due to be ignited, he pulled it out as quickly as possible.

This seems unlikely because examples of the phrase are comparatively recent and they seem to originate in Australia. It appears first in Sidney Baker, *A Popular Dictionary of Australian Slang* (1941). It is defined as meaning 'Hurry up!' and is used mainly to demand effort from a lazy or inactive person. It seems to come from the notion of idleness characterised by having one's finger inserted in a particular bodily orifice.

In German, the term is very specific in the military phrase said to be current in the 1960s: 'Mann, nimm die Finger aus dem Arsch.' (Man, take your finger out of your arse.)

Temple Sutherland, *Green Kiwi* (1956): '"They're tigers for toil," he went on. "The bloke that takes a job with them wants to be able to pull his finger out."'

Whatever the provenance, eyebrows were certainly raised when the Duke of Edinburgh was reported in *The Times* (1961): 'I think it's about time we pulled our fingers out.'

Pull one's weight – *to do the very best one can, to play one's proper part, to share the responsibility*

This is a rowing expression which demands that every member of the crew do his best by putting all his weight into the stroke. An oarsman who does not pull his weight is a drag on the rest of the crew.

E.F. Norton, *The Fight for Everest* (1925): 'No members of the climbing party pulled more weight in the team than these two by their unostentatious, unselfish gruelling work.'

Pull out all the stops – *to make a supreme effort to achieve an objective, to do one's best*

An organ has stops to bring into use various pipes. When all the stops are pulled, the organ will be played at its loudest and most powerful.

Anthony Price, *Other Paths to Glory* (1974): '"But they have no idea who did it?" – "Not from what I heard ... I know they're pulling out all the stops, though."'

Pull someone's leg – *to tease a person, to chaff someone, to make fun of them*

Originally this phrase had a less humorous meaning. It probably meant to trip up, to pull the legs from under someone, in order to rob them. The sense remains of trying to put something over on someone but the intent in the modern phrase is jocular, not malicious.

William B. Churchward, *Blackbirding in the South Pacific* (1888): 'Then I shall be able to pull the leg of that chap Mike. He's always trying to do me.'

Later variations are 'Pull the other one' or 'Pull the other leg, it's got bells on!'

Michael Butterworth, *The Man in the Sopwith Camel* (1974): '"Pull the other leg, it's got bells on!" she said. "A bank's a bank, and you've got yourself charge of a bank for no other reason but to dip your fingers into the till."'

Pull the chestnuts out of the fire – *to retrieve a difficult situation for someone, to undertake the dangerous part of an enterprise, to save the day*

An old fable from France says that a monkey and a cat lived in the same family, and it was hard to tell which of them was the greater thief.

One day, as they were roaming together, they spied some chestnuts roasting in the ashes of a fire. 'Come', said the cunning monkey, 'we shall not go dinnerless today. Your claws are better than mine for the purpose; pull the chestnuts out of the ashes, and you shall have half.'

The cat pulled them out, burning her paws severely in doing so. When she had stolen every one, she turned to the monkey for her share of the booty, but, to her chagrin, she found no chestnuts, for he had eaten them all.

The same fable gives rise to the phrase 'to make a cat's paw of someone', to get someone to do one's dirty work.

Economist (1957): 'The Germans cannot be expected to pull our chestnuts out of the fire.'

Samuel Richardson, *The History of Sir Charles Grandison* (1754): 'He makes her fight his battles for him; and become herself the cat's paw to help him to the ready roasted chestnuts.'

Pull the wool over someone's eyes – *to make blind to facts, to hoodwink, to deceive*

Since the 17th century, 'wool' has been a standard slang word for hair, and this phrase probably means pulling the hair over someone's eyes. Some argue that it refers to a wig, but this seems unlikely.

'Cuthbert Bede', *The Adventures of Mr Verdant Green* (1853): 'He'd got no wool on the top of his head – just the place where the wool ought to grow, you know.'

William D. Howells, *The Rise of Silas Lapham* (1884): 'I don't propose he shall pull the wool over my eyes.'

Purple patch or passage – *highly coloured and florid writing in a literary work that is generally undistinguished*

Quintus Horatius Flaccus, known in English as Horace, first used the phrase 'purple patch' in *De Arte Poetica* (68–65 BC) to describe a piece of poetry which he deemed so ostentatious that it should be sewn and displayed on someone's clothes.

> Inceptis gravibus plerumque et magna professis
> Purpureus, late qui splendeat, unus et alter
> Adsuitur pannus.

This is translated as: 'Often to weighty enterprises and such as profess great objects, one or two purple patches are sewn on to make a fine display in the distance.'

Samuel Taylor Coleridge, 'Revue de Litérature Comparée' (1834): 'Admirably reasoned as this Essay is, I yet regard it but as one of the rich Purple Patches of the Robe of Casuistry.'

Gramophone (1977): 'One is grateful to be spared one of Wilde's purpler passages.'

Push the boat out – *to be extravagant or over-generous*

A mid-20th-century boat-building expression, it refers to the launch of a ship with a bottle of champagne and the celebrations which followed.

John Le Carré, *A Murder of Quality* (1962): "'Fielding's giving another dinner party tonight." – "He's pushing the boat out these days."'

Push the envelope – *to go to the limit; to stretch the limit*

In use since the 1940s, this expression originated in the aerospace industry, in which the limits of safe performance were marked on a two-dimensional graph, called the 'envelope'. This represented safe usage, and to 'push the envelope' is to go beyond those recommended limits.

In 1979, Tom Wolfe's bestseller *The Right Stuff* vividly described the life of test pilots during the 1950s and 60s. It appears that this book, and the subsequent film, did much to popularise the notion of 'pushing the envelope'.

The idea of an envelope as a kind of enclosing boundary is not new. In 1899 Arnold Bennett wrote: 'My desire is to depict the deeper beauty while abiding by the envelope of facts.'

Sunday Times (1995): 'Messrs E. and V. want you to know that if you thought *Basic Instinct* was pushing the envelope, this year's trendy phrase for taking a risk, *Showgirls* is according to the publicity material "pushing the edge of the envelope".'

Put a sock in it – *be quiet, shut up, make less noise*

It is thought that this expression refers to the late 19th century and the earlier years of the 20th, when gramophones or phonographs amplified the sound through large horns. Woollen socks were often stuffed in them to muffle the sound.

However, it could equally be a military expression. When a colleague snored too loudly, someone was invited to put a sock in his mouth.

Malcolm Lowry, *Ultramarine* (1933): 'Aw, put a sock in it. Well, I'm going to sleep, chaps, and if you wake me again, the fellow that does it I'll slip him thirteen inches of saltpetre.'

Put a spoke in someone's wheel – *to prevent someone from doing something*

This is an odd expression today. It conjures up a bicycle wheel, which already has spokes. The reference is, however, to earlier times when carts had solid wheels and no spokes in the modern sense. The 'spoke' then was a pin which could be inserted into a hole on the wheel to act as a brake.

The expression has been known since 1583. 'Spoke' may be a mistranslation of *spaak* (meaning bar, stave) in the Dutch expression *een spaak in 't wiel steeken*, to put a bar in a wheel.

Mary Meeke ('Gabrielli'), *The Mysterious Husband* (1801): 'If you was to attempt to make your escape, I should be obligated to put a spoke in your wheel.'

Put on one's thinking cap – *to consider something carefully*

This is probably a reference to the judge's cap, which he donned when passing judgements. It was latterly reserved for passing the death sentence.

However, it may also refer to the time when most people wore hats to go about their daily work. It was at their work that people were required to do their thinking. When they were asked to put their thinking cap on, they were being encouraged to think seriously about something, probably in their professional capacity.

The term 'thinking cap' originated in the late 1800s and replaced 'considering cap', which dates from the early 1600s.

Charles Dickens, *Great Expectations* (1861): 'I'll put on my considering cap, and I think all you want to do may be done by degrees.'

Put one's dukes *or* dooks up – *to put one's fists up as though preparing to fight*

The origin of 'dukes' meaning fists is uncertain. One theory is that because the Duke of Wellington had such a large nose, a 'duke' came to mean a nose. A man's fists were known therefore as 'duke busters', abbreviated through usage to dukes.

An alternative theory prefers another duke, the Duke of York, and claims the origin as Cockney rhyming slang meaning 'fork' or finger, standing for the whole hand or fist. (See **Fork out**.)

J.D. Brayshaw, *Slum Silhouettes* (1898): "E could 'andle 'is dooks an' no error: the way 'e set abaht Bill was a fair treat.'

In a public speech in 1909 about House of Lords reform, Winston Churchill said: 'In the absence of any commanding voice, the Tory party have had to put up their "dooks".'

A report of the speech adds: 'Great laughter and a voice: "What about your grandfather?"' (Churchill's grandfather was the Duke of Marlborough.)

Put one's foot in it – *to make a mistake, to blunder, to make a faux pas, to get into trouble*

Authorities usually refer to the common-sense explanation, the embarrassment of putting one's foot in some mess on the pavement.

A more interesting and reasonably plausible explanation is that the present-day idiom comes from a much earlier phrase, 'the bishop hath set his foot in it', which was a common cry when broth or milk was burnt.

Bishops, it seems, were not popular in the Middle Ages. According to William Tyndale in *The Obedyence of a Chrysten Man* (1528): 'If the podech [soup] be burned to, or the meat over-roasted, we say the Bishop hath put his foot in the pot, or the Bishop hath played the cook. Because the Bishops burn who they lust and whosoever displeaseth them.'

John Milton used the expression in *Animadversions* (1641): 'It will be the bishop's foot in the broth.'

Jonathan Swift employed it almost a century later in *Polite Conversation* (1738): 'This cream is burnt too – Why madam, the bishop hath set his foot in it.'

Interestingly, the French had a phrase of similar origin, *pas de clerc*, 'priest's footstep', which was used when someone had committed an indiscretion through ignorance or lack of good sense.

George Orwell, *Coming Up for Air* (1939): 'She lies low till she's found out all the weak points in your alibi, and then suddenly, when you've put your foot in it by some careless remark, she starts on you.'

Put one's shoulder to the wheel – *to make a real effort*

Occasionally also seen as 'lay' or 'set' one's shoulder to the wheel, this is a reference to the carter who would put his shoulder to the wheel to assist his horses in hauling his wagon out of a rut.

Sir Roger L'Estrange, *Fables* (1692): 'Lay your Shoulder to the Wheel, and Prick your Oxen.'

Anthony Trollope, *The Small House at Allington* (1864): 'Putting your shoulder to the wheel when the coach gets into the mud. That's what I've been doing all my life.'

Put the dampers on – *to discourage, to hinder*

A damper is a device in a piano which presses on the strings to stop them vibrating. When the dampers are on, the effect is that of cutting the sound dead. The term is used figuratively to describe the stifling effect that an unhappy event, circumstance or person might exert upon the enjoyment of others.

A link with 'damp' in the sense of cold and wet may also exist, as in Samuel Richardson, *Clarissa* (1748): 'I very early discharged shame, that cold water damper to an enterprising spirit.'

(See also **Pour cold water on.**)

Put the kibosh on – *to put a stop to, prevent from continuing, ruin, spoil, bewilder, knock out (both literally and figuratively)*

The very oddity and exotic feel of the word 'kibosh' have prompted several etymologies, the most plausible being that it comes from the Yiddish *kabas*, *kabasten*, to suppress.

The earliest instance discovered comes from Charles Dickens, *Sketches by 'Boz'* (1836): "'Hooroar" ejaculates a pot-boy … "put the kye-bosh on her, Mary!"'

From around 1860 the word is noted in costermonger use as meaning eighteen pence, from the Yiddish *kye*, eighteen, and 'bosh', meaning pence. If correct, it may be that this arbitrary sum is the answer, and the pot-boy in later parlance would have been saying: 'Give her a fourpenny one, Mary!'

Others have suggested that the expression has an Irish origin. 'Kibosh' may be from the Irish *cie bais*, pronounced 'kye-bosh', referring to the cap that judges wore when they passed sentence of death.

Song, 'Belgium Put the Kibosh on the Kaiser' (c. 1914):

> For Belgium put the kibosh on the Kaiser
> Europe took a stick and made him sore.

Q

Queer someone's pitch – *to make things difficult for someone, to forestall or thwart someone*

To 'queer' is a verb meaning to ruin, and a 'pitch' is the place where someone contracted business or put on an entertainment. The sense is therefore to render a person's efforts useless by underhand means, as a street or market vendor might find his trade spoilt by an interloper.

Mathew Mackintosh, *Stage Reminiscences* (1866): 'The smoke and flames of "blue fire" which had been used to illuminate the fight came up through the chinks of the stage, fit to choke a dozen Macbeths, and – pardon the little bit of professional slang – poor Jamie's "pitch" was "queered" with a vengeance.'

Punch (1890): 'Wy, they'd queer the best pitches in life, if they kiboshed the Power of the Quid!'

(See also **Put the kibosh on.**)

Queer Street – *an imaginary place of financial difficulties*

Using a street name to identify a group is well established in the English language: 'Whitehall' for civil servants, 'Fleet Street' for journalists and so on. It has been suggested that Carey Street, off Chancery Lane, was called Queer Street because it housed the bankruptcy courts. 'Queer Street' was 19th-century slang, an imaginary street where people in difficulties were supposed to reside. A similar coinage was 'Civvy Street', civilian life for soldiers who had left the army.

Charles Dickens, *Our Mutual Friend* (1865): 'Queer Street is full of lodgers just at present.'

R

Rack and ruin – *utter decay or destitution*

'Rack' here means 'wreck' and is therefore synonymous with 'ruin', with which it is paired for alliterative emphasis.

Other pairings have developed in a similar way, with old words retaining their currency only in the alliterative phrase. Examples are 'spick and span', 'might and main', 'kith and kin'.

Elisabeth Blower, *George Bateman* (1782): 'Everything would soon go to sixes and sevens, and rack and ruin.'

(See also **At sixes and sevens.**)

Rack one's brains – *to try very hard to find a solution or remember something*

This is a reference to the instrument of torture, the rack, which stretched a victim's joints to the limit. This, therefore, means to stretch one's brains to the limit until the solution is found.

W. Byrd (1583) in Edward Farr, *Select Poetry Chiefly Devotional of the Reign of Queen Elizabeth* (1845): 'Racke not thy wit to winne by wicked waies.'

Mme Frances d'Arblay (Fanny Burney), *Early Diary* (1768): 'I have rack'd my brains for half an hour – in vain.'

Rain cats and dogs – *to rain very heavily*

There are three possible explanations of this picturesque saying. The most popular is that when it rained very heavily in days of inadequate drainage, the dogs and the cats were swept away by the flood water and drowned.

Jonathan Swift, 'Description of a City Shower' (1710):

> Now from all parts the swelling kennels flow,
> And bear their trophies with them as they go.

The 'trophies' are numerous but among them are:
Drowned puppies, stinking sprats, all drench'd in mud,
Dead cats and turnip tops, come tumbling down the flood.

The expression was used in a slightly different form in the previous century in Richard Brome, *The City Wit* (1653): 'It shall raine … dogs and polecats.'

Daily Mail (1991): 'There was a danger, when the bumpers were raining like cats and dogs, that Viv Richards would end his final Test with English blood on his hands.'

Rat race – *competitive struggle to further one's career*

This probably refers to rats in a laboratory running continuously on a treadmill.

It was also the name of a very popular form of 1930s dancing to jazz music. This is part of the tradition of linking names of animals to dances – the foxtrot, the turkey trot, and the bunny hug, for example.

American Speech (1937): 'Terms for recreations: *rat-race*, dance of low-grade nature.'

Roy Fuller, *Image of a Society* (1956): 'A boy's got to have guts to make his way in this rat race of a modern world.'

Rats leaving a sinking ship – *untrustworthy, unreliable or disreputable people who leave an organisation or a cause as soon as the going gets tough*

Pliny (1st century AD) alleged that mice were able to hear the noise of a collapsing house before humans and so would leave the house first.

Shakespeare in *The Tempest* (1611) applied the idea to rats, and gave the phrase its modern sense.

A rotten carcass of a boat, not rigg'd,
Nor tackle, sail, nor mast; the very rats
Instinctively had quit it …

Sinclair Lewis, *Babbitt* (1922): 'He was not merely annoyed; he was frightened. "Why did she quit, then?" he worried. "Did she have a hunch my business is going on the rocks? And it was Sanders got the Street Traction deal. Rats – sinking ship!"'

Read the riot act – *to quell rowdy or objectionable behaviour by remonstrating and making the consequences clear*

The Act for Preventing Tumults and Riotous Assemblies, or Riot Act, was decreed in 1715 in the reign of George I. The act made it unlawful for twelve or more people to disturb the public peace through riotous behaviour. Such a crowd could be ordered to disperse by a magistrate reading aloud the following proclamation: 'Our Sovereign Lord the King chargeth and commandeth all persons being assembled immediately to disperse themselves, and peaceably to depart to their habitations or to their lawful business.'

Those who had not obeyed the command an hour later were sentenced to imprisonment with hard labour.

Peter Hill, *The Hunters* (1976): 'Read her the riot act, tell her to be a good girl and take her home.'

Real McCoy – *the genuine article*

An expression used in the USA, but formerly in Britain it was 'the real MacKay'. Various stories about an American boxer have been suggested as the origin of the phrase. It is more likely to have dated from the 1880s in Scotland, where it was applied to whisky, men and things of highest quality. The whisky and the phrase were exported to the USA and Canada, where people of Scottish origin kept the phrase alive.

The American boxer was Norman Selby (1873–1940), who had assumed the professional name Kid McCoy. There is no doubt that the name 'The Real McCoy' was applied to him, perhaps to distinguish himself from the other McCoys who were on the professional and amateur circuit. On one occasion in a bar, he was invited to punch a fellow drinker to prove that he was 'the real McCoy'. Selby obliged and flattened him!

Robert Louis Stevenson, 'Letter to C. Baxter' (1883): 'The auld Johnstone, ye ken – he's the real Mackay, whatever.'

American Mercury (1930): 'McCoy, genuine liquor. "This is McCoy. You can't fake Quebec wrappers."'

Leonard Bernstein, *The Joy of Music* (1959): 'The operetta score ... was musically elaborate, closer to opera, even containing finales, with everybody *singing* their way through the plot, vocalising different sentiments at the same time – the real contrapuntal McCoy.'

Red herring – *a subject which diverts attention away from the matter under discussion*

Used metaphorically first in the 19th century, the sense of diverting attention comes from fox-hunting. A red herring is a dried, smoked and salted herring. Drawn across the trail of the fox, its strong odour will destroy the scent and divert the hounds.

Nicholas Cox, *The Gentleman's Recreation* (1686): 'The trailing or dragging of a dead Cat, or Fox (and in case of necessity a Red-Herring) three or four miles ... and then laying the Dogs on the scent.'

Liverpool Daily Post (1884): 'The talk of revolutionary dangers is a mere red-herring.'

Red tape – *excessive bureaucracy, form-filling*

Modern usage has reinforced the phrase as condemnatory, the insult of a frustrated man doing battle with officialdom. It originates in the former practice of tying together papers and official documents with red tape.

This procedure goes back to the 17th century, as instanced by an advertisement in the *Public Intelligencer* (1658) which offered a reward for 'a little bundle of papers tied with red tape which were lost on Friday last ...'.

It was possibly Sydney Smith who first used the phrase to satirical effect. Discussing Sir James Makintosh, he writes: 'What a man that would be, had he a particle of gall, or the least knowledge of red tape! As Curran said of Grattan, "he would have governed the world."'

Daily Mail (1991): 'Council chiefs were accused yesterday of "robbing" schools to spend more on red tape.'

Red-letter day – *a day to remember and celebrate*

On 15th-century calendars, all saints' and feast days were marked in red and all other days in black. Red letter days were therefore days for celebration and rejoicing.

William Caxton, *The Boke yf Eneydos* (translated 1490): 'We wryte yet in our kalenders the hyghe fests wyth rede letters of coloure of purpre.'

T.A. Trollope, *What I Remember* (1887): 'I used to dine and pass the evening with Dr Jeune; and these were my red-letter days.'

Redneck – *a member of the white rural labouring class of the southern USA, one whose attitudes are considered characteristic of this class, frequently a reactionary; a labourer, farmhand, cowboy*

It is most likely that the phrase came from the sunburned necks of white labourers working in the deep south of the USA. Alternatively, one of the most common garments worn by labourers was a neckerchief, usually a red one, and some suggest that the phrase refers to the dye coming off as they sweat in the sun, staining their necks.

New Yorker (1974): 'He seems Southern redneck – a common man who works outdoors in the sun – to the soul.'

Jim Bishop, *The Days of Martin Luther King Jr* (1971): 'The fearful Southern red-neck, committed to the credo that the black man is a bridge between the animal kingdom and the human, derided the speech [King's 'I have a dream …'] as typical "coon shouting".'

Ride roughshod over – *to show no consideration for another's* *feelings or views*

If a horse is 'roughshod', the nails in its shoes protrude to get a better grip in slippery weather. In the 17th century, horses were roughshod so that they could do more damage to the enemy in battle. The idea proved impractical, since the horses cut into not only their adversaries' mounts but those of their own company.

Its metaphorical sense, to domineer, tyrannise over, appeared in the 19th century.

Randle Holme, *The Academy of Armory, or a Storehouse of Armory and Blazon* (1688): 'Rough shod – when the nails are not yet worn that holds on the shoes.'

Thomas Moore, *Intercepted Letters; or the Two-penny Post-bag* (1813): ''Tis a scheme of the Romanists, so help me God! To ride over your most Royal Highness roughshod.'

Right as ninepence – *in good health, perfectly well, in perfect* *condition*

The silver ninepence was common until the year 1696, when all unmilled coin was called in. These ninepences were very pliable and, being bent, were given as love tokens, the usual formula of presentation being: 'To my love, from my love.'

> Like commendation ninepence, crooked,
> With 'To and from my love,' it looked.
>   Samuel Butler, *Hudibras* (1663)

The pliability of the coin gave rise to the phrase 'as nimble as ninepence', and the old proverb: 'A nimble ninepence is better than a slow shilling.'

Alliteration contributed to the popularity of the phrase and led to another, 'as neat as ninepence'. In the 19th century this became 'as right as ninepence', and both phrases were common until the latter half of the century, when only the modern phrase and meaning survived.

James Howell, *English Proverbs* (1659): 'As fine as fippence, as neat as ninepence.'

F.E. Smedley, *Frank Fairlegh* (1850): 'Well, let her say "no" as if she meant it ... and then it will be all as right as ninepence.'

Blackwood's Magazine (1857): 'If I didn't see him whip the picture out of the frame, as neat as ninepence.'

The one phrase, also alliterative, that does not seem to owe its provenance to the silver coin is 'as nice as ninepence', which was a corruption of 'as nice as nine-pins'. It refers to the way in which the skittles in the game nine-pins are arranged in three rows with the utmost exactitude or nicety.

Ring a bell – *to strike a chord, to sound familiar, to remind someone of something*

Speculation abounds as to what kind of bell rings when the memory is jogged. Some say that the bell is one that attracts the attention of a clerk, receptionist or servant and that, in the same way, something seen or said may suddenly focus our attention on a person or event stored away in our memory.

Another suggestion is that the phrase may be related to the bell ringing when one is successful at a fairground stall. The contrary argument is that the phrase would then be 'to ring *the* bell'. Perhaps instead it is a nostalgic sound that triggers the memory, a school or church bell. The fact is, no one really knows.

Margery Allingham, *Coroner's Pidgin* (1945): 'That's where I saw the name then ... It rang only a very faint bell.'

Ring true *or* have the ring of truth – *to give the appearance of being authentic, to feel right*

When coins were made of pure metal and not alloys as they are today, a genuine silver coin would emit a ringing sound when dropped on a hard surface. A counterfeit coin made a dull sound.

Samuel Pegg the Elder, *Anonymiana; or Ten Centuries of Observations on Various Authors and Subjects* (1796): 'Ringing, or sounding money, to try if it be good, is not modern.'

Independent (1992): 'But somehow the idea that undertakers are sensitive souls does not ring true. These undertakers have many fine qualities but they keep their trade-exhibition champagne in mortuary refrigerators. They hold impromptu cocktail parties on stands surrounded by coffins. They leave dishes of Smarties on the bonnets of their hearses.'

(See also **Dead ringer**.)

Rip van Winkle – *a man behind the times*

In Washington Irving's *The Sketch Book* (1820), Rip van Winkle was a happy-go-lucky, hen-pecked husband of a 'well-oiled' disposition.

To get away from his wife he went on a ramble to the Kaatskill mountains north-west of New York. There he met some quaint people, dressed in the old Flemish style, playing at nine-pins. Unobserved, he took a draught of their 'Hollands' (gin) and soon fell asleep.

He slept for twenty years. When he awoke he found the world very much changed, his house deserted, his former companions gone, and instead of being a colonial subject of King George III, he was a free citizen of the United States of America.

Rob Peter to pay Paul – *to benefit one person or enterprise at the expense of another*

The true origin of the phrase is buried in time, but it is suggested that it relates to some old theological debate or rivalry within the Christian Church in which the relative merits of the two apostles were discussed.

Herbert of Bosham in *The Life of St Thomas of Canterbury*, as early as the 1170s, uses a similar phrase relating to the two apostles: 'As one who crucified Paul that Peter may go free.'

Usually it is St Peter who loses and St Paul who gains; here it is the reverse.

In 1380, John Wycliffe wrote: 'Lord, hou schulde God approve that thou robbe Petur and gif this robbere to Poule in the name of Crist?'

On 17 December 1540, the Church of St Peter at Westminster became a cathedral. It enjoyed its elevated status for only ten years before the diocese of Westminster fell once again within that of St Paul's cathedral.

Ill feeling was further exacerbated when a good portion of revenue from St Peter's land was then used to finance repairs at St Paul's. Someone applied this already current phrase to claim that they 'had robbed Peter to pay Paul'.

The expression is not confined to English. Old French has a similar saying, 'descouvrir S Pierre pour couvrir S Pol', strip St Peter to clothe St Paul.

L.T. Hobhouse, *Liberalism* (c. 1920): 'When taxation is utilised to secure healthy conditions of existence to the mass of the people it is clear that this is no case of robbing Peter to pay Paul.'

Round robin – *a petition or protest; a letter addressed to several people; a circular*

In 17th- and 18th-century France, peasants who signed petitions to the King were liable to be severely punished. The leading protagonists ran the risk of losing their lives.

'Round robin' originates in France, and according to some authorities the term is a corruption of the French *rond*, round, and *ruban*, a ribbon. The petitioners found it safer to sign in circular form, like a ribbon, so that the King could not identify the ringleaders and punish them.

The term is also used for a sporting contest in which all participants compete against all others.

The Times (1994): 'Today I returned home with a great sense of satisfaction, having posted our Christmas cards which, because my wife and I have just spent our first year abroad, for the first time contain a round-robin letter.'

Round the bend – *mad*

It has been suggested that this phrase refers to the curve in the driveway to Victorian mental hospitals, which was either to differentiate them from the homes of the gentry or to keep the inmates out of sight from passers-by.

Nevil Shute, *Round the Bend* (1951): 'People are saying that I have been out in the East too long, and I've gone round the bend.'

Rub salt in the wound – *intentionally to make a person's pain or shame even worse*

The allusion is to the days when errant sailors were flogged on their bare back and afterwards had salt rubbed in their wounds.

It has been believed down the centuries that the best way of healing a wound is to reopen it and clean it, often through the application of salt.

The modern saying emphasises the discomfort of the process rather than its healing values.

Guardian (1973): 'Mr Nixon's treatment for war wounds is rubbing salt in them.'

Rule of thumb – *a rough and ready measure, guesswork, practice or experience as distinguished from theory*

The phrase has been in figurative use since the late 17th century. There are three theories for its origin.

Just as a yard may be equal, roughly, to a man's stride, so does the top joint of an adult thumb equal an inch. These are very approximate measurements. Before the metric system was adopted, the French called the inch *un pouce*, meaning a thumb.

An alternative, though not so well known, theory is that the temperature of fermenting ale was checked by dipping the thumb into the brew. It is said that, in Yorkshire, such ale was referred to as 'thumb brewed'.

The third suggestion is that an old English law permitted a man to beat his wife provided that the stick he used was no thicker than his thumb. The idea is traced back to a pronouncement made in 1782 by the judge Sir Francis Buller, which led to a fiercely satirical cartoon by James Gillray, caricaturing Buller as Judge Thumb. Evidence that Buller actually made the pronouncement is disputed.

E.M. Forster in *Harper's Magazine* (1947): 'Virginia Woolf … believed in reading a book twice. The first time she abandoned herself to the author unreservedly. The second time she treated him with severity and allowed him to get away with nothing that he could not justify. After these two readings she felt qualified to discuss the book. Here is good rule of thumb advice.'

Rule the roost – *to be in charge; to demonstrate one's authority*

Conjuring up images of the cockerel proudly strutting among the hens, this phrase surprisingly has nothing to do with the hen coop. The original phrase, dating back to the 15th century, was 'to rule the roast', and it refers to the tradition that the master of the house carves and serves the roast meat.

By the 20th century, 'most unliterary persons', as H.W. Fowler describes them, had never heard the original phrase and assumed it referred to 'a cock keeping his hens in order'.

Charles Kingsley, *Westward Ho!* (1855): 'He had it all his own way and ruled the roast … right royally.'

Stanley Ellin, *Stronghold* (1974): 'My grandfather … ruled the roost, and he was a firm ruler for all his mild manner.'

Run amok – *run out of control, be in a murderous frenzy*

A Malayan word, *amoq* is defined as: 'engaging furiously in battle, attacking with desperate resolution, rushing in a state of frenzy to the commission of indiscriminate murder … Applied to any animal in a state of vicious rage.' (William Marsden, *Malay Dictionary*, 1812)

In the 17th century there were various spellings, but by the 20th century 'amok' or 'amuck' became the accepted form.

Shiva Naipaul, *Black and White* (1980): '"Here," an acquaintance said to me, "you either reach for the stars or you crack up and run amok with a chainsaw."'

Run for one's money – *satisfaction or pleasure from one's expenditure even if the outcome is not entirely successful*

Usually expressed as 'having a (good) run for one's money', or 'giving someone a (good) run for their money', the reference is to backing a horse which performs well but does not win.

Albert E. Petch also points out that to 'get a good run for one's money' has been since about 1925 'a modern humorous reference to patent medicines like Kruschen's Salts' (i.e. laxatives).

Eugene O'Neill, *A Moon for the Misbegotten* (1952): 'You're a wonderful fighter. Sure, you could give Jack Dempsey himself a run for his money.'

Run the gamut – *to cover the whole range, consider all the options*

'Gamut' was originally the lowest note in the musical scale devised by the medieval Italian, Guido d'Arezzo. *Gamma* was introduced in the Middle Ages to represent a note one tone lower than the A which began the scale inherited from classical times. Gamma became *gamut* as a result of the elision with the first note of the scale represented by *ut*. Ut was followed by *re, mi, fa, so, la* and *si* to complete the scale.

These derive from certain initial syllables in the following mnemonic, the 'Hymn for St John the Baptist's Day': 'UT queant laxis REsonare fibris MIra gestorum FAmuli tuorum, SOlve polluti LAbii reatum, Sancte Iohannes.'

'Gamut' was later extended to mean the whole range of notes, not just the lowest. The word was then applied figuratively to mean the whole scale, the full range or compass of a thing.

Charles Dickens, *A Tale of Two Cities* (1859): 'The sounders of three-fourths of the notes in the whole gamut of Crime.'

Dorothy Parker (1893–1967), US author, humorist, poet and wit, speaking of Katharine Hepburn: 'She runs the gamut of emotions from A to B.'

Run the gauntlet – *to be exposed to danger on both sides*

This is derived from a military punishment at the time of the Thirty Years War (1618–48), called 'gantlope'. The word comes from the Swedish *gatlopp*, meaning passageway. The company or crew were provided with rope ends or sticks and drawn up in two rows. The culprit, stripped to the waist, was made to run between the rows and every man dealt him as severe a blow as he could.

The spelling of gauntlet is due to confusion with 'gauntlet', meaning glove, from Old French *gantelet*, a diminutive of *gant*, glove.

Increase Mather, *The History of King Philip's War* (1676): 'They stripped them naked and caused them to run the Gauntlet.'

Francis Parkman, *France and England in North America* (1880): 'They descended the Mississippi, running the gantlet between hostile tribes.'

Run to earth – *to discover someone or something in a hiding place, to get to the bottom of something, to find someone or something after a long search*

This is a fox-hunting expression, alluding to the way in which the quarry is chased or 'run' to its 'earth', so it cannot escape.

Spectator (1888): 'All the men who helped to run to earth the various members of the Ruthven family … were richly rewarded.'

Run-of-the-mill – *ordinary, undistinguished, mediocre*

One suggestion is that this refers to the steady flow of water issuing from the millpond, which keeps the mill running smoothly and normally.

An alternative is that the run of the mill is the total production of that mill, good and bad, before it is examined for quality. It would therefore be average or undistinguished.

The latter seems to be a better reflection of the modern, slightly pejorative meaning.

Robert Ludlum, *The Holcroft Covenant* (1978): 'Althene was not your run-of-the-mill mother, as mothers were understood by this particular son.'

Times Literary Supplement (1980): 'We are left with a pretty run-of-the-mill thriller.'

An equivalent in the USA is 'run-of-the-mine', as in *American Notes and Queries* (1977): 'Prices of run-of-the-mine books are often more difficult to ascertain than those of $500-plus items.'

S

Safe pair of hands – *a reliable person*

A 19th-century cricketing expression for a player upon whom one can rely in fielding and catching.

MCC, *Match Reports* (2004): 'Sadler miss-hit Agarkar to wide long off for another safe-as-houses catch by McGrath; Snape nicked into another safe pair of hands, Ben Scott keeping wicket.'

Independent, 2004: 'Mr Matthews [outgoing finance director of Sainsbury's] is a marathon runner and is fond of rugby, football and cricket. ... He was seen by investors as a safe pair of hands.'

Sail near *or* close to the wind – *to go to the verge of what decency or propriety allows, to act at the limit of legality, to take a risk*

A boat cannot sail directly into the wind, but it can sail towards it, as close as about 45 degrees off the wind's direction. A boat sailing as close as possible into the direction from which the wind is blowing is at high risk of capsizing, but is at the same time capable of making spectacular progress.

Henry Kingsley, *The Hillyars and the Burtons* (1865): 'A certain young kind of English gentleman, who has sailed too close to the wind at home, and who comes to the colony to be whitewashed.'

Salad days – *a time of youthful innocence*

This is a quotation from Shakespeare's *Antony and Cleopatra* (1606–7), in which Cleopatra speaks of 'My salad days, / When I was green in judgement, cold in blood'.

Cornhill Magazine (1865): 'Being in want of a horse at the time – it was in my salad days, reader – I looked through the advertisements in *The Times* and noticed one which at any rate promised well.'

Salt of the earth – *the most reliable, worthy, excellent of people*

Jesus said to his disciples (Matthew 5:13): 'Ye are the salt of the earth: but if the salt have lost his savour, wherewith shall it be salted? It is thenceforth good for nothing, but to be cast out, and to be trodden under foot of men.'

The phrase through the ages has meant worthiness and excellence.

Geoffrey Chaucer, *The Summoner's Tale* (1386): 'Ye been the salt of the erthe and the savour.'

John Lyly, *Euphues, the Anatomy of Wyt* (1579): 'The universities of Christendome which should be ... the leaven, the salt, the seasoning of the world.'

P.G. Wodehouse, *Performing Flea* (1953): 'You dine with the President on Monday, and he slaps you on the back and tells you you are the salt of the earth, and on Tuesday morning you get a letter from him saying you are fired.'

Save one's bacon – *to escape injury or difficulty, to rescue from trouble*

The original meaning was to escape injury, probably in the sense of avoiding a beating for some misdemeanour. 'Bacon' and 'back' are from the same Teutonic root, *baec* being both an Old Dutch word for bacon and Anglo-Saxon for back. There is another connection between back and bacon: it is the pig's back that is usually cured for bacon, while the legs become hams.

Another suggestion is that the phrase alludes to the care formerly needed to save from the dogs of a household the bacon that was stored for winter use.

In the colloquial language of the early 1700s, 'bacon' meant 'prize', and to save one's prize, possibly ill-gotten gains, came to mean any narrow escape. This suggestion is supported by the definition of 'bacon' in 1811 as thieves' cant for 'escape'.

Hilaire Belloc, *Cranmer* (1931): 'Cranmer had just saved his bacon. It had been a very close thing.'

(See **Bring home the bacon**)

Saved by the bell – *saved at the last possible moment, in the nick of time*

The origin of the phrase is generally believed to be the bell rung at the end of a round in boxing. If the bell is rung before a boxer, having been knocked down, can be counted out, he is allowed to return to his corner and continue the next round of the fight. He is said to have been 'saved by the bell'.

An alternative story, perhaps fanciful, tells of a guard on duty in Horse Guards Parade in London during Victorian times. He was accused of being asleep on duty, which he denied, and to support his denial he claimed that he had heard Big Ben chime thirteen times at midnight, instead of twelve.

Such was the seriousness of the charge, the clock mechanism was checked. It was discovered that a cog was out of line and Big Ben would indeed chime thirteen times instead of twelve. On that evidence the guard was freed – saved by the bell.

The Times (1963): 'If, in future, the bell interrupts a count, the count will continue until the boxer is counted out – unless he gets up in the meantime … The expression "saved by the bell" will therefore become an anachronism.'

George Sims, *The End of the Web* (1976): 'Had he been saved by the bell … Was there still a chance of some lovers' games?'

Scapegoat – *someone taking the blame for another's error, misdemeanour or crime*

Part of the ancient ritual among the Hebrews for the Jewish Day of Atonement was for two goats to be led into the tabernacle. The high priest cast lots, one for the Lord and the other for Azazel (Hebrew for 'the power of God'). The goat dedicated to God was sacrificed. The other was the scapegoat, and the high priest having by confession transferred his sins and the sins of the people on to it, the scapegoat was taken to the wilderness and allowed to escape.

Mary Russell Mitford, *Our Village: Sketches of Rural Life and Scenery* (1824): 'Country boys … are patient, too, and bear their fate as scapegoats, (for all sins whatsoever are laid as matters of course to their door …) with amazing resignation.'

Scarlet woman – *a promiscuous woman*

This is a reference to St John the Divine's prophetic vision in the Book of Revelation (17:1–6):

So he carried me away in the spirit into the wilderness: and I saw a woman sit upon a scarlet coloured beast, full of names of blasphemy, having seven heads and ten horns.

And the woman was arrayed in purple and scarlet colour, and decked with gold and precious stones and pearls, having a golden cup in her hand full of abominations and filthiness of her fornication: And upon her forehead was a name written, MYSTERY, BABYLON THE GREAT, THE MOTHER OF HARLOTS AND ABOMINATIONS OF THE EARTH.

St John was probably talking about Rome, which at the time was 'drunken with the blood of saints'. Some controversial Protestants have applied the words in various forms to the Church of Rome, as scarlet lady, scarlet whore or scarlet woman.

H. Havelock Ellis, *Studies in the Psychology of Sex* (1924): 'I sought out a scarlet woman in the streets of — and went home with her.'

Score a duck – *to score no runs at cricket*

The similarity between the '0' on a cricket score-card and a duck's egg led to the original phrase 'to score a duck's egg'. The phrase is now always used in the abbreviated form 'to score a duck'.

If the batsman does score, it is called 'breaking his duck'. This makes more sense in the original unabbreviated form, as in G.H. Selkirk, *A Guide to the Cricket Ground* (1867): 'If he makes one run he has broken his duck's egg.'

A duck in both innings of a game, also because of the '0' on the score-card, is called 'a pair of spectacles', abbreviated to 'a pair'.

St Paul's Magazine, Daily News (1868): 'You see that his fear of a "duck" – as by a pardonable contraction from duck-egg a nought is called in cricket-play – outweighs all other earthly considerations.'

In American football, 'a goose egg' is used for no score in a game.

The Desert-Mountain Times, Texas, 2003: 'Despite the goose egg in the win column, this year's Sul Ross squad represents an improvement over last year's team.'

Scot-free – *without penalty or payment*

'Scot' is an old word for payment, applied to municipal taxes as early as the 13th century. The very poor were exempt from taxes and went scot-free. Tavern bills were also known as scots. A drink on the house was, therefore, 'scot-free'.

William Tyndale, *Exposition* of 1 John 2:2 (1531): 'The poore sinner shulde go Skot fre.'

> Scot-free the poets drank and ate;
> They paid no taxes to the State!
> > John Wolcot ('Peter Pindar'), 'Odes of Condolence' (1792)

Seamy side – *the least pleasant aspect*

The phrase means the wrong or worse side, as in 'the seamy side of life'. In joined fabrics, Brussels carpets, tapestry and the like, the 'wrong' side shows the seams or threads of the pattern exhibited on the right side.

> Some such Squire he was
> That turned your wit, the seamy side without
> And made me to suspect you with the Moor.
>> Shakespeare, *Othello* (1604)

Thomas Carlyle, *Frederick the Great* (1865): 'The splendid and the sordid, the seamy side and the smooth, of Life at Cirey.'

See a man about a dog – *a euphemism when one wishes to keep secret one's purpose and destination*

Originally, to say 'I am going to see a man' was to disguise that one's real purpose was to go out for a drink.

The reference to the dog was first recorded in a little-known play, *Flying Scud* (1866), by Dion Boucicault. To avoid a tricky situation, one of the characters, an eccentric old jockey, says: 'Excuse me, Mr Quail, I can't stop; I've got to see a man about a dog.' This is the only thing that seems to have survived from the play.

In the late 19th and early 20th centuries, it became a euphemism for an assignation with a woman.

See Naples and die – *experience the ultimate pleasure after which one may die happy*

This is an old Italian saying which suggests that once one sees Naples there is nothing more beautiful to be seen on earth. It is also known in Dutch: 'Napels zien en dan sterven.'

Sceptics have pointed to the murderous traffic, Mafia activity, the ever-present threat of a Vesuvius eruption, and the region's history of earthquakes. However, the phrase pre-dates at least the traffic.

It may, however, have been a warning, dating from the time when the city was a notorious centre for typhoid, cholera and other diseases. In 1495 a syphilis epidemic spread from Naples throughout Europe, leading to 'Naples' becoming a common euphemism for this dreaded disease.

Some say that Virgil originated the phrase 2,000 years ago. It is true that his grave is thought to be in Naples.

Finally, others say that the origin lies in the advice to travellers to visit Naples and then go on to the nearby town of Mori (Latin for 'to die')!

J.W. von Goethe, *Italian Journey* (1787): 'I won't say another word about the beauties of the city and its situation, which have been described and praised so often. As they say here, "Vedi Napoli e poi muori!" – "See Naples and die!"'

Sell down the river – *to breach faith with someone, to let someone down, to betray*

This refers to the Mississippi and the transfer of slaves from the north to the harsher south near New Orleans. The modern sense comes from the loss of security, home and family, and the betrayal of trust that this trade implied.

Mark Twain, *The Tragedy of Pudd'nhead Wilson* (1894): 'Ole Marse Driscoll'll sell you down de river.'

Southern Evening Echo (1974): 'Some aspects of Britain's education system needed to be put right but "we should not sell it down the river", Education Secretary Mrs Shirley Williams said last night.'

Sell one's birthright for a mess of pottage – *to accept some small advantage, some triviality, in exchange for something of great and lasting value*

In the Old Testament story, Esau sold his rights as the first-born to his brother Jacob for a bowl of lentil soup and some bread. 'Mess of pottage', at the time of the King James version of the Bible, would have been an everyday phrase meaning a thick soup.

The word 'mess', while not appearing in the text, was used as the chapter heading in the Bibles of 1537 and 1539, and so entered the modern saying.

> And Esau said to Jacob, Feed me, I pray thee, with that same red pottage; for I am faint: …
> And Jacob said, Sell me this day thy birthright.
> And Esau said, Behold, I am at the point to die: and what profit shall this birthright do to me?
> And Jacob said, Swear to me this day; and he sware unto him: and he sold his birthright unto Jacob.
> Then Jacob gave Esau bread and pottage of lentiles; and he did eat and drink, and rose up, and went his way: thus Esau despised his birthright.
>
> Genesis 25:30–34

Send to Coventry – *to ostracise, to ignore someone*

It is said that the citizens of Coventry once had so great a dislike of soldiers that a woman seen speaking to one was instantly outlawed. Hence when a soldier was sent to Coventry, he was cut off from all social intercourse.

A more likely explanation, however, comes from the English Civil War, when Coventry was a Parliamentary stronghold. The King's fury is recorded by John Brown, cleric: 'His Maiesty out of the high indignation of his supposed iniuries, being full and confident in his owne cause, hath with eleven thousand men strongly besieged the City of *Coventry*, and environed them so strongly, that there is no way possible for them to escape, unlesse that they betimes allay the indignation of the Kings designes, which are hitherto so violent, that he intends to make their City the obiect of the thundring Canon.'

Edward Hyde, Earl of Clarendon, in his *History of the Great Rebellion* (1702–04) records that Royalists captured in the 1640s were sent to Coventry, where prisoners could expect no help or sympathy.

The phrase gained common use from the mid-1700s.

Club Book, Tarporley Hunt (1765): 'Mr John Barry having sent the Fox Hounds to a different place to what was ordered ... was sent to Coventry, but return'd after giving six bottles of Claret to the Hunt.'

Separate the sheep from the goats – *to divide the worthy from the unworthy, the good from the evil, the favoured from the disfavoured; to pick out the best from the rest*

This is an allusion to St Matthew's Gospel, in which Jesus prophesies the Last Day of Judgement.

Matthew 25:32: 'And before him shall be gathered all nations; and he shall separate them one from another, as a shepherd divideth his sheep from his goats. And he shall set the sheep on his right hand, but the goats on the left.'

Separate the wheat from the chaff – *to divide the good and the bad*

This refers to threshing corn and separating the worthless husks from the good grain.

Ninian Winzet, *Book of Fourscore Three Questions* (1561): 'Guid and euill, expressit in the Euangell, be the similitude of queit and fitcheis.' (Good and evil, as expressed in Christ's teachings, are similar to wheat and chaff.)

Ira D. Sankey, *Sacred Songs* (1874):

> Let us keep the wheat and roses,
> Casting out the thorns and chaff.

Set off on the right *or* wrong foot – *to start a job well* or *badly, to have an auspicious* or *inauspicious start; to establish good relations, or fail to*

The Romans believed that anything which involved the left (Latin *sinister*) would have evil consequences. Therefore the left foot was always the wrong foot.

The phrase can refer to a job or enterprise, or to the establishing of a relationship with a new acquaintance.

Listener (1958): 'There is that vast number of marriages ... where the marriage takes place to give the baby a name. The whole thing starts on the wrong foot.'

Raymond Chandler, *The Little Sister* (1949): 'I got off on the wrong foot. After that I just had to take my lumps.'

(See also **Ears are burning** and **Get out of bed on the wrong side**.)

Set one's cap at – *to go all out to attract someone*

Known by the early 19th century, this phrase is possibly a reference to a woman wearing beguiling headgear with a view to getting her man.

It may also be a mistranslation of the French nautical expression *mettre le cap à*, to head towards.

Jane Austen, *Sense and Sensibility* (1811): '"You will be setting your cap at him now, and never think of poor Brandon." – "That is an expression, Sir John," said Marianne warmly, "which I particularly dislike. I abhor every commonplace phrase by which wit is intended; and 'setting one's cap at a man' and 'making a conquest' are the most odious of all."'

Settle a score *or* Pay off an old score – *to get your own back*

A 'score', from the Old English *scora*, related to Old Norse *skor*, was a bill notched up on a stick. So it was settled by paying it. The relationship between 'score' and 'notch' is continued in modern English by the phrase 'notching up' a victory.

Sir Thomas Elyot, *Dictionary* (1538): '... the scores which men unlerned do make on styckes for their remembrance.'

Tom Taylor, *The Ticket-of-Leave Man* (c. 1863): 'There's the satisfaction of doing one's duty ... but there's something better than that ... Paying off old scores.'

See also **In the nick of time**.

Seventh heaven – *bliss, supreme happiness*

In the Jewish religion there are seven heavens, of which the seventh, the highest, is the abode of God.

Similarly, in Islam the seventh heaven is the place of divine light and ecstasy. Ruled by Abraham, each of its inhabitants is bigger than the whole earth and has 70,000 heads, each head 70,000 faces, each face 70,000 mouths, each mouth 70,000 tongues; and each tongue speaks 70,000 languages, all for ever employed in chanting the praises of the Most High.

Sir Walter Scott, *St Ronan's Well* (1824): 'He looked upon himself as approaching to the seventh heaven.'

Shanks's pony – *on foot*

This is a Scottish jocular expression from the 16th century, originally 'Shanks's mare', 'nag' or 'naggy', in which Shanks is both the old word for legs and someone's name.

Robert Fergusson, *Poems* (c. 1774): 'And auld shanks-naig wad tire, I dread, / To pace to Berwick.'

Theodore Watts-Dunton, *Aylwin* (1898): 'I'll start for Carnarvon on Shanks's pony.'

Shell out – *to pay up*

Money is encased in a 'shell', in the form of a wallet or purse, and to shell out is to take the money out as one would shell peas from a pod. Another form of the expression, now rare, is to 'shell down'.

Thomas Moore, *Tom Crib's Memorial to Congress* (1819): 'Who knows but, if coax'd, he may shell out the shiners?'

Shilly-shally – *to vacillate, to hesitate, to act in an undecided, irresolute way*

In the 18th century the expression was 'Shill I, shall I', evocative of an indecisive person.

It is one of the many examples in English of reduplicated or ricochet words. Other examples are **Namby-pamby** and **Pell-mell**.

Mme Frances d'Arblay (Fanny Burney), *Cecilia* (1782): 'So I suppose he'll shilly-shally till somebody else will cry snap and take her.'

Ship-shape and Bristol fashion – *everything in order and ready for inspection*

'Ship-shape' means that everything is stowed and in good order and the ship fully ready for sea. Bristol was, before the growth of Liverpool, the main west-coast trading port with very high standards of efficiency.

Bristol had, and still has, one of the largest differences of water level between ebb and flow in the world, around 10 metres. At low tide ships in the harbour, if not properly constructed and laden, would either break their backs or shift their cargoes.

Admiral William Henry Smyth, *The Sailor's Wordbook* (1867): '*Bristol fashion and ship-shape.* Said when Bristol was in its palmy commercial days … and its shipping was all in proper good order.'

Short shrift – *minimum attention*

The verb 'to shrive' means to hear confession. The past tense is 'shrove', hence Shrove Tuesday when people went to confession and then made merry before starting Lenten penances. A condemned man was often given 'short shrift' (i.e. short confession) because he was considered beyond absolution.

W.H. Dixon, *Royal Windsor* (1879): 'Short trial, shorter shrift, had been given to the chief criminals.'

The Times (1887): 'Every argument … tells with still greater force against the present measure and it is to be hoped that the House of Commons will give it short shrift tonight.'

Show a leg – *to get up, get going*

In the days when seamen were refused shore-leave in case they deserted, 'wives' were allowed on board a berthed ship. While the men had to be up early the next day, the women were allowed to sleep a little longer. The traditional formula used by the boatswain, waking the men for work, was: 'Wakey, wakey, rise and shine, the morning's fine … show a leg, show a leg, show a leg.' This confirmed whether a man or a woman was in a particular hammock. (See **Son of a gun**.)

Show the white feather – *to show cowardice*

A fighting cock with a white feather was considered inferior, and therefore became a metaphor for a person lacking fighting spirit. During the First World War, before conscription, white feathers were given to civilians who were thought to be afraid of joining up.

Although he was a serving soldier, the writer Compton Mackenzie complained about the activities of the Order of the White Feather. He argued that these 'idiotic young women were using white feathers to get rid of boyfriends of whom they were tired'.

The pacifist Fenner Brockway claimed that he received so many white feathers he had enough to make a fan.

Sick as a parrot – *extremely disappointed*

This phrase was used frequently in the 1970s by footballers and football managers in post-match interviews. Its over-use was ridiculed by the satirical magazine *Private Eye*, and the phrase became a football cliché.

Two possible explanations have been offered. In the 17th and 18th centuries the phrase 'melancholy as a (sick) parrot' was used, in the play *False Count* (1682) by Aphra Behn, for example.

Alternatively, in the early 1970s several people fell ill with the disease psittacosis or parrot fever, caught from caged birds. The phrase may have been coined by an imaginative footballer prompted by the publicity surrounding the disease at the time.

Private Eye (1979): 'The Mogatollah admitted frankly that he was "sick as a parrot" at the way events had been unfolding.'

Collins Birmingham University International Language Database, BBC World Service (1989): 'The average footballer faced with the stock inquiry: "How did you feel when you had an open goal and missed?" mumbles the stock reply: "I felt sick as a parrot." The caricature hasn't always been that far from the truth, but Lineker is refreshingly different: modest and articulate.'

Sign *or* take the pledge – *to become teetotal*

The 19th-century Temperance Movement required its followers to make a public statement of sobriety by signing a pledge never to touch alcohol again.

Marion Miliband, *The Observer of the Nineteenth Century* (1843): 'Father Matthew … called upon all those who wished to take the "pledge" to kneel down … About 3,000 persons took the pledge … From the appearance of many of them, we should say the total abstinence pledge was very necessary.'

Skeleton in the closet *or* cupboard – *a guilty secret*

There is a tale, of unknown origin, that someone without a single care or trouble in the world had to be found. After a long search, a lady was found who satisfied her inquirers on all points, until she took them upstairs to a closet where she showed them a human skeleton.
'I try', she said, 'to keep my trouble to myself, but every night my husband compels me to kiss that skeleton.' She then explained that the skeleton was once her husband's rival for her affections, killed in a duel.

This story was in common currency earlier, but the first literary expression of the phrase is in William Makepeace Thackeray, *The Newcomes* (1853–5): 'And it is from these that we shall arrive at some particulars regarding the Newcome family, which will show us that they have a skeleton or two in their closets as well as their neighbours.'

Skid row – *a run-down area of a town where the unemployed, vagrants and alcoholics tend to congregate; therefore, 'on skid row', meaning down and out*

A skid row, in the timber industry, was a row of logs down which other logs rolled on their way to processing. Around 1880, Tacoma, near Seattle, was a flourishing timber centre and loggers working there created a community which attracted some of the less desirable members of American society.

Ngaio Marsh, *Photo-Finish* (1980): 'He disguises himself like a Skid Row drop-out.'

Slap-up meal – *a hearty meal*

It has been suggested that this is a variation of the Dickensian expression 'a slap-bang meal', in which the money was slapped down and the food was banged on the table. In 1785 a 'slap-bang shop' was defined as 'a petty cook's shop where there is no credit given, but what is had must be paid down with the ready (cash) slap-bang (immediately)'.

Others say that 'slap-up' existed separately, probably of northern origin, meaning excellent, first-rate. It was not exclusively related to food, and did not distinguish between persons and things. Slap-up had a similar meaning to 'bang-up', as in 'bang-up to the mark'.

In the late 19th and early 20th centuries, the phrase became generally confined to food.

Sporting Magazine (1827): 'Send them to that slap-up work, the *Sporting Magazine.*'

William Makepeace Thackeray, *The Paris Sketch Book* (1869): 'He had some slap-up acquaintances among the genteelest people at Paris.'

W. Somerset Maugham, 'Nash's Pall Mall Magazine' (1931): 'A bottle of pop tonight, my pet, and a slap-up dinner.'

Sleep like a top – *to sleep very well*

The reference is to a child's top which, when it is spinning, appears to be quite still and gives off a soothing hum. When it is not spinning perfectly, winding up or down, it wobbles and falls over.

William Congreve, *The Old Bachelor* (1693): 'Hang him, no, he a dragon! If he be, 'tis a very peaceful one. I can ensure his anger dormant, or should he seem to rouse, 'tis but well lashing him and he will sleep like a top.'

Sleep tight – *sleep well*

It is often said that the phrase comes from old beds, before box springs, which used ropes pulled tightly across the frame to support the mattress. If these ropes became loose, then the mattress sagged, giving an uncomfortable night. The tighter the ropes were tied, the better the prospects for a good night's sleep.

The chronology seems to be at odds with this interpretation. The phrase first appears in a diary by Susan Eppes, *Through Some Eventful Years*: 'May 2nd 1866 – All is ready and we leave as soon as breakfast is over. Goodbye little Diary. "Sleep tight and wake bright," for I will need you when I return.'

The origin is almost certainly the traditional children's rhyme:

> Good night, sleep tight
> Wake up bright
> In the morning light
> To do what's right
> With all your might …

'Tight' was applied to sleep from the end of the 18th century, and meant 'soundly'. The inversion of the phrase 'tight asleep' to 'sleep tight' is a small step.

Mary Annette Von Arnim, *Elizabeth and her German Garden* (1898): 'She had been so tight asleep.'

Doris Lessing, *In Pursuit of the English* (1960): 'When we left him, she patted his shoulder with triumphant patronage, and said: "Sleep tight. And keep your dreams clean."'

Sling one's hook – *to go away; to depart secretly or hastily, or both*

This may refer to weighing the anchor on a ship. The anchor (hook) had to be secured in its sling at the bow before the ship could get under way.

Some have suggested a mining origin. The hook is where a miner would hang his day clothes, to be collected when his work was done.

Rudyard Kipling, *Poetry and Barracks Ballads* (1892): 'Before you sling your 'ook, at the 'ousetops take a look.'

Daily News (1897): 'If you don't sling yer hook this minute, here goes a pewter pot at yer head.'

Slush fund – *usually a secret, separate supply of funds*

This was first used, in its modern sense, by the US Congress in 1866 to refer to a special contingency budget.

However, the word 'slush', probably derived from the Swedish *slask* meaning wet or filth, was the surplus fat from beef and pork boiled aboard ship. When a boat came into port, the slush could be sold to buy extras for the crew.

William Thompson, *The Royal Navy-men's Advocate* (1757): 'Tars whose Stomachs are not very squeamish, and who can bear to paddle their Fingers in stinking Slush.'

Naval Encyclopaedia (1884): '*Slush-fund*, money obtained from the sale of slush. It is to be used for premiums for target-firing etc. and not for ship's purposes.'

The Congressional Record (1874): 'We have had this "slush-fund" since 1866 ... It was divided among these officers to increase their salaries.'

Smart Alec – *a know-all*

Some writers have asserted that this phrase comes from the fertile mind of the humorist J.B. Morton, who wrote the 'Beachcomber' column in the *Daily Express* for more than 50 years. One of his characters was Dr Smart-Allick, headmaster of the notorious public school Narkover.

However, the phrase 'Smart Alec' existed well before Morton was born in 1893. He did no more than borrow it.

For many years, Smart Alec or Smart Aleck was thought to be just a generic character, first cousin to Clever Dick. In fact he was Alex Hoag, a 19th-century American pimp who perfected a trick called the Panel Game.

While his target was otherwise engaged with one his girls, Hoag would enter the room through a secret panel, steal his belongings and be far away by the time his victim woke up. He was nicknamed 'Smart Alex' because he was brilliant at avoiding capture.

Laurence Meynell, *Hooky and the Villainous Chauffeur* (1979): 'Smart alec, aren't you? Smart and smug like all you intellectual lot.'

Smell a rat – *to be suspicious*

Without seeing them, dogs and cats can smell out rats and kill them. This phrase means that, although one is unable to see the danger, one can nevertheless sense it.

'To smell' is often used figuratively, meaning the intuitive way in which one senses something. Shakespeare has 'Do you smell a fault?' (*King Lear*, 1605), and Iago says to Othello: 'One may smell in such a will most rank.' (*Othello*, 1604)

St Jerome said that St Hilarion had the gift of knowing what sins and vices anyone was inclined to by smelling either the person or their garments, and by the same faculty could discern good feelings and virtuous propensities.

John Skelton (c. 1460–1529) in *Skelton's Works* (1843): 'Yf they smell a rat, / They grisely chide and chatt.'

James Shirley, *Andromana, or the Merchant's Wife* (1660): 'I smell a Rat sir, there's jugling in this business.'

Smoking gun – *absolute evidence of guilt*

Attributed to Republican Congressman Barber Conable who, on listening to the Watergate tapes, believed that he heard clear evidence that President Nixon knew of the cover-up.

On 17 June 1972, police apprehended five men attempting to break into and wiretap Democratic party offices in Washington DC. With two other accomplices they were tried and convicted in January 1973. All seven men were either directly or indirectly employees of President Nixon's re-election committee, and many people, including the trial judge, John J. Sirica, suspected a conspiracy involving higher-echelon government officials.

Collier's Year Book (1975): 'After the new transcripts were disclosed ... members of Congress abandoned Nixon in droves. "I guess we have found the smoking pistol, haven't we?" asked Representative Barber Conable.'

Soap opera – *a popular television serial*

In the 1930s, the early popular serials produced for radio were sponsored by soap manufacturers. 'Opera' is jocular, as is explained in the following quotation from Chris Stacey and Darcy Sullivan, *Supersoaps* (1988):

'Soap manufacturers ... sponsored several of the series – perhaps because they were "cleaner" than rough-and-tumble mystery pro-grammes. Radio producers nicknamed the programmes "soaps" and the name caught on with the press. Television began replacing radio as family entertainment in the 1950s, and as the more successful radio soaps jumped from the airwaves to the small screen, "opera" was added to "soap" as a joke on the programme's "heavy" fare.'

Spectator (1958): 'Eugene O'Neill's wordy autobiographical play is an endlessly tragic soap-opera, a sort of Mrs Dale's Diarrhoea.'

Soft soap – *flattery*

Familiar in English since the mid-1800s, the phrase seems to refer, in its earliest form of 'soft sawder', to soldering pieces of metal. It means, therefore, joining and, metaphorically, bringing people together.

Later, 'soap' was added to the phrase, its lubricant qualities being a metaphor for helping people to get along.

Register of Debates in Congress (1830): 'I will not use the vulgar phrase and say he has been pouring soft soap down the backs of the New York delegation.'

Radio Times (1961): '"Nobody likes to watch a soft-soap interview. People *want* the facts and they can take them," says Robin Day.'

Sold for a song – *sold for next to nothing*

Shakespeare, in *All's Well that Ends Well* (1601), makes the first printed comparison between a financial trifle and a song: 'I know a man that had this trick of melancholy hold a goodly manor for a song.'

The phrase was probably already an established notion, because sheet music, very popular at the time, was sold for next to nothing.

Morvan de Bellegarde, *Reflexions upon Ridicule* (1707): 'He retrenches the Number of his Servants or their Wages, and would have them serve, as they say, for a Song.'

Son of a gun – *exclamation of amazement*

This familiar term, originally implying contempt but now used with friendly familiarity, derives from the days when women were allowed to live in naval ships. Children were born in the ship, often near the midship gun, behind a canvas screen. If paternity was uncertain, the child was entered in the log as 'son of a gun'.

William Makepeace Thackeray, *The History of Pendennis* (1849): 'What a happy feller I once thought you, and what a miserable son of a gun you really are!'

(See also **Show a leg**.)

Sow one's wild oats – *to commit youthful excesses or follies*

Wild oats are similar to the cultivated variety but are worthless, being, in effect, tall grass. It is folly and mischief to sow wild oats instead of good grain.

Thomas Newton, *Lemnie's Touchstone of Complexions* (1576): 'That wilfull and unruly age, which lacketh rypenes and discretion, and (as wee saye) hath not sowed all theyr wyeld Oates.'

Spick and span – *very neat and clean*

The phrase is a shortening of 'spick and span new'. A 'spick' is a spike or nail. 'Span new' comes from the Old Norse words *spann*, a woodchip and *nyr*, new, and means 'as new as a shaving cut from a block of wood'. A 'spick and span new' ship is one in which every nail and woodchip is new.

Sir Thomas North, *Plutarch's Lives of the Noble Grecians and Romanes* (1579–80): 'They were all in goodly gilt armours, and brave purple cassocks apon them, spicke, and spanne newe.'

Samuel Pepys, *Diary* (1665): 'My Lady Batten walking through the dirty lane with new spicke and span white shoes.'

Spill the beans – *to divulge a secret*

The phrase may originate from the way in which secret ballots were held in ancient Greece. Votes were cast by means of white beans (in favour) and brown beans (against). The beans were counted in private, and the only way that anyone would know the details of the vote was if the beans were spilled before them.

The phrase, however, is of fairly recent origin, being a US slang expression adopted in the UK in the 1920s.

Elaine Dundy, *The Dud Avocado* (1958): 'Spilling beans of shattering truths and equally shattering lies.'

(See **Blackball**.)

Spin a yarn – *to tell an exaggerated story*

As explained in Peter Barlow's *Encyclopaedia Metropolitana* (1831–3), 'the first part of the process of rope making is that of spinning the yarn or threads'. This was a laborious process and, to pass the time, sailors often told each other seafaring stories, usually exaggerating the details. A yarn therefore became the story itself. It was, generally, long and fanciful and described marvellous, indeed incredible, events.

A variation of the phrase in the late-18th to mid-19th century was to 'spin one's yarn upon one's own winch' which meant to tell one's own story.

J.H. Vaux, *A New and Comprehensive Vocabulary of the Flash Language* (1812): '*Yarning or spinning a yarn*, signifying to relate their various adventures, exploits and escapes to each other.'

Spitting image – *a precise likeness, exact double*

Some writers suggest that this phrase is a corruption of 'spirit and image', meaning that two people are identical in mind and body.

The phrase also appears as 'splitting image'. Dorothy Hartley, in *Made in England* (1939), writes: 'Evenness and symmetry are got by pairing the two halves of the same tree, or branch. (Hence the country saying: he's the "splitting image" – an exact likeness.)'

Neither story is true, though there is some argument about the origin. Variations down the years include 'spitten image', 'spit and image', 'the very spit of', 'dead spit for', and 'spit' by itself. The current 'spitting image' was the last to appear, in 1901, and was at one time considered an error for 'spit and image'.

The core of all these variations is obviously 'spit'. It suggests that one is so like another that he has almost been spat out of his mouth.

French has an exact comparable in *C'est son père tout craché* (he is the very spit of his father). Some writers suggest that 'spit' is actually a euphemism and make a link with seminal ejaculation, which may account for the phrase being used originally only of the son of a father.

The British television programme *Spitting Image* was based around the grotesque puppets created by Peter Fluck and Roger Law. It opened with a puppet caricature of Israel's Prime Minister, Menachem Begin, wearing a magician's outfit. With a flourish, he produced a dove of peace from his top hat, then announced, 'For my first trick …', and wrung its neck. This was the first of many outrages perpetrated on the British public, who were either offended or delighted each Sunday evening from 1984 to 1992.

A.H. Rice, *Mrs Wiggs of the Cabbage Patch* (1901): 'He's jes' like his pa – the very spittin' image of him!'

Splice the main-brace – *to have a drink*

The main-brace is the rope for holding or turning one of the sails on board ship. The expression may come from a comparison between the reviving effect of alcoholic drink and repairing or strengthening ('splicing') the main-brace.

An alternative suggestion is that the tradition of 'splicing the main-brace' was born around the time of the conquest of Jamaica in 1687, when brandy was replaced with a rum issue for ships' crews. After heavy damage at sea or in the aftermath of a battle, the ship would need repair to ensure its seaworthiness. If the main-brace or other braces snapped off, they had to be repaired with a rope splice, which, in those days, was no mean feat. After such arduous activity, the crew would be rewarded with a double rum issue.

Frederick Marryat, *Peter Simple* (1833): 'Mr Falcon, splice the main-brace and call the watch.'

Spoil the ship for a ha'porth of tar – *to spoil a job by economising on a detail, to mar the final result by saving a small amount*

A demonstration of how usage changes the original sense, this country phrase became a nautical expression.

The original 17th-century saying was to 'lose the sheep for a ha'porth of tar'. It referred to the tar put on a sheep's sores and wounds to protect them from the infection caused by flies. 'Ship' was a dialect pronunciation of 'sheep'.

By the 19th century this rustic expression had become a nautical one, and, as a consequence, the word 'lose' was replaced by 'spoil'.

Captain John Smith, *Works* (1631): 'Rather … to lose ten sheep, than be at the charge of a halfe penny worth of Tarre.'

Review of Reviews (1891): 'To sink the ship by the refusal of the traditional ha'porth of tar.'

See also **Tarred with the same brush**.

Square meal – *a satisfying and nutritious meal*

Various suggestions have been made to explain the use of the word 'square', as in the following examples:

Seafarers when under sail had only one substantial meal a day, usually in the evenings, and this was served on a square tray which could be easily stacked and cleaned, and which kept the food safe if the ship lurched unexpectedly.

A dinner plate was once a square piece of wood with a bowl carved out to hold a serving of the perpetual stew cooking over the fire.

In the US military, soldiers when eating were required to sit bolt upright with arms at right angles to the body, forming a square shape.

There is no evidence to support any of these theories. 'Square' has the sense of right, fair, honest and straightforward, and it is probably this sense that applies here.

'Square meal' was originally American, and the earliest examples come out of miners' slang. An article in *Harper's New Monthly Magazine* (1865) about the gold-mining town of Virginia City in Nevada quotes the proprietor of a small shanty: '"LOOK HERE! *For fifty cents* you CAN GET A GOOD SQUARE MEAL at the HOWLING WILDERNESS SALOON!"' The writer felt the need to explain this strange phrase: 'A square meal is not, as may be supposed, a meal placed on the table in the form of a solid cubic block, but a substantial repast of pork and beans, onions, cabbage, and other articles of sustenance.'

Stalking horse – *a less acceptable purpose hidden behind a more attractive façade*

The problem for any huntsman is how to get close enough to the game. In the Middle Ages, horses were trained to provide cover for fowlers stalking their quarry. Later these 'stalking horses' were replaced by movable screens made in the shape of a horse.

In modern times the term has been used figuratively, particularly in politics. Sir Anthony Meyer stood as a 'stalking horse' in opposition to Mrs Thatcher in 1989 for the leadership of the Conservative Party. No one expected him to win; the purpose of the challenge was to demonstrate that there was opposition to the incumbent, and perhaps also to prepare the way for a weightier challenger. In the event, Mrs Thatcher was deposed the following year.

Shakespeare, *As You Like It* (1599): 'He uses his folly like a stalking-horse and under the presentation of that he shoots his wit.'

Country Living (1991): 'The cost of building a golf course is staggering. Developers claim they need leisure facilities or housing developments … to make it financially viable. (Hence the accusation that golf is being used as a stalking horse for yet more housing.)'

Stamping ground – *homeland or area*

Deer and sheep stamp the ground to express warning of invasion to their territory. Applied to humans, the phrase describes an area where they are at home or where they have made their mark.

The phrase has long meant a field or park frequented by lovers. It derives from the stamping and mating of animals, but it lost this sexual connotation in the 20th century. The phrase 'to be back in one's old stamping ground' is now quite innocuous.

Edgar Rice Burroughs, *Return of Tarzan* (1915): 'The woman he loved was within a short journey of the stamping-ground of his tribe.'

Start from scratch – *to start again from the beginning*

This phrase has sporting origins. A race was run from a starting line which was scratched in the ground. To start from scratch is to go back to the beginning.

'Scratch' is the starting point of a competitor who receives no handicap. It is sometimes used to describe the competitor himself, as in 'scratch golfer'.

Now obsolete, 'scratch' also meant 'the crease' in cricket. In boxing it was the line drawn across the ring to which the opponents were brought for an encounter.

Phrases like 'come up to scratch' and 'bring (up) to (the) scratch' find their origins here.

George Orwell, *Coming Up for Air* (1939): 'We'd no fishing tackle of any kind, not even a pin or a bit of string. We had to start from scratch.'

Steal a march on – *to gain advantage by stealth*

Military tacticians will calculate the distance that an army can march in a day. It is a huge tactical advantage if they can 'steal a march' on their adversary and arrive unexpectedly.

Horace Walpole, *Letters* (1745): 'The young Pretender … has got a march on General Cope.'

Edgar Allan Poe, 'The Oblong Box', in *Godey's Lady's Book* (1844): 'He evidently intended to steal a march upon me, and smuggle a fine picture to New York under my very nose.'

Steal someone's thunder – *to forestall someone by adopting their ideas as one's own*

John Dennis (1657–1734), the critic and playwright, invented an effective device for producing stage thunder for his play *Appius and Virginia* (1709). The play was a flop and was withdrawn, but shortly afterwards Dennis heard his thunder used in a performance of *Macbeth*. 'Damn them!' he exclaimed, 'they will not let my play run, but they steal my thunder.'

George Orwell, *The Road to Wigan Pier* (1937): 'It is important ... to disregard the jealousy of the modern literary gent who hates science because science has stolen literature's thunder.'

Sterling qualities – *excellent qualities, of sound intrinsic worth*

'Sterling' is a term applied to British money and also to gold and silver plate, denoting that they are of standard value or purity.

The word, first appearing in the 12th century, has been held to be a corruption of *easterling*, a name given to the merchants of the Hanseatic League trading with England, but it is probably from the Old English *steorling*, 'coin with a star', a Norman English silver penny. The quality and purity of this coin was recognised throughout Europe, and earned it extensive currency in foreign countries.

In October 1202, Baldwin, Count of Flanders contracted to pay certain Venetian nobles 'the sum of 121 ounces in marks sterling [*marcas sterlinorum*] at the rate of 13 *solidi* and 4 *denarii* for each silver mark'. (Rawdon Brown, *Calendar of State Papers*, Venice, 1864–6)

From the 17th century, 'sterling' was used as a term of excellence.

> True faith, like gold into the furnace cast,
> Maintains its sterling pureness to the last.
> Thomas à Kempis, 'Meditations' (1767)

Laetitia Hawkins, *Annaline* (1824): 'I know the sterling qualities you have.'

Stick one's neck out – *to take a risk, ask for trouble*

This could refer to the hangman slipping his noose around one's neck, or the risk of a beheading.

Because of its fairly recent coinage, some have suggested an army origin referring to the danger of sniper fire. However, military men with long memories say they have not encountered this usage.

The University of Virginia claims to have invented the phrase. *University Magazine* (1926): 'Absolutely original slang at the University of Virginia includes ... *to stick one's neck out.*'

Stiff upper lip – *self-control, courage, resolution*

The lips, quivering with rage, or trembling with grief, give away one's emotional state. Keeping a stiff upper lip means controlling one's emotion.

It may also be a naval expression involving burial. Seamen who died at sea were wrapped in a weighted shroud which was sewn with the final stitches through the upper lip and the lower part of the nose. Sailors trying to escape the Royal Navy by feigning death would certainly feel this, but if they could stand the pain, then once overboard they could cut themselves free.

Spectator (1887): 'The Financial Secretary, who, it is supposed, will have a stiff upper lip and tightly buttoned pockets.'

Stony broke – *no money, penniless, ruined*

'Stone broke' was the original form. Several phrases in English use stone as a comparison for extremes, for example of cold, 'stone-cold', or of hardness of expression, 'stone-faced', or difficulty, 'like getting blood out of a stone'.

The link between 'stony' (rather than 'stone') and 'broke' is provided by R.C. Lehmann in *Harry Fluyder* (1890): 'Pat said he was stoney or broke or something but he gave me a sov.'

Stool pigeon – *a police informer, a decoy*

The phrase comes from the USA, as defined in John R. Bartlett's *Dictionary of Americanisms* (1859): '*Stool*, an artificial duck or other water-fowl used as a decoy.'

'Stool' is a variant of 'stale' or 'stall', meaning decoy. It is from the Anglo-French *estal* or *estale*, meaning a pigeon which entices a hawk into a net. Old English has *staelrhan*, a decoy reindeer, Northumbrian *staello*, catching (of fish), and German *Stellvogel*, a decoy bird.

G.E. Stevens, *The Wicked City* (1906): 'Under others were inscribed: "He is a 'stool'" … "He was croaked by the cops".'

Storm in a teacup – *a fuss about nothing, a great commotion in a small community or about a trifling matter*

There are many variant examples of this expression, although in its modern form it did not gain currency until the 19th century.

Probably the origin was Cicero's metaphor, *excitabat fluctus in simpulo*, 'he whipped up waves in a ladle'.

The Grand Duke Paul of Russia referred to a 'tempest in a glass of water' (c. 1790) and Lord Thurlow to a 'storm in a wash-hand basin' (1830).

Historical Manuscripts, Reports of the Royal Commission, Ormonde MSS (1678): 'Our skirmish seems to be come to a period, and compared with the great things now on foot, is but a storm in a cream bowl.'

Strait-laced – *prudish, excessively rigid or scrupulous in matters of conduct*

'Strait', not to be confused with 'straight', means tight or narrow. This is the meaning in Matthew 7:14: 'Because strait is the gate, and narrow is the way, which leadeth unto life, and few there be that find it.'

Literally, therefore, to be 'strait-laced' is to wear tightly laced stays or bodice. In the 17th century, a small waist, achieved by whatever uncomfortable means, was much admired. The phrase's metaphorical usage, to mean excessive rigidity of conduct, goes back to the 16th century.

> No Maid here's handsome
> thought, unless she can
> With her two short Palms
> her straight-lac't body span.
>   John Bulwer,
>   'Anthropometamorphosis' (1650)

Sir Robert Dallington, *A Method for Travel* (1598): 'They of the Reformed Religion may not Dance, being an exercise against which their strait-laced Ministers much inveigh.'

Straw poll – *a superficial test of opinion*

This was a form of public opinion poll sponsored by the American press as early as 1824, when reporters from the *Harrisburg Pennsylvanian* were sent to Wilmington to test public opinion of a presidential candidate.

Straw is thrown into the air to see which way the wind is blowing, in this case, the wind of public opinion.

Spectator (1958): 'In my own straw poll I found two electors who were going to vote Liberal for the first time.'

See also **Fly a kite**.

Streets paved with gold – *a place to find fortune*

The source of this idea is the first paragraph of the story of Dick Whittington.

Dick, a poor orphan, went to London to seek his fortune, and ended up working for a wealthy merchant called Mr Fitzwarren.

Although Mr Fitzwarren was kind to Dick, the Cook made his life a misery and Dick decided to run away. He had reached almost the end of the city when he heard Bow Bells chime out the words: 'Turn again Whittington, thrice Lord Mayor of London.'

He returned to become a rich man, to marry Mr Fitzwarren's daughter Alice, and, as the bells had said, to become Lord Mayor of London three times. Metaphorically, the streets of London were paved with gold.

Stuffed shirt – *a pompous fool, an over-formal bore, conservative but ineffectual*

This phrase compares a conservative, over-formal, pompous person with a stuffed shirt, a dummy, in a tailor's window. The dummy may look the part but there is nothing inside and it is ineffectual, unable to do anything.

A.J. Ayer, *Part of My Life* (1977): 'The head of the section, who disliked Cummings for his indifference to spit and polish and his preference for the company of the French cook and the mechanics to that of the more stuff-shirted Americans.'

Stumbling block – *an obstruction*

In 15th-century rural England, 'block' meant tree stump.

William Caxton, *The Historye of Reynart the Foxe* (1481): 'They … drewe hym over stones and over blockes wythout the village.'

Stumbling over a block or a tree stump would have been commonplace in rural England at the time, but the phrase 'stumbling block' may have been coined by William Tyndale. It appears, as one word, in his translation of the New Testament (1526): 'Let us not therefore judge one another any more: but judge this rather, that no man put a stumblingblock or an occasion to fall in his brother's way.'

Stump up – *to pay up with difficulty*

'Stump up' means literally to dig up by the roots. The phrase implies digging deeply in a pocket as if one were trying to dig up a tree stump.

Richard H. Barham, *The Ingoldsby Legends* (1842): 'My trusty old crony, / Do stump up three thousand once more as a loan.'

Stymied – *in a very awkward spot*

This is a golfing expression, describing a situation in which a player's shot is obstructed by his opponent's ball which is in direct line with the hole. A now obsolete rule forbade the removal of the ball. This was called 'laying a stymie'.

Remarks on Golf (1862): 'Steimies … frequently occur, and often cause the hole to be halved which the steimied man felt confident of winning.'

George Ade, *The Girl Proposition* (1902): 'In about 8 minutes he had the Regular Fellow stymied and Hazel was leaning against him.'

Swan-song – *a final performance*

One of Aesop's fables (6th century BC) tells of a swan whose song saves its life.

A certain rich man bought a goose and a swan in the market. He fed the one for his table and kept the other for the sake of its song. When the time came for killing the goose, the cook went to fetch him at night, and in the dark, he was not able to distinguish one bird from the other. By mistake he caught the swan instead of the goose. The swan, threatened with death, burst forth into song, making himself known by his voice, and preserved his life by his melody.

It is a theme to which writers and composers (for example, Tchaikovsky in *Swan Lake*) have returned down the ages.

Thomas Carlyle, *Sartor Resartus* (1831): 'The Phoenix soars aloft … or, as now, she sinks, and with spheral swan-song immolates herself in flame.' (See also **Phoenix from the ashes**.)

Graham Greene, *The Human Factor* (1978): 'Ivan made his swan song as an interpreter in a building not far from the Lubianka prison.'

Swashbuckler – *a romantic adventurer, a swaggering bravo or ruffian, a noisy braggadocio*

A swashbuckler was a 16th-century lout. The expression comes from the antiquated words 'swash' (to make a noise while striking) and 'buckler' (shield). Swashbucklers were noisy bullies and braggarts who were not very good swordsmen or fighters. Today's use of the word has taken on a much more romantic resonance.

Washington Irving, *Knickerbocker's History of New York from the Beginning of the World to the End of the Dutch Dynasty* (1809): 'He had a garrison after his own heart … guzzling, deep-drinking swashbucklers.'

Time (1977): '*Star Wars* is a combination of *Flash Gordon*, *The Wizard of Oz*, the Errol Flynn swashbucklers of the '30s and '40s and almost every western ever screened.'

Sweet Fanny Adams *or* Sweet FA – *nothing at all*

Fanny Adams was a little girl, eight years old, who was murdered in a hop garden at Alton, Hampshire in 1867. Her body was dismembered. The word 'sweet' was probably added in some popular song or poem.

Sailors with gruesome humour called their tinned mutton 'Fanny Adams' after a sailor allegedly found a button in it.

Because 'FA' since 1914 was the services' slang abbreviation for 'fuck all', it was a short linguistic journey from nasty tinned food to something worthless, and then nothing at all.

J.R. Cole, *It Was So Late* (1949): 'What do they do? Sweet Fanny Adams!'

Swing the lead – *to evade work, to malinger, to make excuses*

It has been suggested that a sailor claiming he was unable to work because of a leg injury would 'swing the leg'. This was corrupted to 'swing the lead'.

More likely is an allusion to the leadsman on a ship, charged with the job of taking soundings using a line weighed down by lead. If he was lazy, he could protract the job by idly swinging the lead.

B.K. Adams, 'Letters', in *American Spirit* (1918): 'Lead-swingers are those that stall along, doing as little as they possibly can, hoping the war will be over before they finish.'

Sword of Damocles – *impending doom, an imminent threat*

Damocles' story is an ancient one, recorded in the works of Horace and Persius among others. It was alluded to in English literature in the 16th century but received scant attention until the 19th century.

The story tells of Dionysius, ruler of Syracuse around 400 BC, who, night and day, was compelled to listen to the sycophantic murmurings of Damocles lauding his power and riches. The exasperated Dionysius finally invited him to taste this good fortune and dine with him.

Damocles accepted eagerly and was enjoying the feast when, glancing upwards, he was horrified to see a large sword suspended by a single hair. This, explained Dionysius, was a symbol of the insecurity with which everyone holding power and position is burdened.

The Times (1963): 'In particular, the Damoclesian sword of a veto from General de Gaulle hangs over the proceedings.'

T

Take a _or_ the back seat – _to take up the least prominent position, to occupy a subordinate place, to have little involvement in decision-making_

This phrase originates in the USA and refers to taking a seat at the back of a hall, therefore figuratively a subordinate position.

It is unlikely to originate, as some have suggested, from the British Parliament where ordinary MPs sit on the back benches, and have less influence than the leaders of government and the opposition on the front benches.

James Bryce, _The American Commonwealth_ (1888): 'A leader came to care for his influence within the State chiefly as a means of gaining strength in the wider national field … The State, therefore had, to use the transatlantic phrase, "to take the back seat".'

Take a rain-check – _to reserve the right not to take up a specified offer until such time as it should prove convenient; to postpone something; to delay an assignation or meeting_

In the USA, a rain-check is a counterfoil to a ticket which, if an outdoor sporting event is rained off, enables a spectator to attend the postponed game.

Alan Hunter, _Gently Instrumental_ (1977): '"I couldn't afford what the blackmailer wanted." – "And he settled for a rain-check?" – "No."'

Take a shufti – _to take a look_

Known since 1943, the phrase probably arises from the Arab word _shufti_ which means 'look'. Hence, in military slang, a shufti-scope was the name given to a telescope, probe or similar instrument for looking through.

Richard Adams, _The Girl in a Swing_ (1980): 'Good idea, old boy. I'm game. Let's 'ave a crafty shufti round with that in mind, shall we?'

Take down a peg – *to lower someone a degree in his own or the general estimation, to humble, to snub, to mortify, to make someone less arrogant*

To take, or let, or bring, down a peg (or two) is probably an allusion to a ship's colours, which were raised and lowered by a series of pegs. The higher the colours were flown, the greater the honour. If they were flown too high for the occasion, they had to be taken down 'a peg or two'.

An earlier explanation refers to the ancient practice of sharing drink from a pegged container down to one's allotted peg.

Others have suggested that it refers to the peg on a stringed musical instrument, which is loosened or tightened to alter the pitch.

Pappe with an Hatchet, ascribed to John Lyly or Thomas Nashe (1589): 'To Huffe, Ruffe etc., Now have at you all my gaffers of the rayling religion, 'tis I that must take you a peg lower.'

Mrs Humphry Ward, *Marcella* (1894): 'I must take that proud girl down a peg.'

Take French leave – *to be absent without permission, to depart without intimation or as if in flight*

The reference is to the 18th-century French custom of leaving without saying goodbye to one's host. The French associated the habit with the English, however. Hence their equivalent for 'to take French leave' is *s'en aller* (or *filer*) *à l'anglaise*, to leave in the English way.

England's frequent battles with the French have led to a number of sayings that implied scandalous behaviour by neighbours across the Channel.

However, the original reason for 'French leave' was based on politeness, not discourtesy, as explained in John Trusler's *The Principles of Politeness and of Knowing the World (extracted from Earl Chesterfield's letters to his son)* (1775): 'As the taking of what is called a French leave was introduced that on one person's leaving the company the rest might not be disturbed, looking at your watch does what that piece of politeness was designed to prevent.'

W. Gifford, *Smiles* (1821): 'The few teeth I have seem taking their leave – I wish they would take a French one.'

Take something with a grain *or* pinch of salt – *to take something with a degree of reservation, with some scepticism*

Just as a sprinkling of salt makes one's meal more enjoyable, so a doubtful story or excuse goes down easier with a 'pinch of salt'.

The phrase is held by many to be from the Latin *addito salis grano* by Pliny the Elder (c. AD 77). He had come across a story that King Mithridates VI, King of Pontus, built up immunity to poisoning by fasting and swallowing small, regular doses of poison with a grain of salt (*cum grano salis*) to make them more palatable.

Other authorities, however, are doubtful, pointing out that Pliny intended the phrase to be taken literally and that nowhere in classical Latin does the word 'salt' appear as a figurative expression of scepticism.

The expression does not seem to date back further than the Middle Ages, and the likelihood is that *cum grano salis* is a piece of medieval Latin.

Roger Lockyer, *Tudor and Stuart Britain* (1964): 'John Foxe, the martyrologist, reports that Cromwell learned the whole of Erasmus's New Testament by heart while travelling to Rome and back, and although this story should be taken with a pinch of salt, there is evidence that Cromwell was in touch with Miles Coverdale when Coverdale was still a friar at Cambridge.'

See also **Not worth his salt**.

Take the bull by the horns – *to confront a problem directly; to screw up one's courage and cope with a dangerous or unpleasant situation decisively, head on*

This phrase may have its origins in the Spanish proverb: 'Take a bull by the horn and a man at his word.'

Since the earliest quotation yet found is 1873, it seems unlikely that it has its roots in bull-running, a brutal English sport popular from the reign of King John until it was outlawed in the mid-19th century.

A more likely origin is the Spanish bullfight, where *banderilleros*, having planted darts in the neck of the bull, tire him more by seizing him by the horns, trying to hold the head down.

Early ranchers in the American south-west also wrestled bulls, or steers, in a popular sport called 'bull-dogging' that is still seen in rodeos.

Henry B. Tristram, *The Land of Moab* (1873): 'Determined to take the bull by the horns … I stepped forward.'

Take the cake *or* the biscuit – *to carry off the honours, to be the best, to deserve merit*

'Take the cake' came from the USA in about 1880 and some have said that it relates to the 'cake walk', a popular late-19th-century pastime by black slaves in southern US plantations. Couples would walk arm in arm and those judged to walk most gracefully and with greatest style won the prize of a cake. 'That takes the cake' therefore means 'That wins the prize'.

Others dispute this on the grounds that the cake walk came later. They suggest that it is a jocular reference to the Greek *puramous*, the prize of victory, originally a cake of roasted wheat and honey awarded to the person of greatest vigilance in the night-watch.

'Take the biscuit' is the earlier expression, dating from medieval times. Wilfrid J.W. Blunt in *Sebastiano* records that the innkeeper's daughter at Bourgoin, a famous beauty, was present, in 1610, as a delegate at an

International Innkeeper's Congress held at Rothenburg-am-Tauber. Against her name the Secretary wrote *Ista capit biscottum*, 'that one takes the biscuit'.

The phrase in the 20th century also came to mean a piece of impudence or effrontery, as in the colloquial phrase: 'Well, if that doesn't just about take the biscuit …!'

Arnold Bennett, *A Great Man* (1904): 'My bold buccaneer, you take the cake … There is something about you that is colossal, immense and magnificent.'

Georgette Heyer, *A Blunt Instrument* (1938): 'I've met some kill-joys in my time, but you fairly take the cake.'

Take the mickey – *to make fun of someone, to jeer at, to deride*

The origin is Cockney rhyming slang, 'Mike Bliss', shortened to Mike or Mickey, meaning piss. The sense is of the deflation, as of a bladder, of conceit.

It is usually said that the phrase derives from an older one, 'piss-proud', which refers to having an erection when waking up in the morning, usually attributed to a full bladder. 'Proud' here is an obvious pun on its two senses of something raised or projecting and of something in which one may take satisfaction.

It is first recorded, as so many such indecorous expressions are, in Francis Grose's *A Classical Dictionary of the Vulgar Tongue*; in the second edition of 1788 he wrote: 'Piss-proud, having a false erection. That old fellow thought he had an erection, but his – was only piss-proud; said of any old fellow who marries a young wife.'

This developed into a figurative sense of somebody who had an exaggerated idea of his own importance. So to 'take the piss' is to deflate somebody, to disabuse them of their mistaken belief that they are special. It is not recorded before the beginning of the 20th century.

The phrase has also been further elaborated, as in: 'Are you by any chance extracting the Michael?'

Observer (1958): '*Tonight* is not only a tough and irreverent programme, but glib and smart and anxious to take the mickey.'

Take umbrage – *to take offence*

The word 'umbrage' has its roots in the Latin *umbra* meaning shade, from which 'umbrella' is also derived.

'Umbrage' in its literal meaning of shade is now obsolete, as are the other figurative phrases 'under the umbrage of', meaning under the cover of something else, and 'to stand in umbrage', meaning to be in disfavour with someone.

Only 'to give umbrage', and more often 'to take umbrage', have survived into modern parlance. The sense is to cast a shadow of resentment, displeasure or annoyance.

> Our stout Knight …
> Took umbrage that a friend so near
> Refused to share his chase and cheer.
> > Sir Walter Scott, 'Rokeby' (1813)

Taken aback – *shocked, surprised*

In the days of sailing ships, if the wind unexpectedly whipped the huge sails back against the masts, the ship was taken aback, and its progress was abruptly halted. This could happen either through faulty steering or a swift change in wind direction.

The shock involved relates now to a person's reaction when suddenly stopped short by something unexpected.

Andrew Morton, *Diana: Her True Story* (1992): 'He wasted no time with social niceties, asking her immediately how many times she had tried to commit suicide. She was taken aback, but her reply was equally forthright: "Four or five times."'

Taken to the cleaners – *to have lost all one's money, to be ruined*

In the 19th century, people were 'cleaned out' when they were stripped clean of everything of value, either through gambling or as victims of dishonest practice. This use is still current. To be 'taken to the cleaners' is a more recent term which expresses the same thing.

Daily Mail (1991): '"I was taken to the cleaners", sobs Royal Designer.'

Talk gibberish – *to talk unintelligibly*

There is much debate about the origin of this phrase. 'Gibberish' may come from an 11th-century Arabian alchemist called Geber who, fearing that he could be charged with heresy, developed his own language to keep his scientific notes secret.

Others suggest that gibberish comes from 'gibber', a verb allied to 'jabber', meaning to speak rapidly and unintelligibly. The word gibberish however seems to pre-date the verb gibber.

> What me thynke ye be clerkyshe
> For ye speak good gybbryshe.
> > Anon., 'The Enterlude of Youth' (1554)

> The graves stood tenantless and the sheeted dead
> Did squeak and gibber in the Roman streets.
> > Shakespeare, *Hamlet* (1604)

Talk the hind legs off a donkey – *to talk incessantly, to talk too much; to talk persuasively*

Originally an expression of praise for a person's ability to achieve the impossible through the power of persuasion, it became a complaint that someone talked too much.

There are many variations on this theme, which appear as talking the hind leg off a bird, a cow, a dog, a horse and a jackass, and even talking the hind leg off a brass pan or a saucepan. A 20th-century Australian variant is 'talk the leg off an iron pot'.

Cobbett's Weekly Political Register (1808): 'The old vulgar hyperbole of "talking a horse's hind leg off" … will find its verification in the American Congress.'

W. Somerset Maugham, *Of Human Bondage* (1915): '"Doesn't she look like Rubens' second wife?" cried Athelney. "Wouldn't she look splendid in seventeenth century costume? That's the sort of wife to marry, my boy. Look at her." – "I believe you'd talk the hind leg off a donkey, Athelney," she answered calmly.'

Talk turkey – *to discuss business issues frankly and seriously*

The origin of the expression is uncertain, but it may have arisen from the efforts of turkey hunters to attract their prey by making gobbling noises.

An interpretation which reflects the modern meaning suggests that the American Indians, having domesticated the turkey before the Europeans arrived, regularly served this delicious new dish. When the Pilgrim Fathers came, they developed such a taste for the bird that every serious bartering session with the Indians became known as 'talking turkey'.

A more prosaic view might be that the turkey is the main, substantial and succulent part of the (Christmas) dinner. Talking turkey is discussing the main issue.

Aldous Huxley, *After Many a Summer* (1939): "'I'll make it worth your while," he said. "You can have anything you care to ask for." … "Ah," said Dr Obispo, "Now you're talking turkey.'"

Tarred with the same brush – *considered to show the same faults or peculiarities*

This expression seems to originate with the shepherd and his flock. Formerly, sheep sores were treated by dabbing them with tar, the same brush sufficing to dress the sores of every sheep in the flock. A tar brush might also be used to daub a special mark of ownership upon every fleece, so that each sheep was identified as being a member of the same flock.

Sir Walter Scott, *Rob Roy* (1818): 'They are a' tarr'd wi' the same stick.'

W.R. Inge, *More Lay Thoughts* (1931): 'I cannot see, from my reading of history, that there is a pin to choose between the morality of empires and that of republics. They are both tarred with the same brush.'

See also **Spoil the ship for a ha'porth of tar**.

Teach one's grandmother to suck eggs – *to tell somebody how to do something that they already know, to offer help to a much more experienced person*

This expression is about 300 years old and it is probably the absurdity of the phrase which ensured its popularity, rather than its precise meaning. Some have suggested that soft-boiled eggs would have been eaten by grandmothers without teeth, and that they needed no advice from the young on how to eat them.

Others suggest the egg-collector's practice of sucking the fluid of the egg out through a tiny hole in the shell.

There are other similar sayings. 'To teach one's grandma to grope ducks' referred to the way an experienced woman could measure the distance between the duck's pelvic bones, to see whether the bird's egg-laying days were over and the time had come for her to be put in the pot.

These are variations of an older theme that was absurd enough to appeal to the popular fancy. One of the earliest of these is given in Nicholas Udall's translation of *Erasmus' Apophthegmes* (1542): 'A swyne to teach Minerua, was a prouerbe, for which we sai: Englyshe to teach our dame to spyne.' (Don't try to teach a dame to spin.)

John Stevens, translator, *Quevedo's Comical Works* (1707): 'You would have me teach my Grandame to suck Eggs.'

Tell it *or* that to the Marines – *an expression of incredulity*

Regular seamen of the Royal Navy were contemptuous of the marines, the Maritime Regiment of Foot, regarding them as gullible fools with no real understanding of the sea. This led to an expression: 'Tell it to the marines, the sailors won't believe it.'

Major W.P. Drury in *The Tadpole of an Archangel* (1904) constructed a hoax around this idiom in a book of naval stories. He claimed that Charles II was dining with Samuel Pepys when the subject of flying fish was raised. The King said he did not believe in flying fish but an officer in the marines present claimed that he had indeed seen them with his own eyes.

The King was very impressed, and said: 'From the very nature of their calling no class of our subjects can have so wide a knowledge of seas and lands as the officers and men of Our Loyal Maritime Regiment. Henceforward ere ever we cast doubts upon a tale that lacks likelihood, we will first "Tell it to the Marines".'

However, there is no record of the story in Pepys' diaries and Major Drury subsequently admitted that it was a hoax, 'a leg pull of my youth'.

John Davis, *The Post Captain* (1806): 'He may tell that to the marines but the sailors will not believe him.'

Eugene O'Neill, *Ah, Wilderness!* (1933): 'And I suppose you just sat and let yourself be kissed! Tell that to the Marines!'

That's (just) the ticket – *perfect, absolutely right*

Several suggestions have been offered for the origin of this phrase. It may come from US politics, in which the 'ticket' is the manifesto of policies that a political party puts before the electorate.

It could be a variation on the phrase 'that's the ticket for soup', derived from the card given to beggars in the 19th century for immediate relief at soup kitchens. Tickets which could be exchanged for soup, clothing, coal and other basic necessities were issued to the needy by charities.

It may be also a reference to a winning lottery ticket.

Routledge's Every Boy's Annual (1866): 'That's the ticket! That's the winning game.'

There's more than one way to skin a cat – *there are several ways to solve a problem*

This saying appeared in John Ray's collection of English proverbs in 1678, and is first attested in the United States in John Smith's *Letters* (1839) in a slightly different form, as: 'There are more ways to kill a cat besides choking him to death.'

Other variants, 'besides choking him with butter' and 'besides choking him on cream', also appear.

Some authorities say that the expression refers to a boys' gymnastic trick, 'to skin the cat', to hang by the hands from a branch, draw the legs up, and pull oneself up into a sitting position. There do not, however, seem to be many different ways to perform this trick, which after all is skinning *the* cat, not *a* cat.

Another suggestion is that the phrase refers to the catfish, 'cat' being an abbreviation used in the southern states of the USA. The easiest way to remove the skin of the catfish is to put the fish quickly into boiling water. The age and the widespread use of the phrase suggest that this is a local adaptation of the proverb.

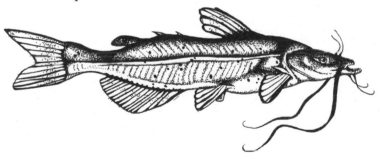

Seba Smith, *Way Down East; or, Portraitures of Yankee Life* (c. 1854): 'This is a money digging world of ours; and, as it is said, "there are more ways than one to skin a cat," so are there more ways than one of digging for money.'

There's no such thing as a free lunch – *everything has a price, one never gets something for nothing*

In the mid-19th century, bars in the USA offered a free lunch with every drink. The lunch was a modest snack, a gimmick to encourage customers to buy drinks. If they wanted to eat anything more substantial, they would have to pay for it.

An article about nationalising industries, in the journal *Ethics* (1952), attributes the saying in its present form to Professor Alvin Hansen (a prominent economist at Harvard University) and quotes the well-known acronym of the phrase, TINSTAAFL.

Now a common business expression, it appeared in Robert Heinlein's *The Moon is a Harsh Mistress* (1966). American economist Milton Friedman, who won the 1976 Nobel Prize, did much to popularise the phrase, and used it as a title for one of his books.

Stephen Hawking, *A Brief History of Time* (1991): 'It's said that there's no such thing as a free lunch. But the universe is the ultimate free lunch.'

Third degree – *intense interrogation*

The 'third degree' is the highest degree, that of Master Mason, in British freemasonry. A candidate must submit himself to a rigorous and exhaustive examination.

The phrase is also used to describe interrogation of a prisoner by police involving the infliction of mental or physical suffering in order to bring about a confession or to secure information.

William Preston, *Illustrations of Masonry* (1772): 'A charge to be delivered at Initiation in the Third Degree.'

Tom Sharpe, *Wilt* (1976): '"You don't think they are giving him the third degree, or anything of that sort?" – "My dear fellow, third degree? You've been watching too many old movies on the TV. The police don't use strong-arm methods in this country."'

Three R's – *the basic subjects taught at school: reading, writing and arithmetic*

This is attributed to Alderman Sir William Curtis (1751–1829), who rose to become Lord Mayor of London. A firm believer in education, he once proposed the toast at a public dinner given by the Board of Education with: 'The three Rs – Riting, Reading and Rithmetic.'

The spelling has been ascribed to Sir William's illiteracy, but while he had limited education, he was very shrewd and contemporary sources say that he chose the particular wording as a joke. It was received with great applause and merriment, and the joke has survived to the present day.

Daily Express (1992): 'Having read the article about Education Secretary John Patten's five-year-old daughter Mary Claire and her state school, I find it worrying that there was no mention of the three Rs. Instead religion, sex and green issues were quoted.'

Three sheets to *or* in the wind – *very drunk*

The sheet is the rope attached to the trailing corner of a sail. It is used to distribute the load so that the ship floats on an even keel. If the sheet is quite free, leaving the sail to flap without restraint, the sheet is said to be 'in the wind', and 'a sheet in the wind' is a colloquial nautical expression for being tipsy. Thus to have 'three sheets in the wind' is to be very drunk.

Charles Dickens, *Dombey and Son* (1847–8): 'Captain Cuttle looking, candle in hand, at Bunsby more attentively, perceived that he was three sheets in the wind, or, in plain words, drunk.'

Tie the knot – *to get married*

A complicated double knot with two interlacing bows on each side and two ends is a symbol of love, and is called a truelove or true-lovers' knot.

Sir Thomas Browne (1605–82) maintained in *Pseudodoxia Epidemica* that the knot owes its origin to the *nodus Herculanus*, a snaky device used for the woollen girdle of Greek brides. This interlacing knot is a symbol of interwoven affection.

Knots are symbols of the union of two people, not only in the Christian but in the Hindu, Sikh, Chinese Buddhist and other marriage ceremonies. They feature in the bridal bouquet and signify love and unity.

> Three times a true-love's knot I tie secure;
> Firm be the knot, firm may his love endure.
> John Gay, *Pastorals*, 'The Spell' (1714)

Tilt at windmills – *to take on imaginary enemies*

Don Quixote by Miguel de Cervantes (1547–1616) is the story of an amiable fellow who has become too fond of ballads and romances and sets off to put the world to rights.

The plot covers Don Quixote's adventures accompanied by his squire, Sancho Panza. Don Quixote is an ordinary Spaniard, a *hidalgo*, the lowest rank of the Spanish nobility. Obsessed with stories of knights errant (*libros de caballerías*), he decides to become one himself, and to wander Spain on his thin horse, Rocinante, righting wrongs and defending the oppressed.

Don Quixote seems mad to most people. He believes ordinary inns to be enchanted castles and their peasant girls to be beautiful princesses. He imagines a neighbouring peasant to be Dulcinea del Toboso, the beautiful maiden to whom he has pledged love and fidelity. He mistakes windmills for oppressive giants sent by evil enchanters, against which he takes up arms, 'tilting at windmills'.

Agatha Christie, *Death on the Nile* (1937): 'Rather eccentric ... inclined to tilt at windmills.'

Tired and emotional – *drunk*

This euphemism was devised to enable British newspapers to operate under libel laws that effectively prevented any direct statement about someone's inebriated state or fondness for alcohol.

The reference was to George Brown, Foreign Secretary (1966–8) who undoubtedly did get drunk. *Private Eye*, the satirical magazine, popularised the phrase. On 29 September 1967, it described George Brown as 'tired and overwrought on many occasions', and the magazine cover showed him gesticulating while Harold Wilson explains to General de Gaulle: 'George est un peu fatigué, votre Majesté.'

Tit for tat – *retaliation in equal measure*

This is a variation of 'tip for tap', in which both words mean 'a light blow'. Dutch has *dit for dat*, this for that. The origin is *lex talionis*, the law of retaliation: 'eye for eye, tooth for tooth, hand for hand, foot for foot' (Exodus 21:24).

J. Quincy, *Life* (1809): 'I shall … give … what politicians call a Rowland for their Oliver, and what the ladies term tit for tat.'

To a T – *perfect for the purpose, exact; typical, characteristic of*

A 'T' is thought to stand for a tittle, a minute and precisely positioned pen stroke or printer's mark. A tiny brush stroke was all that distinguished the two otherwise identical Hebrew letters *dalet* and *resh*, and 'tittle' was the word chosen by John Wycliffe to translate references to this minuscule difference in his version of the New Testament.

D.H. Lawrence, *Sons and Lovers* (1913): 'That's him to a "T" – like a navvy! He's not fit for mixing with decent folk.'

See also **Jot and tittle**.

To boot – *additionally*

The phrase literally means 'to the good' and comes from the Old English *bot*, meaning good or advantage. There was also a verb 'to boot' which meant to make better, to cure, relieve, heal or remedy, or to do a good deed for someone. These words were common currency as recently as the mid-19th century but have fallen into disuse since.

Edward A. Freeman, *The History of the Norman Conquest* (1867): 'One who held all Gaul and all Britain, with seemingly Germany to boot.'

Anon., *Amis and Amiloun* (c. 1330): 'Jesu that is heven king, / Shal bote thee of thy bale.' (Jesus, the king of heaven, will heal your wickedness.)

To the bitter end – *to the very last, until overtaken by death or defeat*

The anchor cable on sailing ships was coiled around the bitts, stout posts set in the deck. The last portion of cable, which was attached to the bitts themselves, was known as the 'bitter end'.

Captain John Smith, *A Sea Grammar with the Plaine Exposition of Smith's Accidence for Young Sea-men Enlarged* (1627): 'A Bitter is but the turne of a Cable about the bitts, and veare it out by little and little. And the Bitters end is that part of the Cable doth stay within boord.'

If it became necessary to let out the cable to the bitter end, the likelihood of disaster would be much greater, since there would be nothing left in reserve.

It is probable, however, that the phrase was influenced by a verse in the Old Testament Book of Proverbs (5:4): 'But her end is bitter as wormwood, sharp as a two-edged sword.'

Graham Greene, *Loser Takes All* (1955): 'A wife ought to believe in her husband to the bitter end.'

Toe the line – *to submit to discipline, to come into line with the rest, to conform, to be obedient*

The phrase also appears as 'toe the mark', 'the scratch', 'the crack' or 'the trig' (meaning the point behind which a player at bowls or curling must stand).

It has been suggested that the expression may be a reference to the line between the two rows of benches in the House of Commons, drawn so that members would neither fight nor strike each other during the heat of debate.

Another suggestion is that it was a line drawn by the executioner on the trap door of the gallows, against which those about to die should stand.

The origin is, however, earlier, referring to the start of a race. The concept was adopted by political parties, particularly in the phrase 'to toe the party line'.

Frederick Marryat, *Peter Simple* (1833): 'He desired us to "toe a line" which means to stand in a row.'

Westminster Gazette (1895): 'The phrase "toeing the line" is very much in favour with some Liberals.'

Tongue-in-cheek – *ironic, insincere, saying one thing and meaning another*

The modern figurative sense harks back to the mid-18th century, when making a lump in one's cheek with the tongue was a sign of contempt.

Listener (1976): 'Someone told Muhammed Ali, tongue-in-cheek, that his book made him come over as a "deep thinker".'

Touch and go – *very close; a risky, precarious, delicate, or ticklish case or state of things; a narrow escape or 'close shave'*

This possibly describes that critical moment in which the wheels of two chariots, racing intensely against each other, touch. This can either spell disaster or survival.

Admiral William Henry Smyth, *The Sailor's Wordbook* (1867): '*Touch-and-go*, said of narrowly to escape rocks etc or when, under sail, she rubs against the ground with her keel, without much diminution of her velocity.'

Hawley Smart, *Cleverly Won – A Romance of the Grand National* (1887): 'She caught [the horse] … by the mane, and though it was touch and go she managed to retain her seat.'

Touch wood – *a superstition to avert apprehended misfortune*

It was traditionally believed that certain trees, such as the oak, ash, hazel, hawthorn and willow, had sacred significance and, if touched, would give blessing and protection. The expression now applies to any wood because the detail of the specific trees has passed into oblivion.

The phrase may also refer to the cross of Christ and to purported 'relics', pieces of the cross which were hawked around in medieval times.

Westminster Gazette (1908): 'On the next occasion when we read of Christmas with spring weather or of the changing seasons, we shall "touch wood".'

Trip the light fantastic – *to dance*

The original phrase comes from Milton's 'L'Allegro' (1632):

> Haste thee Nymph and bring with thee
> Jest and youthful Jollity …
> Sport that wrinkled care derides,
> And Laughter holding both his sides.
> Come, and trip it as ye go
> On the light fantastick toe.

W. Somerset Maugham used the full expression in *Cakes and Ale* (1930): 'The muse does not only stalk with majestic tread, but on occasion trips on a light fantastic toe.'

The modern phrase does not appear until the late 19th century in the USA.

Kingsley Amis, *Lucky Jim* (1954): 'I thought you'd all be on the floor by now. Now, Mr Gore-Urquhart; I'm not going to permit any more of this skulking about in here. It's the light fantastic for you; come along.'

Turn a blind eye – *to pretend not to notice*

This familiar expression became current after the death of Lord Nelson in 1805, when it was recalled that during the Battle of Copenhagen (1801), Nelson was commanded to break off the action but ignored the command, claiming that he had a blind eye and the right to use it.

James Stanier Clarke and John McArthur, *Life of Nelson* (1809): 'Putting the glass to this blind eye, he exclaimed *I really do not see the signal.*'

The Times (1963): 'The police turn a blind eye to this problem because they are only too glad to get lorries from parking on the main road.'

Turn over a new leaf – *to begin again, to resolve to behave better*

The phrase does not refer to the leaves of a tree but the leaves of a book. The image is that of turning over a page of blots and crossings-out to a new, clean white page.

John Galsworthy, *The Man of Property* (1906): 'He intended to take an opportunity this afternoon of speaking to Irene. A word in time saved nine; and now that she was going to live in the country there was a chance for her to turn over a new leaf! He could see that Soames wouldn't stand very much more of her goings on!'

Turn the tables – *to gain the upper hand when previously losing; to reverse one's relationship with another, to one's advantage*

There are several suggested sources for this saying. One claims that it refers to wealthy Roman collectors of antique furniture. When such a man complained about his wife's extravagances, she had merely to turn the tables he had collected and remind him of his own excessive expenditure.

Another story connects it with the parsimonious behaviour of old-time British households. The tops of their tables had only one finished side, a less expensive alternative to having both completed to a high standard.

When the family was alone, they ate on the rough side to keep the finished one in good condition. When company came, they turned the table-top to the good side to impress the visitors.

Both theories seem far-fetched. It is more likely that the phrase comes from gaming.

Backgammon was called 'tables' from medieval times up to about 1750 (derived from the Latin *tabulae*, which may have referred to the 'men' or counters). The board is also divided into four distinct playing tables; to 'turn the tables' referred to a sudden reversal of a player's fortune.

Dudley Digges, *The Unlawfulness of Subjects Taking Arms Against their Soveraigne* (1647): 'The tables are quite turned, and your friends have undertaken the same bad game, and play it much worse.'

Turn turtle – *to turn upside down*

A turtle lying on its back is rendered helpless. Sailors used this expression to describe a capsized boat, which is equally immobile and useless. It now applies to any object which is accidentally overturned.

Henry Pitman, *A Relation of the Great Sufferings and Strange Adventures of Henry Pitman* (1689): 'They, going ashore on the Main to turn Turtle, were set upon by the Indians.'

Daily News (1896): 'An engine and two trucks had turned turtle on the embankment.'

Turn up for the books – *an unexpected piece of good fortune*

The books here are the records of the bookmaker. When a horse performed in a way that nobody expected, so that most bets lost, it was something that benefited the book and so the bookmaker. The classic example would be a rank outsider that won with few bets on it, netting the bookmaker a nice windfall profit.

Craig Hadley, *Slang Dictionary* (1873): '*Turn up* ... an unexpected slice of luck. Among sporting men bookmakers are said to have a turn up when an unbacked horse wins.'

John William Wainwright, *The Jury People* (1978): 'A bit of a turn up for the book, isn't it? Murder, I mean.'

U

Uncle Sam – *personification of US government*

'Uncle Sam' is probably a jocular expression based on seeing the letters 'US' on the side of packages and wagons.

It may also be associated with the supplier of meat to the US Army, Samuel Wilson (1766–1854), who stamped his packing cases 'US'. These letters were new to the soldiers and they therefore thought they referred to Uncle Sam, allegedly Samuel Wilson's nickname.

Some support for this theory is to be found in the first reference to Uncle Sam in the *Troy Post* (Samuel Wilson's local paper) of 7 September 1813: 'Loss upon loss, and no ill luck stir[r]ing but what lights upon Uncle Sam's shoulders.'

Uncle Tom – *a black person who defers to white people*

Uncle Tom was the central character in *Uncle Tom's Cabin* (1852) by Harriet Beecher Stowe (illustrated). This expression is a derogatory reference to a faithful and dignified black slave.

By the 20th century, Uncle Tom had been misrepresented from being faithful to being weak, and then by the 1960s to being branded a 'race traitor' in the minds of black leaders such as Malcolm X.

When *Uncle Tom's Cabin; or, Life Among the Lowly* was first published, no one, least of all its author, expected the book to become a sensation, but this anti-slavery novel took the world by storm. It was to become the second-best-selling book in the world during the 19th century, second only to the Bible, and it ignited criticism and praise.

Stowe's novel tells the stories of three slaves, Tom, Eliza and George, who start out together in Kentucky, but whose lives take different turns. Eliza and George, who are married to each other but owned by different masters, manage to escape to free territory with their little boy, Harry.

On the other hand, Tom fares badly. Taken away from his wife and children, he is sold first to a kind master, Augustine St Clare, but then to the fiendish Simon Legree, at whose hands he meets his death.

Legree has sexually exploited two female slaves. Uncle Tom would rather be whipped to death than give up the location of the two women. He sacrifices his life to protect others. A father of three young children, he chooses, out of his Christian convictions, martyrdom rather than violence to deal with his oppressors.

Up a gum-tree – *stuck, isolated, in real difficulties*

'Up a tree', meaning in difficulty, is an American phrase dating from 1829. It is probably a hunting reference, the allusion being to the gum tree as a refuge for the opossum.

The phrase is also used in Australia, which probably has more gum trees to the square mile than anywhere else. The characteristic of the gum tree, as opposed to other Australian trees, is that it is a long way to the first branch, and therefore difficult to climb, either up or down.

It is said that the Baptist preacher Charles Spurgeon (1834–92) used to exercise his students in extempore preaching. One of his young men, on reaching the desk and opening the note containing his text, read the single word 'Zacchaeus'. He thought for a minute or two, and then delivered himself thus: 'Zacchaeus was a little man, so am I; Zacchaeus was up a tree, so am I; Zacchaeus made haste and came down, and so do I.'

Encounter (1959): 'Until somebody solves the problem of an English idiom we're going to be up a gum-tree.'

Up the spout – *gone, lost, ruined; in real trouble*

The lift by which goods go into storage at a pawnbroker's was called 'the spout'. Anyone who saw their valuables disappearing in those circumstances knew they were in real financial trouble.

The phrase is also a vulgarism meaning pregnant, especially when outside marriage.

Swell's Night Guide (1846): 'And when she saw all hope was up the spout / She spouted everything a spout would take.'

'Simon Troy', *Blind Man's Garden* (1970): 'Up the spout, isn't she? I thought Michel would have had more bloody savvy.'

Up to scratch – *able to do what is required, to be ready or good enough in any test*

In bare knuckle fights, under the London Prize Ring Rules introduced in 1839, a round ended when one contender was knocked down. After a 30-second interval, this fighter was allowed eight seconds in which to get up and make his way unaided to a line scratched in the ground in the centre of the ring. This signified that he was prepared to continue. If he failed to do so, he had not come up to scratch and was declared beaten.

George Orwell, *Burmese Days* (1934): 'If they won't come up to scratch you can always get hold of the ringleaders and give them a good bambooing on the QT.'

Upper crust – *the aristocracy, the cream of society, the élite*

It is suggested that the upper crust of the loaf or pie should be offered to the most honoured guest.

The phrase was first used in Thomas Haliburton, *The Sayings and Doings of Samuel Slick* (1836): 'I want you to see Peel ... Macaulay, old Joe and so on. These men are all upper crust here.'

Two tender babes I nussed:
One was of low condition,
The other, upper crust,
A regular patrician.
W.S. Gilbert (illustrated),
HMS Pinafore (1878)

V

Vent one's spleen – *to express violent ill-nature or ill-temper*

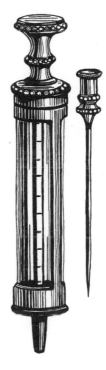

In the concept of the four humours developed by ancient Greek thinkers around 400 BC, the spleen was the seat of melancholy. The temperament of a person was determined by the balance of the humours in the body, and the melancholic temperament associated with the spleen was characterised by despondency and irritability.

Treatments like blood-letting and emetics were used to counter an imbalance of humours, and gave rise to the idea of 'venting one's spleen'.

George Rawlinson, *Egypt and Babylon* (1885): 'This time … he vented his spleen on the Jews by renewed attacks and oppressions.'

See also **Cold-blooded**.

Vice versa – *the other way around; contrariwise, conversely*

This phrase is from the Latin *vicis*, meaning 'change', and *versa*, 'turned'. It sometimes appears in jocular form as 'vicey-versey' or 'vicy-versy'.

Samuel Palmer, *Moral Essays on Some of the Most Curious … English, Scotch and Foreign Proverbs* (1710): 'Nor can we ask his favour upon occasion, and so vice versa he can make no use of us.'

Kenneth O'Hara, *The Searchers of the Dead* (1979): 'Actors work on directors as well as vicey-versey.'

Voice crying in the wilderness – *a lone voice, a person whose warnings are ignored*

This was a phrase used in the Gospels. It refers to John the Baptist, who recognised Jesus as the Messiah and fulfilled the prophecy in Isaiah 40:3: 'The voice of one crying in the wilderness: Prepare ye the way of the Lord, Make his paths straight.'

The quotation is used to assert that John was preparing the way for Jesus, as foretold by the prophecy of Isaiah.

John the Baptist did not, as the modern idiom suggests, go unheard.

W

Walk over one's grave – *a saying to someone who has an involuntary shiver*

In full, the phrase is 'someone is walking over my grave', alluding to an old wives' tale which says that when the spot where one will be laid to rest is walked over, one feels an involuntary shiver.

'Holme Lee', *Basil Godfrey's Caprice* (1868): 'Joan shuddered – that … convulsive shudder which old wives say is caused by a footstep walking over the place of our grave that shall be.'

Warm the cockles of your heart – *to warm and gratify one's deepest feelings*

It is thought that the 'cockles' of the heart are the ventricles, from their Latin name, *cochleae cordis* (*cochleae* meaning 'snails' and *cordis* 'of the heart'). The ventricles are called the 'heart's snails' because of their shape.

Charles Darwin, *Life and Letters* (1858): 'I have just had the innermost cockles of my heart rejoiced by a letter from Lyell.'

Warp and woof – *tight interweaving of different strands*

In weaving, the 'warp' is the thread running lengthwise in the loom, usually twisted harder than the 'weft' or 'woof' which runs across the fabric.

J. May, *The True Estate of Clothing in the Realm* (1613): 'A common thing it is for the weaver to cover a course warpe with a fine woofe, the warpe being spon hard and small, and the woofe soft and round to cover the warpe from sight.'

Frederick W. Robertson, *Sermons* (1849): 'Sorrow is … the … woof which is woven into the warp of life.'

Warts and all – *making no attempt to hide defects*

Oliver Cromwell, a Puritan, would have none of the portrait painter's skill in disguising natural defects. His instructions to Sir Peter Lely were: 'I desire you would use all your skill to paint my picture truly like me, and not flatter me at all; but remark all these roughnesses, pimples, warts, and everything as you see me, otherwise I will never pay a farthing for it.' The portrait now hangs in the Saloon of Kimbolton Castle, near Huntingdon in Cambridgeshire.

Sunday Telegraph (1992): 'The write-ups give warts-and-all descriptions of the property itself and its location.'

Wash one's dirty linen in public – *reveal something discreditable in public which should be kept private*

This is normally used in the context of domestic quarrels or grievances, the discussion of which is best confined to the family circle.

'It is at home, not in public, that one washes one's dirty linen', said Napoleon on his return from exile on Elba in 1815.

Law Times (1891): 'It is ridiculous that grave disputes … should be kept waiting while the dirty linen of high society is … washed in public.'

Wear one's heart on one's sleeve – *to show one's feelings openly, to reveal one's secret thoughts or intentions to others*

The reference is to the old custom by which a young man tied a favour – a handkerchief or a ribbon – to his sleeve to show his beloved that he cared for her.

> But I will wear my heart upon my sleeve
> For daws to peck at: I am not what I am.
>   Shakespeare, *Othello* (1604)

Wear sackcloth and ashes – *to be penitent*

The phrase alludes to the ancient Hebrew custom of wearing sackcloth and ashes to signify mourning or penitence. As a sign of humility in religious ceremonies, sackcloth – a black, coarse goat-hair cloth used to make grain bags – was worn dusted with, or accompanied by, ashes.

The Hebrew word for sackcloth was *saq*, and the Greek *sakkos*. The English word 'sack' is derived from these.

HRH Princess of Wales, *Daily Mail* (1991): 'I am not advocating a general wailing and gnashing of teeth or sackcloth and ashes. But emotional outbursts might be less dramatic or violent if a little steam were occasionally vented harmlessly.'

Weasel words – *evasive language*

Weasels are particularly well known for being cowardly and cunning. They can literally 'weasel' their way out of a tight corner with their lithe little bodies.

They sneak into the hen yard to steal eggs and suck the contents out, leaving the egg intact. It is not until one picks the egg up that one realises that what looks like a normal, nutritious egg is, in fact, just an empty shell.

'Weasel words are words that suck the life out of the words next to them, just as the weasel sucks the egg and leaves the shell', wrote Stewart Chaplin in his short story, 'Stained-Glass Political Platform' (1900).

It was Theodore Roosevelt who popularised the expression when he used it to attack President Woodrow Wilson in 1916.

He said: 'You can have universal training, or you can have voluntary training, but when you use the word *voluntary* to qualify the word *universal*, you are using a weasel word; it has sucked all the meaning out of *universal*. The two words flatly contradict one another.'

Welsh rabbit – *cheese on toast*

This is a joke against the Welsh. 'Rabbit' is correct, and not 'rarebit', which was an 18th-century misconstruction making the dish sound more exotic and refined than it actually is.

In the same way that condoms are called 'French letters' and frogs 'Dutch nightingales', this was an English joke at the expense of another nationality, the implication being that the Welsh could not afford, or could not cook, rabbit and had to make do with cheese.

The term is on a par with 'mock turtle' and 'Bombay duck', indicating a dish that is a substitute for the real thing.

Mrs Hannah Glasse, *The Art of Cookery. By a Lady* (1747): 'To make a Welch-Rabbit. Toast the Bread on both Sides, then Toast the Cheese on one Side, and lay it on the Toast, and with a hot Iron brown the other Side.'

Wet behind the ears – *immature, naïve, inexperienced*

This is probably a military expression to a raw recruit, implying that he needed his mother to make sure that he had dried himself properly. It derives from the fact that the last place to become dry after an animal's birth is the small depression behind each ear.

The French have a similar phrase: *avoir-encore du lait derrière les oreilles*, still having milk behind the ears.

John Brophy and Eric Partridge, *Songs and Slang of the British Soldier* (1931): 'Wet behind the ears, a term of reproach imputing ignorance or youth.'

John Steinbeck, *The Grapes of Wrath* (1939): 'When you bastards get dry behin' the ears, you'll maybe learn to let an ol' fella sleep.'

What the dickens! – *an exclamation of surprise*

This exclamation is not a reference to Charles Dickens, and pre-dates him by three centuries. It is a 16th-century euphemism for the Devil, adopted from the name Dickin or Dickon, the diminutive of Dick, or the surname

Dickens. It has been suggested that it is a corruption of 'devilkin' or 'deilkin' but no evidence of this has been found.

Shakespeare, *The Merry Wives of Windsor* (1601): 'I cannot tell what the dickens his name is.'

Wheeler-dealer – *a sharp trader*

A person who 'wheels and deals' is an adroit, quick-witted, scheming person. The term comes from the US, where 'wheel' in American slang signifies a leader, one who takes charge, a 'big shot'. He is a shrewd and influential operator in a particular field (usually business or politics).

It has also been suggested that the wheel refers to roulette and the dealing of cards, in other words to someone who chances his luck.

Economist (1963): 'Two Dallas oil millionaires ... described as "a pair of old line Texas wheeler-dealers".'

Louis Heren, *Growing up on the Times* (1978): 'He [Lyndon Johnson] was a shop-soiled old politico, a wheeler-dealer, and past master of consensus politics.'

Whipping boy – *another punished for one's own misdemeanours*

Originally, this was a commoner boy who was educated with a Prince and whipped if the Prince offended. Thomas Fuller in *Church History* (1655) says that Barnaby Fitzpatrick stood in this capacity for Edward VI, and Mungo Murray for Charles I. Edward's affection for his whipping boy was well known at Court and was probably the greatest guarantee of his good behaviour, even after he became King. However, in a letter to Fitzpatrick he priggishly instructed him to apply himself to 'honest games, not forgetting sometimes your learning, chiefly reading of the Scripture'. A disgruntled Barnaby replied: 'Ye make me think the care ye take for me is more fatherly than friendly.'

When Henry IV of France abjured Protestantism and was received into the Roman Catholic Church in 1593, Bishop Duperron and Cardinal d'Ossat were sent to Rome to obtain the King's absolution. They knelt in the portico of St Peter's singing the Miserere. At each verse, a blow with a switch was dealt to their shoulders.

Sir Arthur Helps, *Essays Written in the Intervals of Business* (1841): 'The choice of agents is a difficult matter ... for you have to choose persons for whose faults you are to be punished; to whom you are to be the whipping-boy.'

Whip-round – *an impromptu collection of money, often for some benevolent project*

The 'Whip' in hunting and in Parliament is the person who makes sure the hounds and the Members, respectively, conform.

By the end of the 18th century, the term 'whip' was used in the officers' mess to invite those who wanted more wine to contribute funds.

Any call for money became a whip, and by the end of the 19th century the phrase 'whip-round' among a group of colleagues or friends had become commonplace.

Thomas Hughes, *Tom Brown at Oxford* (1861): 'If they would stand a whip of ten shillings a man, they might have a new boat.'

Daily News (1888): 'A "whip-round" ... for the Robin Dinner Fund for poor children in London.'

Whistle for it *or* whistle for the wind – *to expect, seek, try to get, in vain; to fail to obtain, go without*

At one time, mariners on a becalmed ship would whistle in the impossible hope that their breath would encourage a wind to develop. However, to many sailors whistling was 'the Devil's music', which could raise a gale. It was therefore not tolerated.

Charles Johnston, *Chrysal: or the Adventures of a Guinea* (1760): '"Do you not desire to be free?" ... "Aye! that I do! But I may whistle for that wind long enough, before it will blow."'

Lady Georgiana Bloomfield, *Reminiscences* (1882): 'She ... rode off, telling him he might whistle for his money.'

White elephant – *a possession that is of little use and costly to maintain, something no longer wanted or practical*

The kings of Siam (now Thailand) gave a white elephant to courtiers who had fallen out of favour. The gift was not all that it seemed, for the King's intention was to ruin the courtier. White elephants remained the property of the King, and were sacred. They could not therefore be put to work to recover the cost of their upkeep.

John Galsworthy, *Swan Song* (1928): "'You look so well in that hat, Uncle.' Soames took it off again. "White elephant," he said. "Can't think what made Fleur get me the thing!'"

Whited sepulchre – *a hypocrite, something outwardly presentable but inwardly corrupt*

This is a biblical expression from Matthew 23:27, where Jesus condemns the scribes and the Pharisees for being outwardly orthodox and beyond reproach but inwardly corrupt, full of self-indulgence and greed: 'Ye are like unto whited sepulchres, which indeed appear beautiful outward, but are full of dead men's bones and of all uncleanness.'

Jewish tombs were considered ritually unclean and therefore painted white to warn the passer-by. However, Jesus was probably referring to the ornamental plaster-work which adorned the sepulchres of the rich.

Whole caboodle – *the whole lot*

The word has long been a common term among New England longshore-men to mean possessions or property. It probably originates from a shortened form of the more general American expression, 'the whole kit and boodle', which has the same meaning. 'Boodle' may derive from the Dutch *boeltje*, meaning 'possessions'.

Barry Pain, *De Omnibus* (1901): 'I was forced to give 'im eleven coppers, which 'e took and then dropped the 'ole caboodle.'

Whole nine yards – *all the way*

Theories for the meaning of 'the whole nine yards' abound: the capacity of a cement truck, the length of a hangman's noose, the size of a soldier's pack, the area of canvas on a fully rigged ship.

The most appealing suggestion is that it refers to the ammunition belts in Spitfire fighter aircraft of the Second World War, which measured exactly 27 feet. When you had fired off the whole belt, you had gone the whole nine yards. This clearly has the advantage of explaining why it became popular only in the 1960s in America. However, the theory has its detractors. Some argue that the belts of bullets were of variable length.

Washington Post (1981): 'A Japanese disaster film, *Virus*, goes the whole nine yards, showing the city as a deserted freeway underpass.'

Widow's weeds – *a widow's black mourning clothes*

The word 'weeds' comes from an Old German word, *waediz*, meaning clothing. In his translation of Boethius (AD 888), Alfred the Great used it in the singular form to mean an article of clothing.

By the 13th century it related to a person's profession, as in 'a priest's weeds', 'a beggar's weeds' and so on. It was only in the late 16th century that the phrase 'widow's weeds' gained its current meaning and the other meanings began to fall away.

Samuel Richardson, *Clarissa* (1748): 'What a charming widow would she have made! How would she have adorned the weeds!'

Wild goose chase – *a foolish quest or pursuit, a hopeless enterprise*

This referred originally not to a chase *after* a wild goose but a chase *in the manner of* a wild goose. In the 16th century, a 'wild goose chase' was the name of a cross-country horse race in which competitors followed the leader, none of them knowing the route he had taken. The scattered competitors looked like a flight of wild geese.

By the time the phrase was used figuratively by Shakespeare in *Romeo and Juliet*, the origin had been forgotten and it came to mean a pursuit of something as unlikely to be caught as a wild goose.

> Esteeme a horse, according to its pace,
> But loose no wagers on a wild-goose chase.
> > Nicholas Breton,
> > 'The Mother's Blessing' (1602)

MERCUTIO: Nay, if thy wits run the wild-goose chase, I have done; for thou hast more of the wild-goose in one of thy wits than, I am sure, I have in my whole five: was I with you there for the goose?
> Shakespeare, *Romeo and Juliet* (1596)

'Mrs Alexander', *At Bay* (1885): '"I see you have found nothing," exclaimed Lady Gethin ... "It was a wild goose chase," he replied with a weary look.'

Will o' the wisp – *an elusive person; a delusive aim or object; an utterly impractical scheme*

'Will o' the wisp' was the popular name for *ignis fatuus*, medieval Latin meaning 'foolish fire', the phosphorescent light over marshes caused, as is now known, by the spontaneous combustion of methane gas from decaying organic matter.

The expression is its personification, 'Will' being short for William and 'the wisp' a twisted straw used as a torch.

It is also known by a number of other names, such as 'elf-fire', 'jack-o'-lantern', 'peg-a-lantern', 'kit o' the canstick', 'spun-kie', 'walking fire', 'fair maid of Ireland' and 'John in the wad'.

The original metaphor had a sense of hope and ambition, but the modern meaning is that of elusiveness.

William Greener, *The Science of Gunnery* (1858): 'Proof positive, that we have been on the wrong scent, and running after a "Will o' the Wisp".'

Willy-nilly – *whether one likes it or not, willingly or unwillingly,* nolens volens

'Willy-nilly' is a contraction of the Old English words *wile he, nyle he*, meaning 'will he or will he not'.

Arthur Griffiths, *The Chronicles of Newgate* (1884): 'He … conceived an idea of carrying her off and marrying her willy-nilly at Gretna Green.'

Sir Walter Besant, *The Orange Girl* (1898): 'Let us have no more shilly-shally, willy-nilly talk.'

See also **Shilly-shally**.

Win hands down – *to win easily, with little effort*

When a jockey is way out in front, he rides with his hands held loosely down, the horse requiring no more pressure through the reins to win the race.

> There were good horses in those days, as he can well recall
> But Barker upon Elepoo, hands down, shot by them all.
> 'Pips', *Lyrics and Lays* (1867)

The Times (1958): 'Double this speed, however, and the submarine wins hands down.'

Win one's spurs – *to gain public recognition, to attain distinction, to achieve one's first honours*

When a young man was raised to the rank of knight, he was presented with a pair of gilt spurs to mark his achievement.

Penny Cyclopaedia of the Society for the Diffusion of Useful Knowledge (1837): 'His father nevertheless took him [the Black Prince] along with him to win his spurs … in July, 1346.'

George Walter Thornbury, *The Life of J.M.W. Turner* (1862): 'The painter … executed his task with patience … worthy of one who had to win his spurs.'

Wind of change – *a feeling of changing opinion*

'The wind of change is blowing through this continent. Whether we like it or not, this growth of political consciousness is a political fact.' These words were spoken by British Prime Minister Harold Macmillan when he addressed the South African Parliament on 3 February 1960. While this phrase was not coined by Macmillan, he may be credited with popularising it. The records of the *Oxford English Dictionary* show a marked increase in the frequency of the phrase after 1960.

Stanley Baldwin, before he became Prime Minister, had spoken in 1934 of 'the wind of nationalism and freedom blowing around the world'.

J.H. Clapham, *An Economic History of Modern Britain* (1932): 'The [gas] companies or municipal works with their comfortable monopoly areas … began to find a little wind of change blowing among their retorts and coke-heaps.'

Wing and a prayer – *hoping to succeed in unlikely or desperate circumstances*

This First World War expression arose after an American pilot returned to base with a badly damaged wing. He explained that he had prayed all the way home. One of his colleagues, surprised that he had not crashed, said 'a wing and a prayer brought you back'.

> Tho' there's one motor gone,
> We can still carry on
> Comin' in on a wing and a pray'r.
>   Harold Adamson (song, 1943)

Economist (1967): 'The ITA's problem is to decide which applicants give most promise of maintaining an improvement over six years ... This is largely a wing and a prayer decision.'

With bated breath – *with breathing subdued or restrained under the influence of awe, terror, anxiety or other emotion*

'Bate' is a 14th-century verb meaning to lessen or deprive. It was used in many contexts: as 'abate' (c. 1325) in *Early English Alliterative Poems in the West-Midland Dialect* (1864): 'The rayne ... bated as fast'; as 'depress' in Samuel Rogers, 'An Inscription at Strathfieldsaye' (1834): 'On he went, / Bating nor heart nor hope'; or as 'reduce', as in John Locke's 'Raising the Value of Money' (1691): 'He must bate the Labourer's Wages.'

Edward A. Freeman, *The History of the Norman Conquest* (1872): 'It was whispered with bated breath that the vengeance for the blood of Waltheof had begun.'

With flying colours – *triumphantly, easily*

The allusion is to a victorious fleet sailing into port with flags still flying at the mastheads. The colours of a regiment or ship were the point about which the men could rally during the tumult of hand-to-hand warfare. They had to be defended at all costs, and their loss was a disgrace. While the colours were flying, victory was within one's grasp.

Augustus Jessop, *Arcady for Better or Worse* (1887): 'The tenant farmers …
do they come out of it with any flying colours?'

Wolf in sheep's clothing – *someone who is not as pleasant and harmless as first appears*

Aesop tells a fable about a wolf who, wrapped in a fleece, manages to sneak
into a sheepfold. Once inside he falls upon the sheep and devours them.

Matthew, 7:15: 'Beware of false prophets, which come to you in sheep's
clothing, but inwardly they are ravening wolves.'

Henry Fielding, *Amelia* (1751): 'There is the meekness of the clergyman.
There spoke the wolf in sheep's clothing.'

Wooden spoon – *a booby prize, last place*

A wooden spoon was traditionally given to the last of the Junior Optimes,
i.e. the lowest candidate of those taking honours in the Mathematics
Tripos at Cambridge University.

> Sure my invention must be down at zero
> And I grow one of many 'wooden spoons'
> Of verse (the name with which we Cantabs please
> To dub the last of honours in degrees).
> > Lord Byron, *Don Juan* (1820)

Westminster Gazette (1900): 'The international matches … have now all been
played … Ireland, who won the championship last year … have only 1
point and take the "wooden spoon".'

World is one's oyster – *the world offers one limitless opportunities, the chance to make one's own fortune*

The sense is that from the world can be extracted success and profit, as a
pearl can be extracted from an oyster. One can make of the world whatever one chooses through hard work and endeavour.

FALSTAFF: I will not lend thee a penny.
PISTOL: Why, then the world's mine oyster
Which I with sword will open.
>> Shakespeare, *The Merry Wives of Windsor* (1600)

Jonathan Gash, *The Judas Pair* (1977): 'The world was my oyster. My uneasy mood had vanished.'

Would not say 'bo' *or* 'boo' to a goose – *very timid*

The original phrase first appeared in writing in 1572 as 'shoo' to a goose, the expression used to drive away animals.

'Bo' or 'boh' was a combination of consonant and vowel especially fitted to produce a loud and startling sound. There is a link with the Latin *boare* and Greek *boaein*, both meaning to cry aloud, roar or shout.

Martin Marprelate, *Epitome of the First Book Written Against the Puritanes* (1588): 'He is not able to say bo to a goose.'

R.D. Blackmore, *Cradock Nowell* (1866): 'Bob could never say "bo" to a gosling of the feminine gender.'

Would not touch with a barge-pole – *wish to keep well away from, keep one's distance from someone or something one loathes or distrusts*

This is a 20th-century adaptation of an established saying. The earlier phrase (17th century) was 'would not touch with a pair of tongs'. The effect is to pile on the emphasis. Even a barge pole is too short a distance from this detestable or distrusted object.

Unknown author, *Wit Restor'd* (1658): 'Without a payre of tongs no man will touch her.'

Daily Mail (1991): 'A third former Foreign Secretary could stroll into the post to everyone's delight at Westminster, Hong Kong and Peking. But the ever-popular Lord Carrington has let it be known he would not touch it with a barge pole.'

Writing is on the wall – *calamity is imminent*

The Book of Daniel, chapter five, tells the story of Belshazzar, the last king of Babylon, who held a great feast. Wine was drunk from the vessels which his father had taken from the temple in Jerusalem.

During the feast, a man's hand appeared and wrote on the plaster on the wall, 'Mene, mene, tekel, upharsin', in Aramaic literally 'It has been counted and counted, weighed and divided', and thought to mean 'You have been weighed in the balance and found wanting'. The King asked Daniel to interpret the writing. Daniel prophesied that, because he had defiled the temple's vessels, Belshazzar would be overthrown. That night the King was killed and his kingdom divided.

Elizabeth Coxhead, *A Wind in the West* (1949): 'Just try to see the thing with your famous detachment, and you'll soon recognise the writing on the wall. You've had your fling.'

X

X marks the spot – *a specific location identified*

In ancient maps, the location of buried treasure was marked by a cross. However, the earliest recorded reference to the phrase is believed to be a letter from the novelist Maria Edgworth (1813): 'The three crosses X mark the three places where we were let in.'

The actual phrase, 'X marks the spot', appears to have originated with Chicago newspapers in the early days of gangsters. In 'Chicago Gang Wars, X Marks the Spot' (1930), it is clear that 'X' indicated the position of a dead body in a newspaper photograph of a murder scene. This was a time when newspapers shrank from publishing pictures of dead bodies.

As a result, in the slang of the period, 'spotted' came to mean murdered and 'to be put on the spot' took on a specific and sinister implication.

Barry Norman, *The Hounds of Sparta* (1968): 'A message from our alcoholic friend. X seems to mark the spot where he lives.'

Y

You scratch my back and I'll scratch yours – *if you help me, I will help you*

Apart from the self-explanatory literal meaning, it is suggested that the phrase may have originated with the harsh discipline in the British navy in the 17th and 18th centuries.

For often minor offences, a sailor was tied to the mast and flogged with the 'cat o' nine tails', nine lengths of thin knotted rope bound at one end into a handle. The punishment was administered by another member of the crew, who might himself, at another time, be on the receiving end of the flogging. He would therefore be lenient with his victim, applying light strokes and merely 'scratching' his back, so that, when his turn came, he would receive equally lenient treatment.

Alternatively, it may have a connection with an older phrase, 'Claw me and I'll claw thee', itself derived from Homer. 'Claw' in this sense means to flatter, and it appears in the form of 'to claw the back of' or 'to claw by the back'. The transition to 'scratch' would have been simple.

Sir Thomas Wyatt, 'Of the Feigned Friend' (c. 1541): '"Take heed of him who by the back thee claweth:" / For none is worse than is a friendly foe.'

Thomas Heywood, *Pleasant Dialogues and Drammas* (1637): 'These two betwixt themselves use Homer's phrase, / Claw me, I'le claw thee; / Let's live many days.'

Joseph Heller, *Catch-22* (1961): 'A little grease is what makes this world go round. One hand washes the other. Know what I mean? You scratch my back, I'll scratch yours.'

Appendix: Sources

(Numbers cited refer to list of sources key on pp. 342–5.)

A

A little bird told me – 13
Abominable snowman – 47, 51
Above board – 1, 2, 5, 10, 11
Ace in the hole – 1, 47
Achilles heel *or* tendon – 1, 2, 8, 11, 50
Acid test – 1, 58
Across the board – 1, 4, 11
Adam's ale – 13
Add insult to injury – 1, 2, 11
Adonis – 1, 2, 11
Against the grain – 1, 2, 11
Albatross around one's neck – 1, 2, 3, 11
Alive and kicking – 1, 2, 5, 11
All hell broke loose – 2, 3, 6, 11
All mouth and trousers – 5, 7, 11
All my eye and Betty Martin – 1, 13
All over bar the shouting – 47
All things to all men – 1, 11
Also ran – 1, 2, 5
Ambrosia – 1, 2
Annus mirabilis – 1, 2, 11
Answer's a lemon! – 1, 47, 83, 84
Any Tom, Dick or Harry – 1, 2, 11
Anyone we know? – 47
Apple of one's eye – 1, 2, 11, 13
Apple pie bed – 13
Apple pie order – 13
Arcadian – 1, 2, 11
Armed to the teeth – 1, 2, 11
Arms akimbo – 1, 2, 7, 11

As sure as eggs is eggs – 1, 2, 11
As the actress said to the bishop – 5, 11
As the crow flies – 13
At a loose end – 1, 2, 11
At one fell swoop – 1, 11
At sixes and sevens – 1, 2, 7, 11
At the drop of a hat – 1, 2, 11
At the eleventh hour – 1, 2, 11
At the end of one's tether – 1, 2, 11
Aunt Sally – 1, 2, 11
Axe to grind – 1, 2, 6, 11

B

Back to square one – 1, 2, 11
Back to the wall – 1, 2
Badger – 1, 2
Bag and baggage – 1, 2, 11
Baker's dozen – 1, 2, 11
Balloon goes up – 1, 2, 8, 11
Ballpark figure – 1
Balls to the wall – 11, 37
Ballyhoo – 1, 2, 7, 11
Baloney – 1, 11
Bandy words – 1, 2, 11
Bank on – 1, 2, 11
Bark up the wrong tree – 1, 2, 11
Barmy – 1, 2, 47
Barrack – 1, 2, 11, 94
Basket case – 47, 58
Battle-axe – 1, 11, 69
Be at large – 1, 58
Be at loggerheads – 1, 2, 11

Be on the side of the angels – 13
Bean-feast – 1, 2, 9, 11
Beat around the bush – 1, 2, 11
Beck and call – 1, 11
Bedlam – 1, 2, 11, 70
Bee in one's bonnet – 1, 2, 5
Bee's knees – 1, 8, 11
Before *or* quicker than you can say Jack Robinson – 1, 43
Beg the question – 7
Believe that all one's geese were swans – 1, 2, 11
Bells and whistles – 11
Below the salt – 1, 2
Best bib and tucker – 1, 13
Best laid plans of mice and men (go oft astray) – 6, 22
Between a rock and a hard place – 1, 11
Between the devil and the deep blue sea – 1, 2, 5, 8, 11
Between you, me and the gatepost – 1, 2, 11
Beware Greeks bearing gifts – 47
Beyond the pale – 1, 7, 11
Big cheese – 1, 2, 11
Bill stickers will be prosecuted – 47
Black hole of Calcutta – 1, 2
Black Maria – 7
Black sheep – 1, 2, 11
Blackball – 1, 2, 11
Blackguard – 1, 2, 11
Blackleg – 1, 2, 11
Blacklist – 1, 2, 11
Blaze a trail – 1, 2, 11
Blighty – 1, 2, 8, 11
Blot on the landscape – 1, 47
Blow hot and cold – 1, 2, 5, 11
Blow the gaff – 1, 2, 5, 11
Blow to smithereens – 1
Blue blooded – 1, 2, 11

Blue Ribbon – 13, 64
Blue stocking – 1, 2, 11
Blue-chip – 13
Blurb – 1, 2, 11
Bob's your uncle – 1, 2, 11
Boffin – 1, 2, 11
Bog-standard – 7
Bold as brass – 1, 58
Boot is on the other foot – 13
Born on the wrong side of the blanket – 1, 13
Bottle – 1, 5, 11
Brand (spanking) new – 1, 2, 11
Break a leg – 7, 11
Break the mould – 47
Bring home the bacon – 1, 2, 9, 11, 47
Broken reed – 2, 11
Bucket shops – 1, 5, 11
Buggins' turn – 1, 2, 5, 11
Bulldog breed – 47
Burn the candle at both ends – 39, 48
Bury the hatchet – 2, 8, 10, 11
Busman's holiday – 1, 7, 11
By and large – 1, 58
By hook or by crook – 1, 2, 11
By Jingo – 1, 5, 11
By Jove – 1, 5, 11
By the seat of one's pants – 1, 5, 11
By the skin of one's teeth – 2, 11

C
Cack-handed – 1, 5, 11
Call a spade a spade – 1, 2, 7, 11
Call one's bluff – 1, 5, 11
Carry the can – 1, 2, 5, 11
Carte blanche – 1, 2, 8, 11
Cast aspersions – 1, 11
Cat has nine lives – 47, 49
Catch red-handed – 1
Catch-22 – 1, 2, 8, 11
Chalk and cheese – 1, 11

Chance one's arm – 1, 2, 5, 11
Charity begins at home – 1, 2, 11
Che sera sera – 47
Cheap at half the price – 7, 11
Cheesed off – 2, 11
Chew the fat – 7
Chinese fire drill – 11, 39
Chip off the old block – 13
Chip on one's shoulder – 1, 11
Chock-full; chock-a-block – 1, 2, 5, 11
Chopping and changing – 1, 2, 11
Clapped out – 1, 5, 11
Clean bill of health – 1, 11
Cleanliness is next to godliness – 1, 2, 11, 12
Climb on the bandwagon – 13
Close your eyes and think of England – 1, 13
Cloud-cuckoo-land – 1, 2, 11
Cock a snook – 1, 13
Cock and bull story – 2, 11
Cock a hoop – 1, 2, 11
Codswallop – 1, 2, 5, 11
Cold enough to freeze the balls off a brass monkey – 7, 11
Cold feet – 2, 5, 11
Cold shoulder – 1, 2, 5, 11
Cold turkey – 2, 5, 11
Cold-blooded – 1, 2, 11, 36
Come a cropper – 1, 5, 11
Come Hell or high water – 26, 47
Cook someone's goose – 13, 24
Cost an arm and a leg – 5, 11
Cotton on – 1, 2, 5, 11
Couldn't run a whelk stall – 1, 47
Criss-cross – 1, 2, 5, 11
Crocodile tears – 1, 2, 11
Cross the Rubicon – 47
Cuckoo in the nest – 1, 11
Curate's egg – 26
Curry favour – 7, 13

Cut and dried – 1, 2
Cut and run – 13
Cut no ice – 13
Cut the mustard – 1, 2, 7, 11
Cut to the chase – 11, 40
Cut to the quick – 1, 2, 11

D

Dark horse – 1, 2, 5, 11
Davy Jones's locker – 7, 66
Dead as a dodo – 1, 2, 11
Dead as a door-nail – 1, 2, 11
Dead ringer – 1, 2, 5, 11, 58, 65
Dead to the world – 1, 2, 11
Devil to pay – 1, 11
Devil's advocate – 1, 2, 11
Die is cast – 47, 85
Die-hard – 1, 2, 11
Disgusted of Tunbridge Wells – 47
Dog in a manger – 14, 71
Dog days – 1, 2, 11, 72
Dog's life – 1, 2, 11
Donkey's years – 1, 13
Doolally *or* Doolally tap – 1, 2, 5, 11, 26, 58, 73, 74
Dot the i's and cross the t's – 1, 2, 11
Double whammy – 1, 11, 35
Double-cross – 7
Doubting Thomas – 1, 11
Down in the dumps – 1, 2, 11
Dressed up like a dog's dinner *or* breakfast – 1, 5, 47
Dressed (up) to the nines – 1, 2, 5, 11, 75
Drinking a toast – 1, 2, 11
Dumbing down – 47
Dutch courage – 1, 2, 11

E

Eagle-eyed – 1, 2
Ear to the ground – 1

Earmark – 1
Ears are burning – 1, 2
Eat humble pie – 1, 2, 5
Eat your heart out – 1, 2
Egg on – 1, 2
Egg on one's face – 13
Emperor's new clothes – 11
Essex girl – 47, 86
Exception proves the rule – 7, 61

F

Face the music – 1, 2
Fag-end – 1, 2
Fair game – 1, 2
Fall on deaf ears – 1, 2
Feather in one's cap – 13
Feet of clay – 1, 2
Fiddle while Rome burns – 2, 41
Filthy lucre – 13
Finger in the *or* every pie – 13
First-rate – 1
Fit as a fiddle – 1, 2, 5
Flash Harry – 1, 47, 52
Flash in the pan – 1, 2
Flotsam and jetsam – 1, 2, 13
Fly a kite – 1, 2, 5
Fly in the ointment – 1, 13
Fly off the handle – 1, 13
Foot the bill – 1, 2, 5
Footloose and fancy free – 1, 13
Fork out – 1, 2, 5
Forty winks – 1, 2, 5
Fresh as a daisy – 1
From pillar to post – 1, 2
From the horse's mouth – 1, 13
Full Monty – 7
Full of beans – 9, 18, 25

G

Get down to brass tacks – 13
Get down to the nitty-gritty – 1, 5, 11

Get hold of the wrong end of the stick
    – 1, 76
Get on one's wick – 1, 47
Get out of bed on the wrong side – 1, 2
Get someone's goat – 14, 47, 49
Get the bird – 1, 47
Get the sack – 1, 2
Gird up your loins – 1, 2
Give a tinker's dam *or* damn – 1, 12
Give one a break – 5
Give one the willies – 1, 2, 5
Give the thumbs up *or* down – 1, 2
Go AWOL – 11
Go bananas – 1, 2, 5
Go berserk – 1, 2
Go by the board – 1, 2
Go for a Burton – 13
Go haywire – 1, 2, 5
Go on a Cook's tour – 47, 53
Go the whole hog – 1, 2, 5, 10
Go to the wall – 1, 58
Go with the flow – 58, 59
Gone to pot – 2, 5, 9, 10, 11, 13
Gone west – 1, 58
Good egg – 13
Good health! – 58
Goody Two-Shoes – 1, 2
Gordon Bennett – 5, 26, 42, 43, 67
Got my dander up – 1, 2
Grasp the nettle – 1, 2
Grass widow – 7
Great Scott! – 2, 44
Green with envy – 2
Grin like a Cheshire cat – 7
Groggy – 1, 2, 68
Guinea pig – 7
Gung-ho – 1, 5
Gutter press – 1, 2

H

Had one's chips – 1, 58

Hail from – 1, 2
Hair of the dog – 1, 2
Halcyon days – 13
Ham actor – 1, 7, 13
Hang fire – 13
Hangdog look – 13
Hanged, drawn and quartered – 1, 2
Hanky-panky – 13
Happy as a clam – 7
Happy as a sand-boy – 1, 2
Happy as Larry – 1, 2, 5
Hat trick – 1, 2
Haul somebody over the coals – 1, 2
Have a beef – 1, 58
Have a dekko – 1, 58
Have one's work cut out – 1, 2
Heath Robinson – 47, 54
Hide one's light under a bushel – 1, 2
High jinks – 13
Hobson's choice – 1, 2
Hocus-pocus – 1, 2, 13
Hoi polloi – 1, 2
Hoist with one's own petard – 1, 2
Hold the fort – 1, 58
Holy Grail – 1, 2
Hook, line and sinker – 13
How the other half lives – 58, 77
Hunch – 1, 2

I

If the cap fits – 1, 2
If the mountain will not come to
    Mohammed – 1, 2
Illegitimi non carborundum – 47, 88
In a cleft stick – 1, 2
In a jiffy – 58, 60
In a pickle – 1, 2
In a shambles – 1, 58, 78
In cahoots – 1, 58
In clink – 1, 2, 5, 87
In limbo – 1, 2

In one's black books – 1, 2
In the bag – 1
In the cart – 1, 2
In the dog-house – 1, 2
In the doldrums – 1
In the nick of time – 1, 2
In the offing – 1, 58
In the pink – 1, 2
In two shakes of a lamb's tail – 24,
    47
Indian giver – 1, 2
Indian summer – 1, 2, 89
Irons in the fire – 1, 2
It just growed like Topsy – 1, 2
It's not *or* it ain't over until the fat lady
    sings – 2, 26
Ivory tower – 1, 2

J

Jerry-built – 12, 38
Jot and tittle – 11

K

Kangaroo court – 1, 2, 26, 38
Keep at bay – 1, 2
Keep mum – 1, 2
Keep one's pecker up – 1, 2, 5
Keep the wolf from the door – 1, 2, 13
Keep up with the Joneses – 2, 5
Keep your shirt on – 1, 2, 5
Kick the bucket – 1, 2, 5
Kill the goose which lays the golden
    eggs – 13
Kilroy was here – 62
Knock into a cocked hat – 1, 2, 5
Knock off work – 1, 47
Knock seven bells out of – 47
Knock the gilt off the gingerbread –
    1, 2
Knuckle down *or* under – 47, 55
Kowtow to – 1, 2

L
La-di-da, Lah-di-dah – 1, 2, 5
Lame duck – 1, 2, 5
Lark about – 1, 2, 5
Last *or* final straw – 1, 2
Laughing up one's sleeve – 1, 2
Lead someone up *or* down the garden
   (-path) – 1, 2
Leave in the lurch – 1, 2
Let the cat out of the bag – 2, 5
Lick into shape – 1, 2
Life is just a bowl of cherries – 47
Like Billy-o *or* Billio *or* Billyoh – 1, 2
Lion's share – 47, 56
Live the life of Riley – 2
Load of cobblers – 2, 5
Lock, stock and barrel – 1, 2
Look a gift horse in the mouth – 1, 2
Loose cannon – 11
Lose one's marbles – 47
Lynch law – 1, 2, 7

M
Mad as a hatter – 2
Make a bee line – 13
Make a hash of something – 1
Make a mountain out of a molehill – 1,
   2
Make a pig's ear – 2
Make bricks without straw – 1, 2, 79
Make ends meet – 1
Make no bones about – 1, 5
Make the grade – 5
Male chauvinist (pig) *or* MCP – 47
Man in a grey *or* dark suit – 47
Man on the Clapham omnibus – 47
Mata Hari – 1, 2
Mealy mouthed – 1, 58
Mickey Finn – 5, 58
Might as well be hanged for a sheep as
   a lamb – 1

Mind one's P's and Q's – 2
Miss the bus – 1, 2, 5
Moaning Minnie – 1, 2, 5
Molly-coddle – 1, 2
Moot point – 1, 2
More … than you can shake a stick at
   – 1, 2
Mount a boycott – 1, 47, 57, 58
Mumbo-jumbo – 1, 2, 80
Murphy's law – 1, 2, 5

N
Namby-pamby – 1, 2, 5
Name is mud – 1, 5, 81
Neck and crop – 1, 2, 5
Neck of the woods – 1, 58
Nine days' wonder – 11
Nineteen to the dozen – 1, 5
No flies on (someone) – 1, 58
No great shakes – 1, 12
No man's land – 1, 2
No names, no pack-drill – 1, 47
No stone unturned – 1, 2, 58
Nose to the grindstone – 1, 2
Nosey parker – 1, 2, 5
Not a sausage – 1, 2, 5
Not enough room to swing a cat – 1, 2
Not fit to hold a candle – 1, 2
Not on your Nellie *or* Nelly – 1, 2, 5
Not to mince words *or* matters – 1, 2
Not worth his salt – 1, 2
Nutty as a fruitcake – 1, 2, 5

O
Of the first water – 1, 2
Off the cuff – 1, 2
Old Bill *or* the Bill – 1, 2, 5
Old chestnut – 14
On cloud nine – 1, 2, 5
On one's beam-ends – 1, 2, 5
On one's hobby-horse – 1, 2

On one's tod – 1, 2, 5, 82
On tenterhooks – 1, 2
On the cards – 1, 2
On the grape-vine – 1, 2, 5
On the horns of a dilemma – 1, 2
On the treadmill – 1, 58
On the wagon – 1, 5
Once in a blue moon – 1, 2, 5, 45
One over the eight – 1, 2, 5
One swallow does not make a summer
   or a summer make – 1, 2
Open Sesame – 1, 2
Over a barrel – 13
Over the moon – 1, 2
Over the top *or* OTT – 47, 90

P
Paddle one's own canoe – 1, 2, 13
Paint the town red – 1, 2
Palm off – 1, 2
Pandora's box – 1, 2
Pardon my *or* the French – 1, 5
Pass the buck – 1, 2
Pay on the nail – 1, 2
Pay through the nose – 2
Pear-shaped – 9
Pecking order – 1, 2
Peeping tom – 1, 2
Pell-mell – 1
Penny has dropped – 1, 2, 13
Phoenix from the ashes – 1, 2
Pidgin English – 1, 2
Pie in the sky – 1, 2
Piece of cake – 1, 2, 5
Pie-eyed – 1
Pig in a poke – 1, 2
Pigeon-hole – 1, 2
Pin money – 1, 2
Pipe down – 1, 2
Pipe dream – 1, 2
Piping hot – 1, 2

Pissed as a newt – 1, 5
Plain as a pikestaff – 1, 13
Plain sailing – 1, 2
Play ducks and drakes – 1
Play fast and loose – 1, 2
Play havoc – 1, 2
Pleased as Punch – 1, 2
Ploughman's lunch – 1
Plug a song *or* book – 1, 58
Plumb the depths – 1, 2
Point-blank – 1, 58
Possession is nine points of the law – 1,
   11, 47
Post-haste – 1, 58
Pour cold water on – 1, 11
Pour oil on troubled waters – 1, 2, 63
Pretty *or* fine *or* rare kettle of fish – 1,
   2, 5
Pull one's finger out – 1, 2, 14
Pull one's weight – 1, 2
Pull out all the stops – 1, 2
Pull someone's leg – 1, 2, 5
Pull the chestnuts out of the fire – 1, 2,
   15
Pull the wool over someone's eyes –
   1, 2
Purple patch *or* passage – 1, 2
Push the boat out – 1, 2
Push the envelope – 16
Put a sock in it – 1, 2, 5
Put a spoke in someone's wheel – 1, 47
Put on one's thinking cap – 1, 2, 5, 17
Put one's dukes *or* dooks up – 1, 47
Put one's foot in it – 13
Put one's shoulder to the wheel – 1, 2
Put the dampers on – 13
Put the kibosh on – 1, 5

Q
Queer someone's pitch – 1, 58
Queer Street – 1, 11

R

Rack and ruin – 1, 2
Rack one's brains – 1, 2
Rain cats and dogs – 2, 13
Rat race – 1, 2
Rats leaving a sinking ship – 1, 11
Read the riot act – 1, 58
Real McCoy – 1, 2, 5
Red herring – 1, 2
Red tape – 1, 13
Red-letter day – 1, 2
Redneck – 1, 2
Ride roughshod over – 1, 2, 13
Right as ninepence – 1, 2
Ring a bell – 1, 2, 13, 18
Ring true *or* have the ring of truth – 1, 2
Rip van Winkle – 2
Rob Peter to pay Paul – 1, 2, 13
Round robin – 1, 2
Round the bend – 1
Rub salt in the wound – 1, 2
Rule of thumb – 1, 2, 7, 13
Rule the roost – 1, 58, 61
Run amok – 1, 2
Run for one's money – 1, 2, 5
Run the gamut – 1, 2
Run the gauntlet – 1, 2
Run to earth – 1, 2
Run-of-the-mill – 1, 2

S

Safe pair of hands – 30
Sail near *or* close to the wind – 1, 2
Salad days – 1, 2
Salt of the earth – 1
Save one's bacon – 2, 13, 19
Saved by the bell – 1, 58
Scapegoat – 1, 2
Scarlet woman – 1, 2
Score a duck – 1, 2

Scot-free – 1, 2, 13
Seamy side – 1, 2
See a man about a dog – 5
See Naples and die – 47, 91, 92
Sell down the river – 1, 2
Sell one's birthright for a mess of pottage – 1, 2
Send to Coventry – 1, 2, 5
Separate the sheep from the goats – 31
Separate the wheat from the chaff – 1
Set off on the right *or* wrong foot – 1, 2
Set one's cap at – 1, 2, 47
Settle a score *or* Pay off an old score – 1, 2
Seventh heaven – 1, 2
Shanks's pony – 1, 2, 5
Shell out – 1, 2
Shilly-shally – 1, 2
Ship-shape and Bristol fashion – 1, 2, 95
Short shrift – 1, 2
Show a leg – 1, 2
Show the white feather – 1, 2, 20
Sick as a parrot – 13
Sign *or* take the pledge – 1, 2
Skeleton in the closet *or* cupboard – 1, 2
Skid row – 1, 2, 5
Slap-up meal – 1, 2, 5, 19
Sleep like a top – 1, 2
Sleep tight – 1, 2
Sling one's hook – 1, 2, 5
Slush fund – 1, 2, 5, 93
Smart Alec – 1, 2, 7
Smell a rat – 1, 2
Smoking gun – 1
Soap opera – 1, 2
Soft soap – 1, 2, 5
Sold for a song – 1, 2
Son of a gun – 1, 2, 5
Sow one's wild oats – 1, 2

Spick and span – 1, 2
Spill the beans – 1, 2, 5
Spin a yarn – 1, 2
Spitting image – 1, 2, 5, 46
Splice the main-brace – 47
Spoil the ship for a ha'porth of tar – 1, 2
Square meal – 7
Stalking horse – 1, 13
Stamping ground – 1, 5
Start from scratch – 1, 2
Steal a march on – 1, 2
Steal someone's thunder – 1, 2
Sterling qualities – 1, 2
Stick one's neck out – 1, 2
Stiff upper lip – 1, 2, 8
Stony broke – 1
Stool pigeon – 1
Storm in a teacup – 13
Strait-laced – 1
Straw poll – 1
Streets paved with gold – 21
Stuffed shirt – 1
Stumbling block – 1
Stump up – 1
Stymied – 1
Swan-song – 32
Swashbuckler – 1
Sweet Fanny Adams *or* Sweet FA – 1, 5
Swing the lead – 1, 8
Sword of Damocles – 1, 2, 13

T
Take a *or* the back seat – 1
Take a rain-check – 1, 5
Take a shufti – 1, 47
Take down a peg – 1, 2, 8
Take French leave – 1, 2
Take something with a grain *or* pinch of salt – 1, 2, 58
Take the bull by the horns – 1

Take the cake *or* the biscuit – 1, 5
Take the mickey – 1, 5, 26
Take umbrage – 1, 58
Taken aback – 13
Taken to the cleaners – 13
Talk gibberish – 1
Talk the hind legs off a donkey – 1, 2
Talk turkey – 1, 2, 5
Tarred with the same brush – 1, 13
Teach one's grandmother to suck eggs – 1, 13
Tell it *or* that to the Marines – 1, 2, 5
That's (just) the ticket – 1, 2, 5, 25
There's more than one way to skin a cat – 24, 26
There's no such thing as a free lunch – 27, 28
Third degree – 1, 2, 5
Three R's – 13
Three sheets to *or* in the wind 1, 2
Tie the knot – 1, 2
Tilt at windmills – 29
Tired and emotional – 47
Tit for tat – 1, 2
To a T – 1, 11
To boot – 1, 2
To the bitter end – 1, 13
Toe the line – 1, 2, 5
Tongue-in-cheek – 1, 2
Touch and go – 1, 2
Touch wood – 1, 2
Trip the light fantastic – 13
Turn a blind eye – 1, 2
Turn over a new leaf – 1, 13
Turn the tables – 1, 7
Turn turtle – 1, 2
Turn up for the books – 1, 2, 26

U
Uncle Sam – 1, 2
Uncle Tom – 33

Up a gum-tree – 1, 2, 47
Up the spout – 1, 2
Up to scratch – 1, 2
Upper crust – 1, 2

V
Vent one's spleen – 1
Vice versa – 1, 2
Voice crying in the wilderness – 11

W
Walk over one's grave – 1
Warm the cockles of your heart 1, 2
Warp and woof – 1
Warts and all – 1, 13
Wash one's dirty linen in public – 1, 2
Wear one's heart on one's sleeve – 2
Wear sackcloth and ashes – 1, 13
Weasel words – 12
Welsh rabbit – 1, 2, 7
Wet behind the ears – 1, 2, 5
What the dickens! – 2
Wheeler-dealer – 1, 2, 7
Whipping boy – 1, 2
Whip-round – 1, 2, 7
Whistle for it *or* whistle for the wind –
    1, 2, 7
White elephant – 1, 2

Whited sepulchre – 13
Whole caboodle – 1, 2, 34
Whole nine yards – 1, 5
Widow's weeds – 1, 2
Wild goose chase – 1, 2
Will o' the wisp – 1
Willy-nilly – 1, 2
Win hands down – 1, 2
Win one's spurs – 1, 2
Wind of change – 1
Wing and a prayer – 1
With bated breath – 1
With flying colours – 1, 2
Wolf in sheep's clothing – 1, 13
Wooden spoon – 1, 2
World is one's oyster – 1, 2
Would not say 'bo' *or* 'boo' to a goose
    – 1
Would not touch with a barge-pole – 1,
    13
Writing is on the wall – 1, 2, 4

X
X marks the spot – 47

Y
You scratch my back and I'll scratch
    yours – 1

Key

1 *Oxford English Dictionary*, 2nd edition, 1989
2 *Brewer's Dictionary of Phrase and Fable*, 15th edition, 1995
3 *Oxford Companion to English Literature*, 4th edition, 1969
4 *Webster's Dictionary*, 2nd edition, 1950
5 *Dictionary of Slang and Unconventional English*, Eric Partridge, 8th edition,
    ed. Paul Beale, Routledge, 1984
6 *Bartlett's Familiar Quotations*, 14th edition, Little, Brown, 1968
7 *POSH*, Michael Quinion, Penguin, 2004
8 *Swinging the Lead and Spiking his Guns*, Past Times, 2000
9 *Bringing Home the Bacon and Cutting the Mustard*, Past Times, 2000

10 *The Whole Hog*, Oliver Dalton and Gray Jolliffe, Corgi Books, 1987

11 www.users.tinyonline.co.uk

12 www.phrases.org.uk

13 *Dictionary of Idioms*, Linda and Roger Flavell, Kyle Cathie, 1992

14 Copyright © 1995–2004 WordWizard Ltd; info@wordwizard.com

15 www.geocities.com

16 Mark Israel, *alt.usage.english FAQ file* (line 5211), 29 Sept 1997

17 *The American Heritage ® Dictionary of Idioms*, Christine Ammer; copyright
    © 1997 The Christine Ammer 1992 Trust; Houghton Mifflin Company

18 *Heavens to Betsy! and Other Curious Sayings*, Charles Earle Funk, Harper
    Resource, 1955

19 *A Classical Dictionary of the Vulgar Tongue*, Francis Grose, Barnes and Noble,
    1963

20 www.spartacus.schoolnet.co.uk/FWWfeather.htm

21 www.longlongtimeago.com

22 www.bartleby.com

23 *Encyclopedia of Word and Phrase Origins*, Robert Hendrickson, Facts on File, 1997

24 *Hog on Ice*, Charles Earle Funk, Harper and Row, 1948

25 *The Slang Dictionary*, John Camden Hotten, Chatto and Windus, 1859, 1860

26 www.worldwidewords.org; copyright © Michael Quinion 1996–2004

27 www.businessballs.com

28 www.jstor.org

29 www.brainyencyclopedia.com

30 www.middlesexccc.com

31 www.godsview.com

32 www.aesopfables.com

33 *The New Dictionary of Cultural Literacy*, 3rd edition, E.D. Hirsch, Jr, Joseph F.
    Kett, James Trefil (eds); copyright © 2002 by Houghton Mifflin Company;
    all rights reserved

34 www.freedict.com

35 www.bbc.co.uk/election97

36 www.en.wikepedia.org

37 *The Random House Historical Dictionary of American Slang*, two volumes 1994–1997

38 www.wordorigins.org

39 www.randomhouse.com

40 www.yaelf.com

41 http://fbc.binghamton.edu/commentr.htm

42 *The Scandalous Mr Bennett*, R. O'Connor, Doubleday, 1962; *The James Gordon
    Bennetts*, D.C. Seitz, Bobbs-Merrill, 1928, 1973

43 www.peevish.co.uk

44 www.ngeorgia.com/other/scottinmexico.html

45 www.sfgate.com/cgi-bin/article.cgi?f=/c/a/2003/10/26/MO305198.DTL

46 www.museum.tv/archives/etv/S/htmlS/spittingimag/spittingimag.htm

47 *Cassell's Dictionary of Word and Phrase Origins*, Nigel Rees, Cassell, 1996

48 *An Universal Etymological English Dictionary*, Nathan (or Nathaniel) Bailey, printed for E. Bell, J. Darby, A. Bettesworth, etc., 1721

49 *The Book of Why*, Robert L. Shook, Hammond, 1983

50 www.wordexplorations.info/Achilles-heel-story.html

51 www.occultopedia.com/a/abominable_snowman.htm

52 www.bach-cantatas.com/Bio/Sargent-Malcolm.htm

53 www.suite101.com/article.cfm/3550/32110

54 www.bpib.com/illustrat/whrobin.htm

55 www.computerweekly.com/Article103000.htm

56 www.pacificnet.net/~johnr/aesop/aesop3.html

57 www.con-suming.com/Keys_of_successful_boycott.htm

58 *Red Herrings and White Elephants*, Albert Jack, Metro, 2004

59 http://campus.northpark.edu/history/WebChron/Mediterranean/MAurelius.html

60 www.unc.edu/~rowlett/units/dictJ.html

61 *Modern English Usage*, H.W. Fowler, Clarendon Press, 1926

62 www.kilroywashere.org/001-Pages/01-0KilroyLegends.html

63 www.lindisfarne.org.uk/general/aidan.htm

64 www.debretts.co.uk/etiquette/order_of_the_garter.html

65 www.randomhouse.com/wotd/index.pperl?date=20010515

66 http://ask.yahoo.com/ask/20000831.html

67 http://en.wikipedia.org/wiki/James_Gordon_Bennett_Jr.

68 www.vernon-arms.co.uk/The_History.ihtml

69 www.amazonation.com/BattleAxe.html

70 www.newadvent.org/cathen/02387b.htm

71 www.clearyworks.com

72 www.souledout.org/cosmology/sirius/siriusgodstar.html

73 www.wordsmith.org/words/doolally.html

74 www.far-eastern-heroes.org.uk/alberts_war/html/doolally_tap.htm

75 www.thewardrobe.org.uk/wiltshireregiment.php3

76 www.crystalinks.com/romebaths.html

77 www.spartacus.schoolnet.co.uk/USAriis.htm

78 www.britainexpress.com/cities/york/shambles.htm

79 www.keyway.ca/htm2000/20000926.htm

80 www.fvza.org/mungo.html

81 www.law.umkc.edu/faculty/projects/ftrials/lincolnconspiracy/mudd.html

82 www.imh.org/imh/kyhpl5b

83 www.defect.com/Lemonlaw.htm#state_law

84 Copyright © 2000, 2001, 2002, 2003 by Law Offices of T. Michael Flinn

85 www.phrases.org.uk/bulletin_board/7/messages/741.html

86 Copyright © Germaine Greer, 2001. Taken from article 'Long Live the Essex Girl', first published in the *Guardian*, 5 March 2001

87 www.london-se1.co.uk/attractions/clink.html

88 *Safire's New Political Dictionary*, William Safire, Random House, 1993

89 www.jamestownri.com/library/museum.htm

90 http://news.bbc.co.uk/1/hi/special_report/1998/10/98/world_war_i/194197.stm

91 www.succulent-plant.com/ephemera02.html

92 www.kirjasto.sci.fi/virgil.htm

93 *Safire's Political Dictionary*, William Safire, Random House, 1978

94 www.anu.edu.au

95 http://timworstall.typepad.com

Index of Key Words

A

Aback, *see* Taken aback
All to pot, *see* Gone to pot
Amok, *see* Run amok
Angels, *see* Be on the side of the angels
Arm and a leg, *see* Cost an arm and a leg
As happy as a clam, *see* Happy as a clam
As happy as a sandboy, *see* Happy as a sandboy
As happy as Larry, *see* Happy as Larry
As mad as a hatter, *see* Mad as a hatter
Aspersions, *see* Cast aspersions
At bay *see* Keep at bay
At large, *see* Be at large
At loggerheads, *see* Be at loggerheads
AWOL, *see* Go AWOL
Axe to grind, *see* Have an axe to grind

B

Back, *see* You scratch my back and I'll scratch yours
Back seat, *see* Take a back seat
Bacon, *see* Save one's bacon
Bananas, *see* Go bananas
Bandwagon, *see* Climb on the bandwagon
Barge-pole, *see* Would not touch with a barge-pole
Barrel, *see* Over a barrel
Bated breath, *see* With bated breath
Beam-ends, *see* On one's beam-ends
Beans, *see* Spill the beans
Beef, *see* Have a beef

Bee line, *see* Make a bee line
Bell, *see* Saved by the bell
Berserk, *see* Go berserk
Bill, *see* Old Bill
Billy-o, *see* Like Billy-o
Bird, *see* A little bird told me
Bird, *see* Get the bird
Birthright, *see* Sell one's birthright for a mess of pottage
Biscuit, *see* Take the cake/biscuit
Bitter end, *see* To the bitter end
Black books, *see* In one's black books
Blind eye, *see* Turn a blind eye
Blue moon, *see* Once in a blue moon
Bluff, *see* Call one's bluff
Board, *see* Above board
Board, *see* Go by the board
Boat, *see* Push the boat out
Bones, *see* Make no bones about
Books, *see* Turn up for the books
Bowl of cherries, *see* Life is just a bowl of cherries
Boycott, *see* Mount a boycott
Brass monkey, *see* Cold enough to freeze …
Brass tacks, *see* Get down to brass tacks
Break, *see* Give one a break
Bricks without straw, *see* Make bricks without straw
Broke, *see* Stony broke
Brush, *see* Tarred with the same brush
Buck, *see* Pass the buck
Bull, *see* Take the bull by the horns
Burton, *see* Go for a burton

C

Caboodle, *see* Whole caboodle
Cahoots, *see* In cahoots
Cake, *see* Take the cake/biscuit
Candle, *see* Not fit to hold a candle
Canoe, *see* Paddle one's own canoe
Cap, *see* Put on one's thinking cap
Cat, *see* Grin like a Cheshire cat
Cat, *see* Let the cat out of the bag
Cat, *see* Not enough room to swing a cat
Cat, *see* There's more than one way to skin a cat
Cats, *see* Rain cats and dogs
Change, *see* Wind of change
Chase, *see* Cut to the chase
Chase, *see* Wild goose chase
Chestnut, *see* Old chestnut
Chestnuts, *see* Pull the chestnuts out of the fire
Chips, *see* Had one's chips
Cleaners, *see* Taken to the cleaners
Cleft stick, *see* In a cleft stick
Clink, *see* In clink
Close to the wind, *see* Sail near *or* close to the wind
Cloud nine, *see* On cloud nine
Cobblers, *see* Load of (old) cobblers
Cocked hat, *see* Knock into a cocked hat
Cockles of your heart, *see* Warm the cockles …
Cold water, *see* Pour cold water on
Cook's tour, *see* Go on a Cook's tour
Crop, *see* Neck and crop
Cropper, *see* Come a cropper
Cupboard, *see* Skeleton in the cupboard

D

Damocles, *see* Sword of Damocles

Dampers, *see* Put the dampers on
Dander, *see* Got my dander up
Deaf ears, *see* Fall on deaf ears
Degree, *see* Third degree
Dekko, *see* Have a dekko
Dilemma, *see* On the horns of a dilemma
Dirty linen, *see* Wash one's dirty linen in public
Dodo, *see* Dead as a dodo
Dog, *see* See a man about a dog
Doghouse, *see* In the doghouse
Dogs, *see* Rain cats and dogs
Dog's breakfast *or* dinner, *see* Dressed up like a dog's …
Doldrums, *see* In the doldrums
Donkey, *see* Talk the hind legs off a donkey
Dooks, *see* Put one's dukes *or* dooks up
Door-nail, *see* Dead as a door-nail
Dozen, *see* Baker's dozen
Dozen, *see* Nineteen to the dozen
Duck, *see* Score a duck
Ducks and drakes, *see* Play ducks and drakes
Dukes, *see* Put one's dukes *or* dooks up
Dumps, *see* Down in the dumps

E

Eggs, *see* As sure as eggs is eggs
Eggs, *see* Kill the goose which lays the golden eggs
Eggs, *see* Teach one's grandmother to suck eggs
Eleventh hour, *see* At the eleventh hour
Emotional, *see* Tired and emotional
End of one's tether, *see* At the end of one's tether
Envelope, *see* Push the envelope

F

Fancy free, *see* Footloose and fancy free

Fanny Adams, *see* Sweet Fanny Adams/Sweet FA

Fast and loose, *see* Play fast and loose

Fat lady, *see* It's not (It ain't) over until the fat lady sings

Final straw, *see* Last straw

Fine kettle of fish *see* Pretty kettle of fish

Finger, *see* Pull one's finger out

First water, *see* Of the first water

Flies, *see* No flies on someone

Flying colours, *see* With flying colours

Foot, *see* Put one's foot in it

Free lunch, *see* There's no such thing as a free lunch

Freeze the balls off a brass monkey, *see* Cold enough to freeze …

French leave, *see* Take French leave

Fruitcake, *see* Nutty as a fruitcake

G

Gaff, *see* Blow the gaff

Gamut, *see* Run the gamut

Garden (-path), *see* Lead someone up *or* down the garden (-path)

Geese are swans, *see* Believe all one's geese were swans

Gibberish, *see* Talk gibberish

Gift horse, *see* Look a gift horse in the mouth

Gilt off the gingerbread, *see* Knock the gilt off the gingerbread

Go for a song, *see* Sold for a song

Gold, *see* Streets paved with gold

Golden, *see* Kill the goose which lays the golden eggs

Goose, *see* Kill the goose which lays the golden eggs

Goose, *see* Would not say 'boo' to a goose

Grade, *see* Make the grade

Grain, *see* Against the grain

Grandmother, *see* Teach one's grandmother to suck eggs

Grapevine, *see* On the grapevine

Grave, *see* Walk over one's grave

Great shakes, *see* No great shakes

Grindstone, *see* Nose to the grindstone

Ground, *see* Stamping ground

Growed like Topsy, *see* It just growed like Topsy

Gum-tree, *see* Up a gum-tree

Gun, *see* Smoking gun

Gun, *see* Son of a gun

H

Handle, *see* Fly off the handle

Hands down, *see* Win hands down

Hanged for a sheep *see* Might as well be hanged for a sheep as a lamb

Hash, *see* Make a hash of something

Havoc, *see* Play havoc

Haywire, *see* Go haywire

Heart, *see* Warm the cockles of your heart

Heart, *see* Wear one's heart on one's sleeve

Hell, *see* All hell broke loose

Hind legs, *see* Talk the hind legs off a donkey

Hobby horse, *see* On one's hobby horse

Hold a candle, *see* Not fit to hold a candle

Hook, *see* Sling one's hook

Hook or by crook, *see* By hook or by crook

Horns, *see* Take the bull by the horns

Horns of a dilemma, *see* On the horns of a dilemma

Horse, *see* Stalking horse

Horse's mouth, *see* From the horse's mouth

Humble pie, *see* Eat humble pie

I

Image, *see* Spitting image

Insult, *see* Add insult to injury

J

Jack Robinson, *see* Before you can say Jack Robinson

Jiffy, *see* In a jiffy

K

Kettle of fish *see* Pretty kettle of fish

Kibosh, *see* Put the kibosh on

Kicking, *see* Alive and kicking

Kite, *see* Fly a kite

Knot, *see* Tie the knot

L

Lamb's tail, *see* In two shakes of a lamb's tail

Lead, *see* Swing the lead

Leave, *see* Take French leave

Leave no stone unturned, *see* No stone unturned

Leg, *see* Pull one's leg

Legs, *see* Talk the hind legs off a donkey

Lemon, *see* Answer's a lemon

Life of Riley, *see* Live the life of Riley

Light fantastic, *see* Trip the light fantastic

Limbo, *see* In limbo

Line, *see* Toe the line

Lip, *see* Stiff upper lip

Loggerheads, *see* Be at loggerheads

Loose end, *see* At a loose end

Lunch, *see* There's no such thing as a free lunch

Lurch, *see* Leave in the lurch

M

Main-brace, *see* Splice the main-brace

March, *see* Steal a march on

Marines, *see* Tell it to the Marines

Meal, *see* Square meal

Mess of pottage, *see* Sell one's birthright for a mess of pottage

Mice and men, *see* Best laid plans of mice and men

Mickey, *see* Take the mickey

Mince words, *see* Not to mince words

Moon, *see* Over the moon

Mountain, *see* Make a mountain out of a molehill

Mud, *see* Name is mud

Mum, *see* Keep mum

N

Nail, *see* Pay on the nail

Naples, *see* See Naples and die

Near to the wind, *see* Sail near *or* close to the wind

Neck, *see* Stick one's neck out

Nellie, *see* Not on your Nellie

New leaf, *see* Turn over a new leaf

Newt, *see* Pissed as a newt

Nick of time, *see* In the nick of time

Nine lives, *see* Cat has nine lives

Nine yards, *see* Whole nine yards

Nines, *see* Dressed up to the nines

Nitty-gritty, *see* Get down to the nitty-gritty

Nose, *see* Pay through the nose

O

Off the handle, *see* Fly off the handle

Offing, *see* In the offing

Oil on troubled waters, *see* Pour oil on
troubled waters

Ointment, *see* Fly in the ointment

On the side of the angels, *see* Be on the
side of the angels

One fell swoop, *see* At one fell swoop

Opera *see* Soap opera

Other half, *see* How the other half lives

Over bar the shouting, *see* All over bar
the shouting

Oyster, *see* World is one's oyster

P

P's and q's *see* Mind one's p's and q's

Pale, *see* Beyond the pale

Parrot, *see* Sick as a parrot

Pay off an old score *see* Settle a score

Pecker, *see* Keep one's pecker up

Peg, *see* Take down a peg

Petard, *see* Hoist with one's own petard

Pickle, *see* In a pickle

Pigeon, *see* Stool pigeon

Pig's ear *see* Make a pig's ear

Pikestaff, *see* Plain as a pikestaff

Pledge, *see* Sign the pledge

Poke, *see* Pig in a poke

Poll, *see* Straw poll

Pot, *see* Gone to pot

Q

Quicker than you can say Jack
Robinson, *see* Before you can say
Jack Robinson

R

Rain-check, *see* Take a rain-check

Rare kettle of fish, *see* Pretty kettle of
fish

Rat, *see* Smell a rat

Red, *see* Paint the town red

Red-handed, *see* Catch red-handed

Right foot, *see* Set off on the right *or*
wrong foot

River, *see* Sell down the river

Room to swing a cat *see* Not enough
room to swing a cat

Roughshod, *see* Ride roughshod over

Rubicon, *see* Cross the Rubicon

S

Sack, *see* Get the sack

Sackcloth and ashes, *see* Wear
sackcloth and ashes

Salt, *see* Rub salt in the wound

Salt, *see* Take with a pinch *or* grain of
salt

Scratch, *see* Start from scratch

Scratch, *see* Up to scratch

Scratch, *see* You scratch my back and
I'll scratch yours

Seat of one's pants, *see* By the seat of
one's pants

Sepulchre, *see* Whited sepulchre

Sesame, *see* Open Sesame

Seven bells *see* Knock seven bells
out of

Shake a stick at *see* More … than you
can shake a stick at

Shambles, *see* In a shambles

Sheep, *see* Might as well be hanged for
a sheep as a lamb

Sheep, *see* Separate the sheep from the
goats

Sheep's clothing, *see* Wolf in sheep's
clothing

Sheets, *see* Three sheets to *or* in the
wind

Ship, *see* Spoil the ship for a ha'porth of
tar

Shirt, *see* Stuffed shirt

Shoulder to the wheel, *see* Put one's shoulder to the wheel

Shufti, *see* Take a shufti

Sinking ship, *see* Rats leave a sinking ship

Skin a cat, *see* There's more than one way to skin a cat

Skin of one's teeth, *see* By the skin of one's teeth

Sleeve, *see* Wear one's heart on one's sleeve

Smithereens, *see* Blow to smithereens

Soap, *see* Soft soap

Sock, *see* Put a sock in it

Song, *see* Sold for a song

Spade, *see* Call a spade a spade

Span, *see* Spick and span

Spleen, *see* Vent one's spleen

Spoke, *see* Put a spoke in someone's wheel

Spoon, *see* Wooden spoon

Spot, *see* X marks the spot

Spout, *see* Up the spout

Spurs, *see* Win one's spurs

Square one, *see* Back to square one

Stops, *see* Pull out all the stops

Suck, *see* Teach one's grandmother to suck eggs

Sure as eggs is eggs, *see* As sure as eggs is eggs

Swallow, *see* One swallow does not make a summer

T

Tables, *see* Turn the tables

Teacup, *see* Storm in a teacup

Teeth, *see* Armed to the teeth,

Teeth, *see* By the skin of one's teeth

Tenterhooks, *see* On tenterhooks

Thinking cap, *see* Put on one's thinking cap

Thumbs up *or* down, *see* Give the thumbs up *or* down

Thunder, *see* Steal someone's thunder

Ticket, *see* That's (just) the ticket

Tinker's dam(n), *see* Give a tinker's dam(n)

Tod, *see* On one's tod

Topsy, *see* It just growed like Topsy

Town, *see* Paint the town red

Treadmill, *see* On the treadmill

Turkey, *see* Talk turkey

Turtle, *see* Turn turtle

Two shakes of a lamb's tail, *see* In two shakes of a lamb's tail

U

Umbrage, *see* Take umbrage

W

Wagon, *see* On the wagon

Wall, *see* Writing is on the wall

Water, *see* Of the first water

Weeds, *see* Widow's weeds

Weight, *see* Pull one's weight

Wheat, *see* Separate the wheat from the chaff

Whelk-stall, *see* Couldn't run a whelk-stall

White feather, *see* Show the white feather

Whole hog, *see* Go the whole hog

Wick, *see* Get on one's wick

Wild oats, *see* Sow one's wild oats

Wilderness, *see* Voice crying in the wilderness

Willies, *see* Give one the willies

Wind, *see* Three sheets to *or* in the wind

Wind, *see* Whistle for it *or* whistle for
the wind
Windmills, *see* Tilt at windmills
Wolf, *see* Keep the wolf from the door
Wood, *see* Touch wood
Wool, *see* Pull the wool over one's
eyes
Work, *see* Have one's work cut out

Worth his salt *see* Not worth his salt
Wrong end of the stick, *see* Get the
wrong end of the stick
Wrong foot, *see* Set off on the right *or*
wrong foot

Y

Yarn, *see* Spin a yarn